The Algerians

The Algerians

by Pierre Bourdieu

Translated by Alan C. M. Ross

With a preface by Raymond Aron

Beacon Press Boston

First published in France in 1958 under the title
Sociologie de L'Algérie
Revised edition 1961
Copyright © 1958 by Presses Universitaires de France
English translation copyright © 1962 by Beacon Press
All rights reserved
Published simultaneously in Canada by
S. J. Reginald Saunders and Co., Ltd., Toronto
Library of Congress catalog card number: 62-15604
Printed in the United States of America

Maps and graphs by Françoise Mallet

Preface

This book by my friend Pierre Bourdieu concerns itself
with Algeria, not with the war in Algeria. Bourdieu, a sociologist
and philosopher, has lived in that country for many years. He
has the ability to observe with detachment and to understand
with sympathy, to reconstruct the outlook and system of values
of different communities at the same time that he perceives the
growing unity of those communities as they ranged themselves
against the colonial condition.

For almost eight years the drama of Algeria weighed upon
the French like an obsession, a guilt, and also like a duty. It
precipitated the fall of a regime, split a nation asunder. It im-
periled domestic peace and spread throughout the mother country a climate of passion and crime. It could no longer be considered a simple episode in a historically irresistible movement
called "decolonization"; it became a tragic moment in the history
of France. Those who care about the destiny of France and of
the West cannot remain indifferent to Algeria; they will find
in this volume the necessary data for reflection and judgment.

The population of Algeria is neither ethnically nor cul-
turally homogeneous: Kabyles, Shawia, Mozabites and Arabic-
speaking peoples—although all Islamized to a certain extent—
share neither the same traditions, the same way of life, nor the
same social structure. For many reasons, geographical as well as
psychological, the Algerian communities throughout the cen-
turies have been unable to build a nation comparable to the
ones that existed to the east and west, in Tunis and Morocco.
The idea of the "clean board of 1830"—i.e., that before the
French conquest nothing would have existed in Algeria—is un-
questionably a legend. But it is true that political unification
was far from being achieved throughout the territory that is
to be the Algerian republic. The immigration of Frenchmen
and Europeans into an Algeria officially assimilated into the

v

metropolitan territory and divided into *départements* has progressively created the situation that Pierre Bourdieu analyzes
at the end of his book.

Between the traditional culture of all the peoples of Algeria
and the culture—French and modern—that the *colons* brought
with them, there is a radical incompatibility. The Europeans
did not understand and did not wish to understand the authentic nature of the traditional culture. As the dominant minority, they feared that they would be swamped by the majority
if they accorded to the vanquished the civic equality which the
latter had long demanded. The Moslems, for their part, sus-
tained the shock of both a foreign culture and a humiliating
status. Their culture was shattered, partially broken up by contact with the modern culture of the dominant group. The swift
growth of the Moslem population (2.5 per cent annually) also
helped to upset the traditional pattern, to increase the number
of those who had no regular work and who felt themselves lost
in a hostile world, without meaning in an incomprehensible
society. Thus, all the conditions were joined to a pitiless war,
in which nationalists fought for the independence of their
country-to-be and for their dignity, and in which the European
minority defended its right to live on the land which their
fathers' toil had made productive. As for the French in the
homeland: some wanted to hang on to the last segment of
empire, others wished to protect their compatriots who had
settled on the opposite shore of the Mediterranean, and still
others hoped passionately that France would pursue her voca-
tion of liberty to its ultimate end.

We already know what the horrors of the Algerian war
have been. What the future will bring, no one can tell. But,
in spite of the blood that has been spilled and the crimes that
have been committed, the mere fact of a final agreement between the Algerian republican government and the French
government does not permit us to conclude on a note of despair. Precisely because the struggle has given them an awareness of their own worth, the Moslems of Algeria henceforth are
open to modern civilization. The French, on the other hand,
do not feel that they have been defeated. They realized finally

that the conflict itself had lost its meaning and that the accession of Algeria to the status of nation was both inevitable and just. Will Algeria's European minority resign itself to living in an Algerian republic, or will its members return to the mother country? What proportion of Europeans will make the decision one way or the other? Will the government of an independent Algeria that emerged from revolution tolerate in actuality the preservation of a European minority? Will the association with France be anything more than a brief and precarious transition between the colonial condition and a socialism more or less totalitarian, a neutralism more or less positive?

We shall not attempt to predict what course of action will be followed. But let us continue to hope and, above all, let us continue to perpetuate the firm bonds which the dialogue, alternately peaceful and bellicose, has forged between the two peoples.

RAYMOND ARON

Maps and Graphs

Figure   *Page*

1. Plan of a Kabyle House 6
2. Plan of a Kabyle Village: Aït Hichem 14
3. Social Organization of the Tribe of the Aït Yahia and of the Village of Aït Hichem 18-19
4. The Tribe of the Aït Yahia 21
5. The Tribes of the Aurès 26
6. Simplified Plan of the City of Ghardaïa 52-53
7. Growth of the Principal Cities Between 1954 and 1960 63
8. Plan of a Part of the Domain (*haouch*) of the Ben Chaoua 76-77
9. Family Tree and Social Organization of the Tribe of the Ouled Rechaïch 86-87
10. Dynamics of the Social Groups in Kabylia 100
11. Distribution of Farm Properties According to Size and Ethnic Category 124
12. Statistical Tables According to *Département* 126-127
13. Distribution of the Male Algerian Population According to Type of Activity and Age Group 136
14. Population Shifts Within Algeria Between 1954 and 1960 142-143
15. The Military Situation in 1957 166-167
16. Population Shifts in the North of the *Département* of Constantine 168
17. The "Resettlements" in the Territory of Aïn Arbel 173
18. The "Resettlement" of Aïn Arbel (detail) 177
19. The "Resettlement" in the Kerkera Region (Collo) 180-181

Contents

Preface, *by Raymond Aron* v

Introduction xi

Chapter 1. The Kabyles 1
    The Social Structures 2
    The Gentilitial Democracy 16

Chapter 2. The Shawia 25
    Domestic Organization 27
    The Social Structures 32

Chapter 3. The Mozabites 37
    The Challenge of the Desert 37
    Social Structure and City Government . . . 40
    Puritanism and Capitalism 45
    The Interaction Between Permanence and Change 50

Chapter 4. The Arabic-Speaking Peoples . . . 56
    The City Dwellers 59
    Nomads and Semi-Nomads 65
    The New Sedentary Peoples 70

Chapter 5. The Common Cultural Heritage . . 92
    Cultural Interpenetration and Kaleidoscopic
      Mechanism 92
    The Economy and Attitude Toward Life . . 102
    Islam and North African Society . . . 107

Chapter 6. Disintegration and Distress . . . 119
    The Colonial System 120
    The Colonial Society 129
    The Total Disruption of a Society . . . 134

x

Contents

Chapter 7. The Revolution Within the Revolution   145

Special Form and Meaning of the War . . . 147

War as Cultural Agent 155

The Resettlement Policy 163

End of a World 184

Glossary of Arab and Berber Terms 193

Selected Bibliography 202

Index 204

Introduction

Arab writers relate that Caliph Omar used to say (with a pun on the Arabic root word *frq,* meaning "division"): "Ifriqiya [North Africa] stands for breakup!" Certainly the past and the present of northwest Africa—the Maghreb—would appear to support this statement. Which condition, then, confronts us: Diversity or unity? Continuity or contrast? If we note only the existing differences, are we not liable to overlook the underlying identity which prevails? [1]

There are so many criteria, so many lines of cleavage that rarely coincide, so many cultural areas that overlap. For example, according to climate and topography, there is contrast between the Tell coastal region and the "Sahara," between mountain dwellers and the inhabitants of the plains and hills. According to the way of life, contrast exists between nomads and sedentary peoples, but with varying intermediate degrees of semi-nomads and semi-sedentary peoples. According to the type of habitation, there is opposition between those who live in different types of dwellings: terraced houses in the Saharan Aurès and Mzab, houses with tiled roofs in Kabylia, Moorish houses in the cities, but again with a series of transitional types, of which one of the most common is the humble earthen *gourbi;* opposition between the grouped dwelling places of the "old sedentary peoples" and the dispersed dwelling places of the people that have

[1] It is obvious that Algeria, when considered in isolation from the rest of the Maghreb, does not constitute a true cultural unit. However, I have limited my investigation to Algeria for a definite reason. Algeria is specifically the object of this study because the clash between the indigenous and the European civilizations has made itself felt here with the greatest force. Thus the problem under investigation has determined the choice of subject. This study, which is a conceptual outline of more extensive analyses, includes a description of the *original* social and economic structures (Chap. 1-5) which, although not the main purpose of the book, is indispensable for an understanding of the breakdown of the social structures caused by the colonial situation and the influx of European civilization.

only recently become sedentary. According to the anthropo-
logical criterion, one finds antithesis between the local stock and
the additions from the east (but a checkered history has brought
about such a great intermingling that one can rarely and with
difficulty distinguish any perfectly pure types). According to
language and culture, opposition exists between Berber-speaking
and Arabic-speaking peoples, but among the latter are a great
many Arabicized Berbers. According to different culture traits,
such as women's right of inheritance, there is antithesis between
Berber and Moslem law, but on both sides a system of counter-
acting balances which tends to abolish these differences. According to the degree of legislative power of the group, there is
a similar opposition, but with transitions of varying degree.
According to artistic techniques, you discover contrast between
the bold, rectilinear ornamentation of Berber art and the fine,
flowing lines of Arab decoration. One could go on in this way
contrasting the sharecroppers and the wage earners, the varying
relationship of man to the soil, the magic-religious nature of the
oath, the judicial system, the degree of penetration of Islam.
All these lines traced on a map would form an almost inextricable maze, since no two marked areas would overlap exactly
—for example, areas indicating Berber-speakers and sedentary
peoples, or those indicating Arabic-speakers and nomads—and
since too the borders of these areas are seldom clearly defined.

Certain relatively distinct "cultural areas" do, however, stand
out from this maze in strongly marked patterns. Indeed, where-
ever the Berber dialects have been maintained, principally in
the mountain massifs (Kabylia, Aurès), there have been conserved
not only special culture traits but a special mode of life. Here
may be noted, among other features, a certain independence in
regard to Islam (with the exception of the Mzab) which is particularly evident in the judicial system, a peasant love of the
soil and of the desperately hard work required to make it fertile,
the predominance of direct farming of the land by its owner,
a social structure with strong, equalitarian features based on
the concept of the territorial patrimony. While it is true that the
nomadic Arabs have introduced a different system of values—a
disdain for the land and direct farming that is characteristic of a

pastoral civilization, an aristocratically minded society—it would be dangerous to exaggerate the opposition between Arabs and Berbers. Between these two ways of life there are frequent transitions and deeply rooted affinities. Is it possible to imagine the Arab tribe, for example, as being separated from its territorial patrimony, lands that are strictly defined to guard against rival encroachment? On the other hand, is it not true that the social structures of the Berbers, like those of the Arabs, have been developed in accordance with the genealogical pattern? Between the two systems there is a constant interaction based on a close affinity but characterized by a conflicting motivation: the temptation to adopt the ways of one's neighbor and the desire to retain one's own identity.

Algeria is a long, narrow strip of land broken up into a tangle of small sections, with plains of any appreciable size only at its western and eastern tips. By reason of its geographical multiplicity this country has, no doubt, always seemed predisposed to social particularisms. Certain factors, however, have opposed this tendency: the intense movement that animates the whole territory, the migrations of shepherds, the cycle of markets which are the occasion for cultural and judicial exchanges (the role of the *meddah* comes to mind in this connection); the far-reaching influence of the cities which are centers of religious orthodoxy and Eastern civilization; the unity of faith; the fact that the many dialects use the one sacred language of the Koran as an implicit reference. The result is that these two antithetical aspects—unity and plurality, continuity and division—can be understood only when considered in relation to one another. No completely closed and, therefore, pure and intact society exists in the Maghreb; however isolated and withdrawn into itself a group may be, it still thinks of itself and judges itself by comparison with other groups. Each group seeks to establish and base its own identity on the ways in which it differs from others; the result is diversification rather than diversity. Thus, while our analyses will define these differences, it will be only to discover above and beyond them the basic identity that these differences conceal or seek to conceal.

We have no intention of reducing to this pattern either the

contacts between the European and the indigenous civilizations
or the upheavals caused by colonization, and we are not ignorant
of the fact that, just as the old dialogue between Berbers and
Arabs was unequal, so the new dialogue is unequal, but for
other reasons and with more absoluteness. Nevertheless, one of
the keys to the present drama may be found in the painful
debate of a society which is compelled to define itself by reference to another, is torn between self-doubt and complacent self-
pride, between adherence to others and the fierce defense of its
besieged self. Its drama is the acute conflict within an alienated
conscience, locked in contradictions and craving for a way to
re-establish its own identity, even by means of excess and violence.

1. The Kabyles

Settled in very heavy densities (267 inhabitants to the square kilometer in the *arrondissement* of Fort National) in regions of hilly, rugged terrain, the Kabyles are primarily arboriculturists. Their dwellings are grouped in villages. The backs of these dwellings face outward and are connected to form a sort of walled enclosure that is easily defended. Inside the village the houses face on rough, narrow lanes. The threshing floors, the barn for storing hay, the millstones and the rustic presses for the production of olive oil are found at the entrance to the village, at which point the paths leading to the village divide, so that the stranger who has no business within may proceed on his way without entering. Thus, at the first approach, the village reveals its determination to remain a closed and secret unit, resolutely united against the outside world. Perched above its lands, which extend down the slopes to the bottom of the narrow valleys, with its vegetable gardens maintained by the women in the vicinity of the houses, its tiny fields at the next lower level, and its olive groves at the bottom of the valley, the village is both watch-tower and fortress, from which the Kabyle can easily survey his fields and orchards.[1]

The economy depends mainly on two trees, the olive and the fig, together with a few complementary crops (hard wheat and barley) and some small-scale stock raising. The land was formerly held jointly by the large family, but in the last twenty years the breaches in this system have become much more frequent. There are also certain lands held in common by the clan or village (*mechmel*) which usually serve as pasture land. The small holding

[1] It is in the Kabylia of the Djurdjura that the customs have been best preserved. The valleys of the Soummam, the Guergour and the Babor, although Berber-speaking, present characteristics that are foreign to the Kabyle culture and have been borrowed from the Arabic-speaking populations. In various islands of peasants living in the mountainous regions there may be observed a way of life that is similar, with a few variations, to that of Kabylia.

1

predominates: nine-tenths of the families own less than twenty-five acres, the average holding being three to five acres usually divided into several small plots. The *métayage au quint* (share-cropping system) is rare. Aided by the members of his family, and on certain occasions by the whole clan or the whole village, the head of the family farms his own land, which, thanks to the legal custom of joint possession, remains sufficiently large to support the family community. Because of the scanty production, however, a strict control of consumption must be maintained. In a society where money is scarce and interest rates high, and where truly efficient technical methods are lacking, it has been found necessary to combat a singularly sterile natural environment by the coordinated effort of all members of the community. So there has been a wide development of pacts (plowing associations, farming leases, etc.) which are mutually profitable and are of such variety that all possible combinations seem to have been effected.

It becomes evident how sharp and strained is this struggle between man and his environment. By a sort of phenomenon of compensation, to the imperfection of techniques there is a corresponding exaggerated perfection of the social order—as if the precariousness of the adjustment to the natural environment were counterbalanced by the excellence of the social organization; as if, to counteract his powerlessness in regard to things, man had no other recourse than to develop associations with other men in a luxuriant growth of human relationships. But one would be no less justified in considering that the underlying intention of this society is perhaps to devote the best of its energy and its genius to the elaboration of relationships between man and man, at the risk of giving secondary importance to the struggle of man against nature.

The Social Structures

The Kabyle society, which is composed of what might be described as a series of interlocking communities, may be repre-

sented by concentric circles of allegiances which have their
own name, their own property and their own honor. The smallest social cell is the extended family (*akham*, the "large house").
The families join together to form the *takharroubt*, whose members generally bear the same name and consider themselves to be
"brothers," since they descend from a common ancestor to the
fourth or fifth generation. Sometimes, however, the *takharroubt*
joins together families of different names and origins. There may
also generally be found attached to the descendants of the common ancestor dependent groups who have been adopted and
integrated. Each *takharroubt* has its *t'amen*, its spokesman, chosen by common consent, who represents it at assemblies and who,
at the time of the *timechret'*, receives the share of the meat that
is intended for the members of his group. The *takharroubt* may
join with others in varying numbers to form a larger group called,
in Greater Kabylia, the *adroum*. The village, *taddart*, with its
amin (the executive agent of the decisions of the *tajmaât*, the
council chosen by the elders), is made up of several *iderman*
(plural of *adroum*). Each of these social units occupies its own
quarter so that the plan of the village shows the social structure.
Several villages compose the tribe, *ârch*, which bears the name of
a mythical ancestor and which formerly had its own assembly
composed of a representative from each village. The confederation, *taqbilt*, is an extremely vague unit with ill-defined limits.

   Domestic organization.—The extended family is the basic
social cell, the focal point where converge the most varied orders
of facts—economics, magic, customary law, ethics, religion—the
model on which all social structures have been developed. It is
not restricted to the group made up of the married couple and
their direct descendants, but brings together all the agnates (descendants from a common male ancestor), thereby uniting several
generations in intimate association and communion under a single chief. The father, who is leader, priest and judge, assigns a
precise place within the community to each household and to
each bachelor. His authority is generally unquestioned. He has
two greatly feared sanctions at his disposal—the power to disinherit and the power to call down curses—the latter being un-

doubtedly the more powerful weapon, since it is deemed to bring down divine punishment upon the ungrateful, the prodigal or the rebel. His omnipotence is displayed each day in connection with any event concerning family life or organization (the making of purchases, the allotment of tasks, management of the family budget, etc.). He decides upon and presides over all family ceremonies. Thus, for marriages, it is he who decides the date and the amount of solemnity to be accorded to the ceremony. On certain grave occasions he summons a family council comprised of his sons and brothers, and sometimes he has a marabout (priest) participate in its deliberations. The father has the right to compel members of the family to marry. On his death, the eldest son inherits his authority and, even when the property has been divided, he continues to watch over the conduct of his brothers and sisters, giving them aid and acting as their representative in certain circumstances. The mother, for her part, has charge of all the domestic tasks and of certain farm chores (the garden, gathering wood, the fetching of water). She usually helps her husband in the management of the family provisions and is responsible for their safeguarding and thrifty distribution to members of the family. Finally, she represents the power of the father within the female society (allotment of tasks, etc.) so that she often is regarded as "the pillar of the community."

The family cell is a fundamental unit: an economic unit of production and consumption, a political unit within the confederation of families that makes up the clan, and finally a religious unit, since each dwelling is the site of a common cult (rites of the threshold, of the hearth, of the guardian spirits of the family, etc.). This cohesion is strengthened by the fact that the group lives in a single area—the houses of the descendants of a common ancestor being generally grouped around a common courtyard—and by the custom of commensality, or that of eating together (see Fig. 1). The family is also a unit with common interests and occupations: the outdoor tasks, those of both the men and women (construction, sowing, harvests, pottery making, and the like), are the business of all members of the group. This involvement extends to anything that affects the head of the family,

particularly in anything that affects his honor, which they must
defend at all costs.

The families own the houses and cultivated lands and are
represented by their chiefs, who have power to act for the corpo-
rate body. In actual fact the law of joint possession prevails
among the Kabyles (the essential foundation for both the economic and moral balance of the group), so that each member
(household and even individual) has a share which grants him
tenure but not right of ownership. The fact that each household
has its own property does not give it any excuse to disobey the
moral imperative which prescribes that the family property must
be conserved and increased. Moreover, the customary law protects
the landed inheritance. For this purpose was established the
chefâa, the right of repurchase or pre-emption of real estate, to
which custom has given an exorbitant development and which
allows any strangers to the group to be deprived of rights of
ownership. Also working to safeguard the landed inheritance are
the *habous*, charitable foundations which may be set up for a
wife's advantage and which allow her a life interest in the property, although as a "haboused" property it cannot be transferred
and must return to the male heirs on the death of the beneficiary.

This summary analysis has so far described only features that
are common to all types of family in North Africa. The principal
originality of the Kabyle system concerns the status of women.
Unlike Moslem law, which grants a woman the right to inherit,
ab intestat, a third of a legal share, Berber law disinherits women
by virtue of the agnatic principle, according to which the suc-
cessional choice depends primarily on the degree of kinship in
the male line and exists to the exclusive profit of the male heirs.
The disinheritance of women is in the first place an economic
necessity. Given the heavy density of population and the extreme
scarcity of arable land, the excessive dividing up of the property
that would ensue from the intervention of too great a number of
heirs would ruin the family. It must also be realized that the
wife remains a stranger to her husband's group, among whom she
has the status of an invited guest; thus she would not be justified
in laying claim to an inheritance from ancestors who are not her

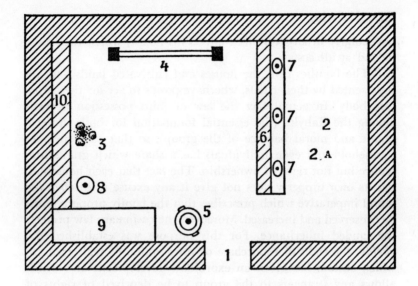

Fig. 1. Plan of a Kabyle House

A Kabyle house is generally rather small: 23 to 25 feet long and 16 feet wide. The walls are from 10 to 12 feet in height and from 1½ to 2 feet thick. They are constructed by laying two parallel rows of stones cemented together by clay or mud.

The house is divided into two parts, the stable, *adainin* (2), and the *taqaats*, the area reserved for the humans. Above the stable is the loft, *taaricht* (2A), made of planks and partly hidden by jars (7), *ikufan*,

own. It is logical, then, that if the husband dies intestate the property should go to the closest male descendant. This ruthless favoring of the male line is, however, tempered in several ways. As a result of the resolutions of 1748, the Kabyles refused to obey any longer the prescriptions of the Koranic law concerning inheritance and returned to the custom of the disinheritance of women. Since that time the *habous*, which previously served to disinherit women (as they do in Arab communities), have permitted them to enjoy a life interest in the lands of their husbands. Furthermore, the code of honor requires a man to assume responsibility for any of his female relatives who may be orphaned, widowed, or repudiated by their husbands.

In the domain of family rights, the same brutal inequality apparently prevails. Marriage liberates a woman from the abso-

placed along the *tadekuant* (6), a small wall two or three feet in height, which separates the stable from the living quarters. Hollowed out in the lower part of this wall are the mangers for the cattle. Against the wall opposite the stable is a narrow, low wall about three feet in height called the *adekuan* (10), on which are placed the kitchen utensils and the oil lamp and in which are niches to hold the cooking pot, the pan for frying the griddle cakes, and the other soot-blackened pots of terra cotta. Along the front wall between the *adekuan* and the doorway is a sort of wide, raised step under which is placed the mutton or the veal for the festival of the Aid. At the base of the *adekuan* is the hearth, *kanun* (3), dug out at ground level and plastered over with a coating of lime and gravel. The handmill (8) occupies one corner of the house. The water jug (5) is placed behind the door. The women set up their weaving loom opposite the door (4). The house has only one small window, which serves to let out the smoke and give light to the loft. The door (1), which provides an entry for both humans and cattle, opens on the inner courtyard. The Kabyles give the name of *lhara* to the group of houses that open on the same inner courtyard. This courtyard is closed in by a wall and has a common gateway which is often covered by a roof.

The house with the roof of round tiles is typical of Kabylia. It is found particularly in the Djurdjura region of Kabylia and in part of the Babors region (from the Isser Valley to the Wadi Agrioun). In the south it extends as far as the chain of the Bibans and to the Guergour, then gives way to the terraced house. On the other frontiers it is replaced by the *gourbi*—a hut with walls either of uncemented stones or of clay covered with thatch, esparto grass or diss—which is found throughout all of the Tell, except in the regions mentioned above, and in the area of Dahra and the Traras.

lute authority of her father only to hand her over to the complete domination of her husband, or, more precisely, to the domination of her husband's family group and particularly of her mother-in-law. She must be both an obedient and faithful wife. With marriage, her former fear of losing her virginity is replaced by the fear of sterility, which she seeks to ward off by amulets, pilgrimages, votive offerings and all sorts of magic rites. The husband has complete liberty to end the marriage. He merely has to pronounce the formula of repudiation in the presence of friends, of a marabout, of the assembly or, at the present time, before the cadi (a minor judge or magistrate).

The status given to women is, in fact, a consequence of the absolute primacy of the family group or, more precisely, of the agnatic group. "The whole social organization of Kabylia," write

Hanoteau and Letrouneux, "all the Kabyle institutions (political, administrative, civil . . .) converge on this single goal: to maintain and develop the solidarity between the members of the same community, to give to the 'group' the greatest possible strength." Hence there is found, among other characteristics, the right of matrimonial compulsion. As a social necessity from which no one can escape, marriage is the affair of the group and not of the individual. Furthermore, the absolute separation of the sexes, which excludes the wife from participation in any outside activity, deprives her of the possibility of living elsewhere than in her lawful abode. The investigation of matrimonial prospects is then very logically the business of the family, since the union of two individuals is merely the occasion for effecting the union of two groups. The fathers seek out a "good family," meet one another, come to an agreement, all without the knowledge of the individuals concerned. The young lad may be betrothed by his father at any age; however, once he has reached majority he is consulted, through the intermediation of a friend, in order that he may freely express his opinion. If he refuses (a rare possibility) his father may make another choice. The girls, on the other hand, are usually informed only after the marriage has been decided upon. In actual fact marriage is often arranged by the women, with the head of the family merely intervening to authorize agreements that have already been reached. Moreover, the Kabyle girl has been prepared by her whole education for her future legal and social condition. Everything is done to impress upon her the fact of male superiority: for example, the importance given to the different ceremonies that mark the main stages of a boy's life (birth, first haircut, first trip to the market, circumcision, etc.).

Nor is it surprising that a marriage should in no way change the family. Married or unmarried, the individual remains bound to the agnatic group and subject to the same paternal authority; the wife, for her part, is considered as a means of increasing the size of the family and of tightening its ties. Such is the true context in which marriage and the matrimonial compensation must be interpreted. Certain authors have seen in the Kabyle marriage (and in the Moslem marriage in general) a kind of sale, with the compensation (paid by the father of the groom to the father of

the bride) constituting a true purchase price; others, a sort of
contract for hiring out of services; others, an original contract
designed to make the father take an interest in the good conduct
of his daughter (thereby allowing him to keep the marriage payment); still others consider this payment as a sort of joint guarantee both for the husband—the bride's father being induced to
watch over the conduct of his daughter—and for the wife, who
may, according to certain customary laws, demand the use of the
marriage payment when her family appears to be deserting her.
The first interpretation must be rejected; the others appear to be
stressing certain "secondary functions," to which should be added
the economic function (circulation of capital). The marriage
payment should really be understood in the context of the "honorable exchange" which implies the exchange of gifts and coun-
tergifts: one example of this institution is the *taousa,* the gift
that the guest makes to his host with great fanfare on festive or
ceremonial occasions. These gifts create a moral and religious
bond and imply the duty of giving back more than has been
received in the way of deferred exchanges. Note, however, the
"marriage by exchange" in which an individual gives his sister
in marriage to another whose sister he in turn marries without
any marriage payment. Marriage is just one more occasion for
such reciprocal exchanges, which are requisites of social existence
and the normal method of transferring goods and chattels, among
which wives must be included. These transactions do not belong
in the logic of economic calculation; the marriage payment is
a countergift and marriage is an exchange which creates alliances
between groups (consequently, the simulated struggles which, in
the rites connected with the marriage ceremony, portray the
opposition of the clan of the groom to that of the bride) and takes
the form of reciprocal gifts, because the relationship between the
marriage and the matrimonial compensation is not an arbitrary
one, the marriage being considered as an integral part of the gifts
that accompany it.

The matrimonial compensation restores a broken balance
in that it is used as a pledge, a substitute for the woman who
should have been provided by the bridegroom's family in exchange for the bride. The continuity of the gift and countergift

mechanism is thus maintained by the matrimonial compensation. Proof of this is the fact that if the husband dies first the marriage payment is returned and the wife goes back to her family, but there is no return of this money if the wife dies first, the husband's family thereby standing definitely as the loser. Hence the extremely insulting nature of the *berrou bat'el* (repudiation of the wife without asking for return of the marriage payment), which breaks the system of reciprocity by giving without receiving in return as honor demands. The wife thus repudiated, a gift that has been returned and for which there is no possible counter-gift, is excluded from the cycle of matrimonial exchanges (*tamaouokt*). On the other hand, to return the matrimonial compensation when the husband dies, or the wife is repudiated, shows that the "contract" is broken but that the system of reciprocity instituted by the marriage continues unchanged.

The marriage payment is also a pledge in another sense: the wife remains a member of her original group which, through her, secures a hold over the magic power of the group that accepts her, since the gift still remains attached to the giver; the payment of matrimonial compensation thus restores the balance in magic powers. In the same context it appears also to be a compensation intended to atone for the violation of the sexual taboo. Thus, in the Aurès, the nuptial gift consists of a *"douro,"* called the *haqd-dkhoul* (right of entry) among the Beni-Bou-Slimane and a *"douro lahlâl"* (*douro* making lawful) among the Touaba. Likewise, the Mozabite jurists maintain that "the nuptial dowry is the condition that actually makes the marriage legitimate and confers the right to intercourse with the bride." And finally, should it not be considered that this gift made to men is in reality being offered through them to the powers of nature, in order that they may grant as a supreme blessing a fruitful marriage?

It is not surprising, then, that the family group should be the focal point of Kabyle society: primacy of the family group, which rules out celibacy and which, through the father, exercises the right of matrimonial compulsion and arranges for the girls to be married at the early age of twelve or thirteen; primacy of the group, which grants absolute authority to the husband and invests him with the right of repudiation because of the fact that it is not the married couple, but the continuity of the family group, that must above all be protected; primacy of the group, which through various legal devices ensures the protection of the family patrimony against any outside intrusion, and which excludes women from inheriting in order to prevent a reduction in the size of the property.

The superior role of the group also appears clearly in the matter of emigration. Indeed, if in North Africa those who emigrate for temporary periods are for the most part sedentary Berbers and particularly Kabyles, it is because the strong cohesion and the solidarity of the agnatic group guarantees to the emigrant that the family he has left behind on the communal property—which provides subsistence for each member of the group—will be protected in his absence by those of his male relatives who have remained on the land. It is the thought of the family that sustains him during his exile, that inspires him to work desperately hard and save his money. Finally, it has been noted that when they are joined together in France to form communities which are patterned on the family structure and which recreate that system of solidarity and mutual support which animates Kabyle life, the emigrants will undergo severe privation in order to send back to their families the greater part of their earnings.

Since it is aware of the extremely important function of the agnatic family, the group does everything in its power to defend it and to continually proclaim those values on which it is based, particularly the virtues of solidarity and mutual aid which cannot be abandoned without threatening the ruin of the entire social organism and the destruction of that balance between man and his environment which is maintained only by coordinated effort. In addition to the mutual loans and contracts of all types, certain tasks (construction of houses, road building, weeding, harvesting, gathering of the olive crop, etc.) are carried out through the cooperation of the whole clan or village; labor that is given gratuitously but which has been made mandatory by custom—a mutual lending of services, a fraternal system of mutual aid involving for the beneficiary only the necessity to provide food and the obligation to reciprocate—the *tiouizi* is a gift of labor to which a countergift will later correspond. The conclusion of those tasks which are accompanied by acts of ritual is celebrated by ceremonies and by a common repast. Thus the collective task becomes both a form of collective celebration and prayer and, above all, an occasion for the solemn reaffirmation of family, clan or village solidarity. In all these customs is expressed the strong desire to keep the ties of the group tightly drawn. Doubtless their limited methods of production have necessitated this collaboration and association, but in a deeper sense this cult of solidarity may be regarded as the reverence of this society for their common ancestor, whether real or mythical, from whom all solidarity and fertility emanate and through whom this society worships itself.

The family as structural model.—The most restricted as well as the widest social units have been conceived on the model of the family unit. Genealogy is resorted to in an attempt to rationalize the social structure by showing that it is rooted in the past. Hence there is a certain lack of precision in the political nomenclature, particularly in regard to the groupings of families, the *takharroubt* and the *adroum*; these terms designate social units of a size that varies both with the region and with the social structure and history of the villages. This is because the transition takes place in a gradual and continuous manner from the narrowest to the most extensive units, although potential points of segmentation do exist, any one of which could become real given the proper occasion or situation.

Among these segmentation points there are some, however, which mark out true *thresholds* defining more stable groups. So it is that the most vital unit is the simple or complex clan (*takharroubt* or *adroum*). Up to a relatively recent date the clan was the framework in which social life developed, and a great many of its features proved that it had its own separate existence: it had its *tajmaât*, its cemetery, its own section in the village, its fountains, and sometimes its own festivals and customs, and even its own legend of its origin. The members of the same clan feel joined together in an actual brotherhood that makes for very familiar relationships and leads to attitudes of spontaneous solidarity, whether it be a question of avenging blood that has been shed or carrying out a communal task. The *timechret'*—the communal sharing of meat and the act of commensality, which defines the limits of the community and at the same time asserts its unity—was formerly carried out within the framework of the clan.

The village unit was primarily territorial. One must be on guard against false analogies suggested by what a number of features would seem to indicate: the village, provided with its own council house and with the laws that are laid down by its own council (*qanoun*), which differ from Islamic law and which govern daily behavior in great detail, calls to mind the idea of the rural commune. But in point of fact the clan exists alongside its neighbors rather than uniting with them to form a higher social unit. Consequently, whether grouped together or separated from one another (*toufiq*), the clans form a confederation rather than a community. Different influences have resulted in the fact that a good number of practices and institutions proper to the clan no longer exist today except at the level of the village, which is becoming progressively a true political unit (see Fig. 2).

More fragile and more vaguely defined than the clan, the tribe—a confederation of villages that exists in name only and has no tangible embodiment—is only activated in special circumstances and for special purposes, so that it is defined principally through its opposition to homologous groups. It may be seen, then, that cohesion and a feeling of solidarity are in inverse ratio to the size of the group. Yet a quarrel concerning the larger group will bring to a halt any quarrels among the lesser groups (see Fig. 10).

The complexity of this system, with the varied rights of initiative it confers, is greatly increased by the interaction of the *çoffs*—diffused and abstract organizations, systems of political and agonistic alliances, which may divide the village, the clan or even the family and which are organized into two general leagues, an "upper" and "lower" league; organizations that are primarily onomastic (name-related) in nature and have a potential rather than an actual existence. These "associations" (in the sense of "a social unit that is not based on the factor of kinship") come into action on every occasion and at every level, whenever a quarrel breaks out between members of different *çoffs*, however trifling

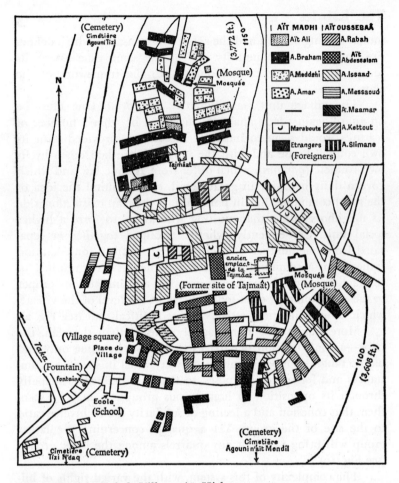

Fig. 2. Plan of a Kabyle Village: Aït Hichem

The situation of this typical village in the Djurdjura region of Kabylia appears to have been decided upon to meet several combined requirements. A fortress and observation post, it is built at the summit of a 4,000-foot crest and, as a result, is completely isolated from other villages, which are also perched on the summit of other peaks. The scarcity of arable land provides an additional reason for choosing this unfertile soil of shale and sandstone as a site for the houses of the

14

village. Moreover, the peasant can watch over the fields and orchards which surround the peak on which the village stands. The proximity of water points and of communication routes does not appear to be a factor determining the position of the settlement: indeed the springs, which are numerous on the hill slopes, are often quite a distance away from the village and communications are provided by paths running along the crest of the hills.

Even the layout of the village is the result of different technical and social requirements. Often, as in the *adroum* of the Aït Mahdi in the present example, the main street follows the crest line with the houses running down the slopes in a herringbone pattern. In the part of the village occupying the side of the crest, the houses are built at right angles to the contour lines, which are marked out, approximately, by alleyways just wide enough to allow a laden mule to pass. In both cases, the arrangement of the houses is such that the stable is naturally sited lower down than the part reserved for human habitation and the liquid manure, the dirty water and the rain can run down towards the gardens (situated behind the houses an in the area of the Aït Madhi) or to the road that serves for drainage.

The main thing to be noted is that the plan reveals the social structure. Marked out by two parallel houses and by thick walls or else by three houses placed at right angles, the courtyard is always common to members of the same large family, namely the families of the father and his married sons or the families of several brothers. The plan then shows up as clearly as would a genealogical tree the sub-divisions of the village community—the extended family, the lineage (*takharroubt*), the clan (*adroum*)—with the neighboring groups all being groups based on blood ties.

The village includes an endogamous family of a marabout and strangers who have found refuge (as the result of a murder, for example) with a related family. The isolated houses have been constructed more recently by individuals who have not found any place within the village.

The village is surrounded by several holy places: (1) "the white stone," the rock on which candles are placed by the women; (2) "the fountain of the well," where lights had been seen by certain people and to which candles are also carried; (3) Sidi Azzab, the tomb of the ancestor of the marabout family of the Azzabène, a holy place surrounded by an enclosure of dry-stone construction to which offerings are brought on the occasion of religious festivals; (4) "the fallow ground of the waterfall," a plot of ground planted with oak trees on which cattle are not pastured and wood is not cut; (5) "the summit," an eminence to which offerings are carried and where candles are lit; (6) "Bou Sehel," a sanctuary situated on a peak (3,600 feet) on the road to Taka, to which pilgrimages are made and offerings taken.

the incident may be, and no matter whether it is on an individual or on a collective scale. This division into opposed and complementary halves appears to constitute one aspect of a deeper structural opposition which dominates the whole social, spiritual and ritualistic life of the people. Different features lead one to think that these conflicts between the leagues assumed an institutional form and that the combats resulted from the logic of the ritual game rather than from a proper war. This "dualist organization" guarantees a balance of forces through strange processes of weighing, a stalemate resulting from the crisis itself. The forces are built up, come into opposition and counterbalance one another. Thus it seems as if equilibrium were being sought under conditions of the greatest tension.

The Gentilitial Democracy

The gentilitial, or genealogical, family, the keystone of this society, is at the same time (as in all of Algeria) the model on which the whole social system has been constructed, without any distinction being made as to a difference in order and kind between domestic organization (the *res privatae*) and political organization (the *res publicae*), since the bonds of consanguinity are considered as the archetype for every social tie, particularly for political ties.[2] If genealogy is used in more or less arbitrary fashion every time that it is important to create or to justify a social unit, it is because it allows a kind of relation of kinship to be created, through the fiction of the eponymous ancestor, between individuals joined together as the result of the operation

[2] It would be easy to demonstrate that the relations of kinship are the model for economic relations, for the relation between man and nature or between master and servant (see *métayage au quint*). This has led, on the one hand, to the great importance and significance that have been conferred on exchange, the things exchanged (gifts, services, etc.) never being merely *things* but also utterances, and, on the other hand, to the fact that the economic domain is never considered as autonomous, as being endowed with its own principles and rules (e.g., the law of interest) and consequently is controlled, at least ideally, by the same system of values (namely the code of honor) as other interhuman relationships.

of quite different forces; it is as if this society could not conceive of any type of relationship existing within a social body other than that which exists between relatives, nor could they conceive of any unifying principle for a political body other than that which makes for the cohesion of the most elementary form of society, the family.

Thus, although numerous features may make us think of our own kind of democracy (a kind of parliamentarianism, an equalitarianism, the concept of the general interest, a roughly defined executive power, and so on) are we entitled to conclude that the Kabyle democracy is the same as ours because of these analogies? How then can we explain that this "democracy" can really function only within the most restricted social unit, the agnatic subgroup, and that the larger units which are brought into being by some exceptional circumstance disappear as soon as the crisis has been overcome? Since they have both been constructed in accordance with the same pattern, the political and the domestic organization are really homogeneous. Thus a number of peculiarities of this system may more easily be understood. The functions of the *tajmaât*, in which only the elders are, in fact, allowed to deliberate, are those which devolve on the "father," acting as head and delegate of the group within a patrilinear society. The council administers, governs, legislates and arbitrates; it has the duty of defending the collective honor; it must see that its decisions are duly executed and has at its disposal a much feared means of coercion, the ostracism or banishment of the offender. If the whole of society is organized around such a restricted basic unit as the consanguineous clan, it is because the clan represents in the political sphere the largest organization in which family solidarity is still an effective influence. The result is that the fundamental social unit finds its own principle of limitation in the very basis on which it has been established. Moreover, since all decisions must be taken unanimously, the political organization is compelled to restrict itself to the maximum limits within which unanimity is practicable—those of the clan whose members are joined together by an intense sentiment of solidarity. In any unit of greater size this sentiment becomes more spurious

Fig. 3. Social Organization of the Tribe of the Aït Yahia and of the
      Village of Aït Hichem

Isolated on a peak between deep ravines which separate it from its
neighbors, the village seems to constitute a social unit that has been
closely defined by the topography itself. But, in fact, is not this appearance of unity rather deceptive? The village is made up of interlocking
groups. The *takharroubt* joins together several patriarchal families
who consider themselves as being descended from a common ancestor.
It must not be thought, however, that its members are always joined
together by real ties of kinship. For example, in the *takharroubt* of the
Aït Issaad, there may be found (as well as the Aït Issaad, properly
speaking) the Aït Abba, the Aït Ferhat, and the Aït Bellil. The members
of the *takharroubt* consider themselves to be brothers; the children
give to all the male adults the name of "father"; they call an older
man "dadda" (big brother), whatever may be the real bond of kinship,
and they call an older woman "nanna" (big sister). The effective ties
are very strong and intimacy is great. The women are not obliged to
hide themselves from the men. The giving of mutual aid is done
spontaneously and is an everyday occurrence. Each *takharroubt* has
a *t'amen,* a "spokesman," who represents it at the meetings of the
tajmaât; who, at the time of the *timechret',* divides up the meat into
as many small amounts as there are "houses"; who offers the gifts of
the group at the time of religious festivals or when alms are requested.
It sometimes happens that the *takharroubt* has its own customs: for
example, among the Aït Abdesselam it is forbidden to set a hen. Sometimes it has a site reserved for the clan cemetery. An individual can
leave his *takharroubt* to join up with another. The *takharroubt* has
no legal jurisdiction nor any political life proper. It may, however, on
rare occasions, hold a secret assembly to decide on internal matters.

The real political unit is the clan, *adroum;* the Aït Madhi and
the Aït Oussebâa each have their own assembly house (the *tajmaât*),
their own mosque, and their separate cemeteries. The vegetable gardens
cultivated by the women are grouped around the houses of each
adroum, since the women of one *adroum* are not permitted to be
seen by the men of the other *adroum.* The Aït Madhi have their own
threshing floor and their own fountain. The members of the *adroum*
consider themselves to be descended from a common ancestor. According to legend, the Aït Oussebâa are supposed to be the descendents of
a woman of maraboutic origin coming from the tribe of the Aït
Menguellet, who remained for a long time without any suitor. Having
married a certain Aït Ouazzoug, she had seven children by him and
the seventh (Oussebâa) gave his name to the clan. The Aït Madhi are
supposed to be the descendents of strangers who came to settle on
the peak which dominates the mountain slope on which the Aït
Oussebâa were already living.

The clan, of which all members claim to be brothers, holds its
own assembly at which are made all the decisions concerning the
community (proclamations as to harvest, religious festivals, the beginning of plowing, collective tasks, etc.). The communal sacrifice, which
was carried out at the beginning of plowing time and through which

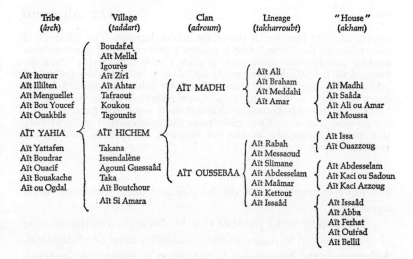

Tribe (ârch)	Village (taddart)	Clan (adroum)	Lineage (takharroubt)	"House" (akham)
	Boudafel Aït Mellal Igourès			
Aït Itourar Aït Illilten Aït Menguellet Aït Bou Youcef Aït Ouakbils	Aït Ziri Aït Ahtar Tafraout Koukou Tagounits	AÏT MADHI	Aït Ali Aït Braham Aït Meddahi Aït Amar	Aït Madhi Aït Saâda Aït Ali ou Amar Aït Moussa
AÏT YAHIA	AÏT HICHEM			Aït Issa Aït Ouazzoug
Aït Yattafen Aït Boudrar Aït Ouacif Aït Bouakache Aït ou Ogdal	Takana Issendalène Agouni Guessaâd Taka Aït Boutchour	AÏT OUSSEBÂA	Aït Rabah Aït Messaoud Aït Slimane Aït Abdesselam Aït Maâmar Aït Kettout	Aït Abdesselam Aït Kaci ou Sadoun Aït Kaci Azzoug
	Aït Si Amara		Aït Issaâd	Aït Issaâd Aït Abba Aït Ferhat Aït Ouïrad Aït Bellil

was affirmed and confirmed the existence of the community, was carried out within the confines of the *adroum*. The latter also had its institutions for giving mutual aid, its own code (more rigorous among the Aït Madhi than among the Aït Oussebâa), its own traditions and beliefs. In the case of the Aït Hichem, the division into *çoffs* coincided with the division into clans, the Aït Madhi being a part of the lower *çoff* and the Aït Oussebâa being part of the upper *çoff*.

The unity of the village *(taddert)* is primarily territorial in nature. However, since about 1930, a number of collective institutions and practices which were formerly peculiar to the *adroum* are now tending to become common to the village. One reason for this is that by making the village into an administrative unit with its *amin,* a sort of mayor, the authorities have favored the development of common village interests. Emigration, schooling and economic changes have also played a decisive role. The new village square near the school is "the neutral ground" on which the village assembly meets. The latter makes all decisions concerning matters of public interest.

The village of Aït Hichem forms a part of the tribe of the Aït Yahia (the *douar* Aït Yahia has the same limits as the tribe). The latter tribe exists primarily through the fact of its opposition to other tribes. Thus it is that a traditional rivalry exists between the Aït Yahia and their neighbors, the Aït Menguellet. The tribe of the Aït Yahia is part of what one might call the confederation of the Igaouaouen, a rather ill-defined and unstable social unit.

The generic names of the social units vary according to regions. One reason for this is that when giving out these names, the Kabyles passed by gradual stages from the patriarchal family to the clan. The intermediate social units are more or less arbitrary and virtual dividing points which become manifest particularly in cases when they must meet opposition. These units are in a constant evolution and transformation;

certain of them increase in size while others decrease. The village, and
even more so the "tufiq," which groups together several hamlets, reas-
sembles a federation more than it does a true community. Thus the
adroum of the Aït Mendil, made up of two *tikharroubin* (plural of
takharroubt), the Ait Bournine and the Aït Said, and situated farther
down the slope, is joined to the *idermen* (plural of *adroum*) of the Aït
Madhi and the Aït Oussebâa although it is separated from them on
the ground. The clan, then, constitutes the fundamental political unit.
(For proper names, the author has followed the spelling used on the
1/50,000 maps.)

and more conventional, as do the political units which are based
upon it.[3]

It is also from the point of view of this logic that the attitude
of the individual in regard to the community must be understood.
Adhesion to the injunctions of the group is assured by the sentiment of solidarity that is indissociable from the feeling of real
fraternity, the sentiment of existing only in and through the
group, of existing only as a member of the group and not as an
individual in his own right. For this reason social regulations
are not comprehended as an inaccessible ideal or as a restraining
imperative, but are rather present in the consciousness of each
individual. Proof of this may be found in the *qanoun*, a collection
of customs peculiar to each village and consisting mainly of a
detailed enumeration of special offenses, or, in other words,
examples of conduct capable of disturbing the communal way
of life—thefts, acts of violence, breaches of solidarity—followed
by the indication of the corresponding penalties. Matters affecting the essential nature of this society are not dealt with in these
qanouns because they are accepted as unquestionable, such essential matters being the sum total of values and principles that are
affirmed by the community through its very existence, the implicit
norms on which are based the acts of jurisprudence, customs
that have been instituted and formulated as circumstances demanded.[4] As Montesquieu has said, "Whatever is defended by

[3] These analyses are very largely true for all other Algerian groups.
[4] For example, the *qanoun* of the village of Agouni-n-Tesellent (Aït
Akbil) out of 249 articles includes 219 "repressive" laws (88 per cent), 25
"restitutive" laws (10 per cent), and five articles concerning the more
general principles (political organization).

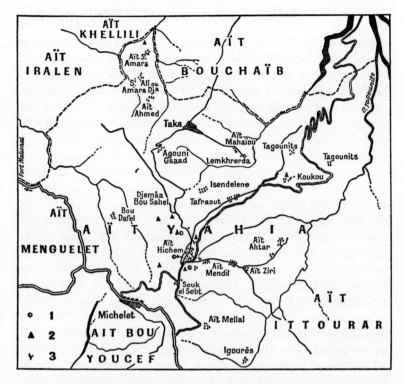

Fig. 4. The Tribe of the Aït Yahia

The symbols represent (1) fountain, (2) consecrated place, (3) cemetery.

honor is even better defended when it is not defended by law; whatever is prescribed by honor becomes even more obligatory when it is not required by law." And why should anyone think of prescribing for something that no one would dream of transgressing?

In reality, the group knows no other code than that of honor, which demands that the crime, whether murder, insult or adultery, should contain within itself its own punishment; it has no court of law other than public opinion; each individual passes sentence on himself in accordance with the common and inwardly felt code of the group, and without interference from any power placed outside and above. It will be objected that the

council of the clan or village acts as a court of law, that it
promulgates "a code of law" (*qanoun*) that is sometimes put
in writing, that it sees to the preservation of law and order and
has at its disposal a whole system of punishments, penalties,
reprisals and banishment. But rather than a court of law in the
sense of a specialized organism charged with pronouncing ver-
dicts in conformity with a system of formal, rational and explicit norms, the assembly is in fact a council of arbitration and
perhaps even a family council. Thus it is that lawsuits concerning an agricultural association or boundary disputes are usually
settled by the judgment of close acquaintances, either neighbors
or relatives, of the two parties. For more serious questions the
assembly often limits itself merely to exhorting the two parties to
come to an agreement. This is because collective opinion is at
once the law, the law court and the agent entrusted with carrying out the punishment. The *tajmaât,* in which all the families
are represented, is the incarnation of this public opinion, whose
values and sentiments it both feels and interprets. The most
dreaded punishment is ostracism. Those who are sentenced to it
are excluded from the *timechret',* from the council and from
all communal activities, so that it is really equivalent to a sym-
bolical putting to death. It is, then, the sentiment either of honor
or justice, which, according to each particular case, dictates both
judgment and punishment, and not a rational and formal justice.
The collective oath, a last resort when all attempts at concilia-
tion and all other methods of proof have failed, merely reveals
with greater clarity the underlying principle of the whole
system. The refusal to take the oath is inspired by the belief that
perjury bears within itself its own punishment, and for this
reason refusal to swear the oath is deemed a confession. The
collective oath is an ordeal, that is to say it is at once a trial,
a proof, a judgment and a punishment, the sentence and the
punishment being an integral part of the trial; the true judge
is not the *tajmaât,* which is a mere witness charged with seeing
that the forms of a debate that exceeds its competence are respected, a debate which brings face to face without intermediary
the two parties swearing the oath and the supernatural powers
charged with ratifying the sentiment of equity that men bear

within themselves by associating punishment with wrong-doing. The collective oath may be understood as the invocatory expectation of the restoration of a hidden unity, that connection between crime and punishment which the innate sentiment of justice experiences as a necessary inner correlation prior to all experience. In short, the foundations on which justice is based are not comprehended as such, nor are they understood as a system of formal and rational standards, but rather they are unanimously lived, acted upon and experienced, the community of sentiment being rooted in the sentiment of the community.

The principles which govern the social organization are similarly affected. The cohesion of the group is based less on an objective and rational organization, as in our society, than on the communal feeling which makes any truly political institutions superfluous. Within the clan or village community the fundamental values transmitted by an indisputable tradition are admitted by all without having to be explicitly and deliberately affirmed. The reason for this is that the political institution is given life and animation through the organic attachment of the individual to the community; it is based on sentiments that are actually felt and not on formulated principles, on common presuppositions which are so intimately admitted and so little debated that there is no need to justify them, to prove them or to enforce them. It can be understood, then, that such a system can only function on the level of the agnatic family group, of which all its members feel themselves to be united by effective ties of kinship and bound by direct and intimate relationships. As the political units grow larger, these sentiments become more superficial and fragile. Thus this type of society has the same limits as those sentiments on which it is based. The transition to a wider form of democracy would presuppose that the mutation by which sentiments are converted into principles had been accomplished. By the very reason of the intensity of communal sentiments, the rules on which the community is based do not need to be made to appear as imperatives. They permeate the living reality of manners and customs. The gentilitial democracy does not have to define itself in order to exist; perhaps it even exists with a much greater vitality in proportion as the senti-

ments on which it is based are less defined. In the Kabyle democracy, the ideal of a democracy seems to have been realized; indeed,
without the intervention of any restraint other than the pressure
of public opinion, the will of the individual is immediately and
spontaneously made to conform to the general will. But this
ideal is put into effect only in so far as it is not realized as an
ideal, not objectively formulated as a formal and abstract principle, but instead felt as a sentiment, as something immediately
and inwardly manifest.

2. The Shawia

A vast mountainous quadrilateral situated between the High Plains and the Saharan borders, the Aurès is cut by deep and parallel valleys (the Wadi el Abiod, inhabited by the tribe of the Ouled Daoud; the Wadi el Abdi, inhabited by the Ouled Abdi) which present varying natural zones corresponding to the different climatic levels: at its base, the desert, with oases and date palms; at the 2,400- to 4,500-foot level, orchards and irrigated cereal crops; in the cool zone of the upper valleys and the northern slope, fruit trees and pasture lands. Except in a few favored regions, the economy of the Aurès, dominated by the scarcity of arable soil and the dictates of climate, is based on a combination of agriculture and stock raising. The prominence and importance given to transhumance (the periodic movement of flocks between regions of varying climate) may be ascribed partly to the role that the flock plays in maintaining the economic balance of the group and partly to the geographical location of these groups. Less poor than the other tribes, and above all more numerous, the Ouled Abdi and the Ouled Daoud take full advantage of the wide range of possibilities offered them by the different levels of terrain and the diversity of climatic regions: culture of cereals on the uplands, in the irrigated valleys and in the oases; horticulture and arboriculture in the valleys; stock raising which involves the transhumance of the animals; and, finally, exploitation of the resources of the zone bordering the Sahara.

The Shawia territory has long existed as a closed economy, with its needs strictly measured to conform to its resources. The primary group lives in almost complete self-sufficiency, as (apart from the difference in the tasks performed by men and women) there is practically no division of labor except for a few semi-specialized or specialized artisans. The man is called upon to do the major part of the work of the fields, while the woman, through her handicrafts, procures for the group certain of its

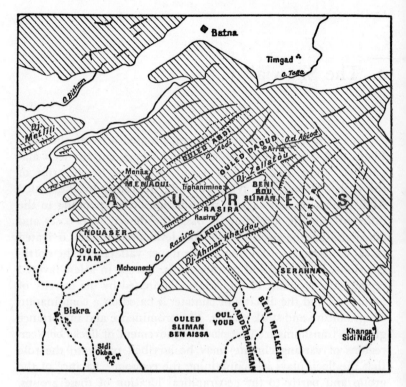

Fig. 5. The Tribes of the Aurès

most needed resources. The great summer markets, which generally coincide with the great pilgrimages (Djebel Bous), were formerly the occasion for the most important exchanges. Any large purchases designed to build up the group's reserves were made in the form of exchanges in kind, "head for head" as the Shawia would say. Besides this commerce directly connected with agriculture, there is the commerce engaged in by itinerant peddlers who are usually Kabyles. Thus has developed an economy of response to needs, established on a principle of "autoconsumption," implying the existence of reserves whose use is controlled by a very rigid discipline. There are relatively few commercial exchanges, and even these few are rarely motivated by the desire to make a profit. The result is that the family group is its own agent of production and distribution and a market for its own goods. In other words, it lives in itself, through itself and for itself.

Two of the southeastern tribes, while having all the characteristics of the other Shawia groups, speak Arabic and call themselves Arabs. The Shawia language is thus strongly marked by Arabic influence. The populations located to the south of the Ahmar Khaddou come down to do business in the markets of the small, Arabicized cities of the Sahara; twice a year Arab nomads cross the massif, making their way through the valleys and trading the salt of the Sahara for cereals and fruit. The Shawia are Moslems; they receive some rudiments of a religious education, are unanimous in practicing the rule of fasting and display a deep reverence for their marabouts, who are often of foreign origin. However, because of its location and particularly because of its physicial structure, the closed country of the Aurès has preserved the Shawia from any ethnic admixture. Their isolation has helped to make them a homogeneous group and has assured the permanence of the ancient social structures. It is principally because of differences in the way of living that a distinction may be made between the sedentary peoples of the fertile valleys of the northwest, who are engaged in the growing of cereals and in arboriculture and who live in large villages, and the semi-nomads of the near-desert valleys of the southeast, herders of goats and sheep, cultivators of wheat and barley, who live sparsely settled in widely scattered dwellings or, for part of the year, in tents. These groups, brought into association by their commercial exchanges, have identical social structures.

Domestic Organization

In addition to being an economic unit the family is also a social and religious unit. Within the family the husband is legally the master, although the wife does, in fact, take the lead in numerous matters; through her influence she plays an important part in the management of affairs and by her work at handicrafts helps the family to be self-supporting.

The grandfather, the chief who is consulted, honored and

obeyed (as in Kabylia), has complete authority over his children and grandchildren, who live under the same roof or in contiguous dwellings, so that people of the same group are quartered in the same area. The extended family of the patriarchal type is the fundamental social unit. Its cohesion is protected and maintained by the system of matrimonial alliances and also by different judicial measures (e.g., the right of pre-emption, the disinheritance of women, etc.) designed to conserve for the males the ownership of an undivided patrimony, as in Kabylia. Solidarity is most strongly displayed between members of the same clan, for the giving of mutual aid is in certain cases restricted to this group (work of the fields, construction of houses; cf. Kabylia). On the family also falls the duty of giving help to the unfortunate, and the hospitality offered to a stranger is considered inviolable. The power and unity of the family is also displayed in affairs of honor: quarrel, fight, lawsuit or crime. The vital principle animating the group is undoubtedly a sense of honor, that gentilitial pride which is the basis for fraternal solidarity in the carrying out of communal tasks or in the avenging of an offense committed against a member of the group.

The primacy of the group is also evident in the question of marriage. According to a Shawia proverb, "For a girl there is only marriage or the tomb." The Shawia woman, like the Kabyle woman, is married very young, and her father has the right to compel her to marry. Although, as in Kabylia, she may be betrothed while still very young, it is not rare, however, for her to make her own choice of a husband after she has reached the age of puberty. In any case the young man prefers to choose a woman from within his own clan (the daughter of a paternal uncle or, failing that, of a maternal uncle) through a desire to draw closer the family ties.

While the group exerts less pressure than it does in Kabylia on matters pertaining to the deciding of the marriage, it nevertheless reacts with vigor when its "honor" is compromised by adultery on the part of the wife. The husband is the sole judge of the punishment to be inflicted, which can be either repudiation or the penalty of death, but his family, through the pressure of threats and through censure, ensures that he carry out a proper vengeance.

The distinctiveness of the system lies in the status of the wife. Since the education of the daughter is entrusted to her mother, who teaches her her household tasks and her social duties, the little Shawian girl is from the outset rapidly initiated into the secrets, intrigues, ruses and tricks of feminine society, and so feels very strongly that sentiment of solidarity, bordering on complicity, which unites women across differences in age and social condition and which is constantly being strengthened by their common cares and toil and, above all, by their need to unite against a "common adversary," man. This society of women, strong in the magic by which it hopes to assure its domination over men, strong in its cohesion and, in both Aurès and Kabylia, in its tireless activity (care of the children, domestic tasks, handicrafts, work in the fields), is one of the characteristics of North African civilization.

Perhaps as a consequence of the above, another paradoxical feature is the separation between woman's very unfavorable legal situation and her relatively favorable actual situation. While the life of the Shawia woman is very hard, primarily because of the many heavy tasks she is called upon to perform, and while, in early marriage, her actual situation corresponds to her legal situation—complete submission to her husband who may exercise over her the "right of correction" and who allows her no say in important decisions—she nevertheless rapidly acquires considerable influence. She will tolerate neither polygamy nor infidelity on the part of her husband and prefers divorce. Within the home the husband and wife are, in fact, equals; the wife has an advisory, if not a decisive, voice in domestic affairs, with the sole exception of the budget and the management of the reserves. Women have even been known to take part in political disputes (quarrels of the çoffs). Another feature is that the marriage payment remains to such a degree her property that she may, if she wishes, reduce its amount by subtracting from it the theoretical sum she might be called upon to contribute to the future almsgiving of her husband, or she may allow her husband complete use of the marriage payment, which thereby becomes a purely nominal sum. She does this to avoid being bound by any conjugal ties and to reserve for herself the possibility of a divorce without restitution of the matrimonial compensation. Moreover, the Shawia woman, who like the Kabyle woman could be arbitrarily repudiated by her husband, has eagerly availed herself of the possibilities offered her by the appointment in 1866 of Moslem cadis judging in accordance with Moslem law, which authorizes a wife to demand the dissolution of a marriage. As happens whenever a cultural borrowing occurs, the borrowed feature is reinterpreted in terms of its receiving context; but the borrowing itself would not have been made except that the receiving context demanded it in the first place. Thus, while women in Kabylia have taken little advantage of the new possibilities offered them, in Aurès on the contrary, because it fulfilled a collective need, this institution has been rapidly adopted. The wife does in fact have the power to obtain a divorce: the reasons given in support of her request are usually only pretexts which hide the desire either to achieve the status of *azriya* (a free woman) or to make a new marriage. The method of obtaining a divorce is quite ingenious: the Shawia wife causes her husband to repudiate her by issuing a sort of challenge to which the husband can reply only by repudiating her. This conduct may be considered symbolic of the relationships existing between the sexes in Shawia society. Legally, only the husband has the right of repudiation, but in this case it is the woman who incites him to use this right and is really using it against him through his own action. Thus, generally speaking, the wife has a strong and real authority, although officially all authority is exercised by the husband.

A final feature is that the repudiated wife or widow becomes *azriya* until she remarries. The *azriya*, literally the wife who has no husband, behaves like a courtesan. Showered with attentions, she wields considerable influence, since she is considered to have certain religious powers. Thus, religious ceremonies and even certain communal tasks could not possibly be performed without the accompaniment of her singing and dancing. The Shawia woman possesses, then, a liberty that is unusual in North African

society, especially when she has the status of a widow or of a
repudiated wife; but it would be wrong to consider her influence as being particularly unusual. It is probable that she owes
her privileged position to her role of sorceress and "agrarian
priestess." The woman alone may enter into communication
with the world of magic, a magic that is primarily amatory but
may also be maleficent, divinatory or medical in nature. Women,
therefore, particularly elderly women, are the object of a super-
stitious respect bordering on fear. Woman is also the guardian
and organizer of agrarian rites, designed either to favor the crops
and fields or to protect them against various dangers, such as the
evil eye and evil spirits.

In short, the situation of the Shawia woman, apparently en-
slaved and without rights but in reality invested with immense
prestige and influence, may perhaps be considered, although as
a borderline case, to offer an enlarged and so more easily interpreted image of the paradoxical status of the North African
woman. To account for this paradox, the hypothesis of survivals
has sometimes been put forward. But while the structure of
an institution does indeed depend on its prior history, its significance depends on its functional position within the social
system of which it forms a part at a given moment. In this way
the opposition between the masculine and the feminine worlds
is illustrated not only in the division of labor between the two
sexes with, for example, the hard work of hoeing the fields fall-
ing to the women while the men handle the team and the plow,
but also in political life and in the legal status of the two sexes,
in the ritual practices, and in the whole social outlook; the
opposition between the two complementary principles, masculine
and feminine, appears to constitute one of the fundamental categories of Shawia thought and of North African thought in general. Similarly certain cultural traits which seem out of place
in a society based on patrilinear descent—the fact, for example,
that the son of the *azriya* who is born out of wedlock is taken into
the mother's clan[1]—could be explained by reference to the am-

---

[1] Observers have noted here a case of filiation on the mother's side
analogous to that which may be observed among the Touaregs in connection
with the *tamesroit*, a free woman whose status is very similar to that of
azriya.

biguous status of the married woman. Does she belong to her
husband's clan or does she remain attached to her clan of origin?
The marriage ceremonies include rites intended to "make her
forget the way to her parents' house," but she continues to bear
her father's name, and, should she become a widow, she returns
to live among her brothers instead of remaining with her
brothers-in-law.

The Social Structures

Each social unit has its own name, which is considered to be
the name of the common ancestor. The members of the most
restricted group, the extended family, consider themselves to be
really descended from the ancestor whose name they bear. In the
larger units, the clan (*harfiqt*) and particularly the tribe (*ârch*),
this name is sometimes that of the most important or the oldest
of the sub-groups, sometimes the result of an arbitrary choice.
The *harfiqt* is the most organic and most distinctive social unit.
It bears the name of the common ancestor who is the object of an
annual ceremony of worship; in the case in which it is made up
of a pure agnatic group, it includes all the male descendants of
the common ancestor, all the "sons of the paternal uncle," as the
Shawia say. It can also be formed by a fragment of an agnatic
group or even by the association of several agnatic groups, in
which case, although the members claim to be related, the bond
uniting them is in reality a fraternity based on mutual agreement. In the latter case, the *harfiqt* is divided into subgroups
of different degrees of relationship. In other words, even when
merely an association of different groups, it is by taking the
extended family, the genealogically based unit, as its model
that the *harfiqt* proves and establishes its own unity. But since
the Shawia may be divided into "sedentary peoples" and "nomads" (in a very relative sense since the "nomads" own land and
the "sedentary peoples" own flocks), can the clan be said to
have the same function and the same structure in both types of
people? While it is true that among the "sedentaries" of the
North living in villages, the *harfiqt* may be compared rather to

a village section, whereas among the nomads it may be compared to a clan which lives in tents the greater part of the time, nevertheless this contrast must not be exaggerated. For even among the sedentary peoples cohesion is never based on the territorial bond alone, as is proven by the cult of the common ancestor and by the fact that marriages are arranged by preference within the clan, preferably with a parallel cousin, with the purpose of strengthening family ties. The clan is then the strongest social unit; the members of the *harfiqt* are obliged to defend its patrimony (women, lands and dwellings) and above all its honor, the supreme value, more precious than life itself.

The council of the clan retained until 1954 the main judicial powers (in spite of the reforms of 1865) and continued to decide lawsuits in accordance with local custom. In addition to handling almost all marriages and divorces, it arbitrated civil differences by using the traditional mode of proof, the collective oath; it imposed penalties, presided over the rulings of the *diia* which were made in accordance with a strict ritual, tried cases relating to inheritances, etc.

The organization of the *guelâa*, the granary-citadel, was also the business of the *harfiqt*.[2] Each agglomeration has several fortified houses in which the harvests are stored during the absences made necessary by the semi-nomadic existence. Formerly these granaries were also fortresses and observation posts; among the Touaba, they formed a sort of defensive line protecting the cultivated lands against the raids of the Abdaoui. The *guelâa*, the cornerstone of the economic life of the group, is also a center for its social life: around the *guelâa*, the many factors relating to the economic life of the group have been combined into what might be called a collective institution—the foresight required to ensure a good harvest at some future date, the right vested in the head of the family to control consumption, the life-long privations that the Shawia must impose upon himself even in

[2] In many regions, the clan *guelâa* was abandoned some years ago in favor of granaries common to a whole village or tribe. As the clan has lost its importance this tendency has increased, particularly in correlation with the development of private property (made possible by the facilities afforded by the *Senatus Consulte*) and with the resulting increase in sales of land.

times of plenty. Conscious of the fundamental role of the collective granary as a regulating force that is indispensable for the
maintenance of a precarious economic balance, the council of
the *harfiqt* decides on its construction and also prescribes with
extreme precision and ingenuity how it will operate and function.
It is the council of the elders who decide on the guardians who
will be responsible for the protection against theft and the upkeep of the building. In a society that lives as a closed economy
cut off from the normal currents of monetary exchange and that
is in any case quite unaccustomed to financial speculation, the
accumulation of goods in kind (barley and wheat, salted meat
and dried fruits, honey or rancid butter), which in such a system
have more value than money, constitutes the only assurance
against the uncertainty of the future and the only possible form
in which reserves may be built up. To add to the importance of
the *guelâa*, it frequently happens, as in the upper valley of the
Wadi el Abiod, that an ancestor is buried either within it or
close to it. The group then is dominated by the granary, which
is also the holy place where a great many family rituals, such
as marriages and circumcisions, formerly took place; the annual
pilgrimages to the tomb of the ancestor were accompanied by
sacrifices and were followed by a communal meal. The collective
granary, as a tangible symbol of the power of the group, of its
wealth and of its cohesion, was invested with a meaning and
function at once social and religious, economic and sentimental.

Thus the *harfiqt* appears to be the widest social unit that
can function properly in a system in which all social groups are
patterned on the model of the family group. The wider social
units are, in fact, less cohesive and less permanent in nature;
so it is with the village, which has little social life of its own and
is rarely provided with an assembly house; so it is also with the
tribe, because of the fact that gatherings of groups belonging to
the same tribe are rarely held, apart from the great assemblies
that meet for war, or for making decisions as to the transhumance
of the animals and the allotment of collective lands, or for the
great annual markets. Political and military units, organizations
which are created only for special circumstances, the tribes are
aligned in accordance with their allegiance to the two great *çoffs*

centered respectively on the Ouled Abdi and the Ouled Daoud. As in Kabylia, the çoffs ensure a balance of power through the interplay of compensating tensions. "A restricted world which becomes conscious of itself as a group only when faced with enemies camped on all its borders" (G. Tillion), each tribe is unable to make war against any of its neighbors without exposing one of its flanks to the attacks of the tribe on its opposite border. Thus it finds itself faced with two tribes which are united in coalition but which are in turn subjected to the same law: beyond these first enemies are allies; farther on, still other enemies. Each çoff controls one valley; the inhabitants of two confluent valleys belong to opposing çoffs. Sometimes the çoff overflows through the passes onto the territory of its adversary. In the Saharan Aurès, among those groups that are attached to the two great leagues of the northern Aurès, the distribution of the two çoffs exhibits this same alternating arrangement, each village being the adversary of the two neighboring villages that are situated above and below it in the valley.

Genealogy appears as the model on which all social units have been conceived. But this model has also been applied to other domains—domains as different as the prescription of festivals or the decisions as to transhumance, the making of survey plans, the distribution of dwellings or the arrangement of the tombs in the cemetery. Thus it was that in the investigations of the *Senatus Consulte* they observed a jumble of habitats and of properties which seemed quite meaningless. "Among the O. Abdi and the O. Daoud," wrote Lartigue, "the organization was so confused that we had no success in attempting to divide these tribes into territorial *douars*"; thus in the Wadi el Abiod, the five clans of the Ouled Daoud have interspersed their properties all along the valley, with the result that lands of two, three, indeed of all the clans may be found in each of the villages. Except in Menâa, the fourteen sub-groups of the Ouled Abdi are mixed up in checkerboard fashion; the same situation prevails among the Beni-Bou-Slimane, whether it is a question of the location of lands under cultivation, of pasture lands or of dwelling places. The statement of a member of the tribe of the Beni Melkem as to the principles that determine the arrange-

ment of the tombs in the cemetery may give us the key to the
way in which the lands are distributed: "There are five cemeteries in the *ârch;* a person may be buried in any of these, but it
must be in the area allotted to his *harfiqt*. The dead are buried towards the east, but in places where the limits of the *hirfiqin*
(plural of *harfiqt*) may be confused, the tombs are built slightly
slanted in order to distinguish them. Every *harfiqt* has an area
in which each family has its own row, and people of the same
family are always buried beside one another in this row" (G. Tillion; a similar organization may be noted in Kabylia). Thus,
since several localities are possible, there is only one restriction
on choice; the site must be selected in the area allotted to the
harfiqt, for its distinctiveness must be maintained at all costs.
Similarly at Mzira, a Saharan village belonging to the tribe of
the Ouled Abderrahmane, the underground dwellings are divided
according to clans, with an empty space being left between
the *harfiqt* areas (T. Rivière). It appears that the same model
is followed in the division of property; it is as though the interlocking distribution of territories were the result of a calculation of maximum and minimum; it allows the different groups
to disperse their territory to the maximum degree (this quest
for dispersion being inspired by the desire to avail themselves as
widely as possible of the range of natural resources), perhaps over
the whole expanse of a valley, but always within the limits imposed by the necessity of giving the strongest possible cohesion
to the *harfiqt,* the very foundation stone of social equilibrium.

3. The Mozabites

In the northern Sahara is situated the unusually desolate *chebka* of the Mzab. The word *chebka,* Arabic for "net," is a good description of this monotonous and fantastic landscape, this rocky plateau, the *hamada,* in which the dried-up valleys of the Saharan wadis stand out like a mesh around the mass of rocky pillars, or *gours,* that have resisted erosion. This "desert within a desert" is cut by the valley of the Wadi Mzab, in which are situated the five cities of the Mozabites.

The Challenge of the Desert

On the whole there are few countries so ill-favored by nature: a soil almost exclusively rocky; in the bottom of the wadis, sandy beds, which were originally unfit for cultivation and which have had to be prepared at the cost of extraordinary and continuous effort; a climate characterized by the torrid excesses of summer, by considerable variations in temperature, and by the extreme dryness of the air; a precarious mode of existence, dependent on the torrential rains that cause the wadi to overflow every two or three years, requiring endless toil to wrest the water from the ground. The good years are those of which they can say, *"L'oued a porté"*—the wadi has overflowed its banks. Thus the very fact of the existence of palm groves presupposes a truly continuous process of creation, or rather a continuing miracle. Day after day amid a grinding of chains, asses and camels must pull the leather containers which pour out into the irrigation basins the water drawn from the depths of the wells. Adaptation to the natural surroundings demands an extremely strong social cohesion, and one of the reasons why such a cohesion is required is to ensure the functioning of the marvelously clever system of irrigation and water supply: the cliffside is ringed by a network of collecting canals which receive the water from the run-off and lead it into reservoirs; in the construction of dams designed to permit the utilization of these periodic overflows, the same skill is displayed.

But this masterpiece of conversion, as well as demanding an enormous output of energy, also consumes the greater part of the revenues. Oases and gardens require enormous quantities of water to "wash the earth." The expenses entailed in the extraction of the water, the pay of the workers and the work of cultivation, are not repaid by the relatively scanty yield. Everything contributes to making a ruinous luxury of these gardens and summer homes. As Gautier has written: "The oases . . . could not long exist on their own resources. . . . The oases system is a vicious circle, a financial paradox, or, more accurately, a millionaire's whim." We shall now attempt to explain the how and the why of this paradox.

The Mozabites are Kharedjite Abadhites (a sect of Islam), who owe their name to the fact that they formed a dissident group against Ali, the fourth caliph, son-in-law of the Prophet, in the name of two principles that they derived from a strict interpretation of the Koran, considered as the unique law to which nothing can be added or taken away, namely, that all believers are equal and that every action is either good or bad, arbitration as to the rightness or wrongness of these acts being allowed only in exceptional circumstances. Thus these equalitarian rigorists, according to whom religion must be vivified not only by faith but also by works and purity of conscience, who attach great value to pious intention, who reject the worship of saints, who watch over the purity of morals with extreme severity, could be called the Protestants and Puritans of Islam.

The prime consideration in the building of the cities of the Mzab was to defend this religious exclusivism. The result has been that the Abadhites have had to impose upon themselves increasingly difficult living conditions during the course of their turbulent history.[1] The first five cities were built within fifty

[1] Since they were considered heretics, the Kharedjites were obliged to flee from persecution; they established in 761 the kingdom of Tahert which fell in 909 to the attacks of the Fatimides. They then moved to Sedrata, near Ouargla, and from there to the Mzab.

years after the founding of El Ateuf in 1011; all are situated in
the same wadi within close range of one another, with the exception of the two more recent (seventeenth century) cities of
Guerrara and Berriane.

It is the history, then, of these "dissenters" that reveals the
reason for this paradoxical settlement, created in defiance of
natural conditions. But how has man managed to have the last
word in this desperate debate with the desert? The explanation
is that the life, the survival, of the cities of the Mzab is dependent on temporary emigration and on the commercial undertak-
ings (one-third of the male population lives outside the Mzab)
which allow the Mozabite to acquire the capital needed to assure
the upkeep of the oases and the expensive cultivation of the palm
groves. But this solution itself poses a problem: if it is true that
"the real Mzab is not in the Mzab," that "all its strength is . . .
in the small groups of Mozabite merchants scattered all through
Algeria," how has the cohesiveness of the whole been maintained
against all the forces of dispersion? How, moreover, have these
rigorous Puritans been able to become financiers, specialists in
big business and high finance, without disavowing their devout
heterodoxy in any way? How can a keen understanding of
capitalistic techniques be united in the same persons with the
most intense forms of a piety that penetrates and dominates their
whole life? How is it that this religious society—tightly closed
upon itself, anxious to assert itself as being different—has been
able to participate in a completely modern economic system without letting itself be affected or impaired in any way and, at the
same time, preserve its own originality intact?

The Mozabite culture finds the basis for its cohesion in the
wealth of its historical, legendary and doctrinal traditions, in
the smooth, harmonious adjustment of the groups within the
different communities, in the ingenious working of the *ittifâqât*,
the written codes that contain many principles of jurisprudence
and, finally, in a doctrine that is both flexible and rigid, and
which determines a way of life that is quite distinctive in North
Africa.

Social Structure and City Government

The cities of the Mzab, built in close proximity to one
another, are the result of the carrying out of a rational plan.
The *h'orm* is the sacred territory in which stand the five cities
of the Mzab proper and in which the observance of the true
faith is maintained, free from any contamination; thus departures
or returns are accompanied by a ritual deconsecration and con-
secration. The city of Ghardaïa is situated on the left bank of the
Wadi Mzab. Downstream on the same bank is Beni Isguen, the
sacred city of the Abadhite doctors and jurists, the city of a
resolute traditionalism set stubbornly against any heretical innovations. Opposite Beni Isguen is Melika, the stronghold of
juridical conservatism. Farther along are Bou Noura and El
Ateuf, whose activity has greatly declined in recent times. Finally,
there are the two eccentric cities of Berriane, the commercial
center, and Guerrara, the center of the reformist movement.

Ghardaïa is laid out in the form of an ellipse: at the highest
point is the mosque; below it are streets which rise up the hill-
side one above the other in concentric circumvolutions and which
are themselves cut by perpendicular streets descending like spokes
to the base of the hill; at the foot of this hill and at the edge of
the city is the market place, cut lengthwise by a main thorough-
fare; beyond this is a polygonal, wide-angled wall. All around
the city extend cemeteries and waste ground. The mosque then
appears to have been the center around which the city was
created, and history confirms this fact. At once a stronghold,
a religious edifice and, in certain cases, a storehouse like the
guelâa, it assures the moral and material protection of the city
living in its shadow. The cities of the Mozabites, like the life of
the people, have two very distinct centers: the mosque and the
market place. The mosque, the center of religious life, has driven
back the market place, the center of economic life and of profane, or secular, activities:[2] the houses are piled up like toy

[2] All business is forbidden in the area of the mosque; on the market
square and in five of the streets adjacent to it are situated 60 per cent of
the business establishments.

building blocks and rise in tiers as if attracted and drawn up
by the mosque, which prolongs their ascent with the skyward
soaring of its minaret. Moreover, the secular part of the city is
shut in, as it were, between the mosque and those immense
necropolises which surround the Mozabite cities, great fields of
anonymous tombs among which stand chapels and sanctuaries,
in which solemn public ceremonies take place and where even
the judicial assizes are held, as if to affirm the solidarity of the
living and the dead. The cemetery, the immense, projected
shadow of the living city, is doubtless, as it is in North Africa
in general, the foundation and the symbol of the unbreakable
bond which unites a man to his soil. It is the religious duty of
the Abadhites to ensure that they are buried in the Mzab. Each
clan has its own separate cemetery, named after the ancestor
who, according to tradition, is buried there. Finally, the plan
of the city gives an indication of the social structure. The extended family, the basic indivisible element, groups together
people of the same name, descended to the fourth or fifth
generation from a common ancestor. The clan, which unites
several extended families, generally has its own district, its own
cemetery, its eponymous ancestor and its own patrimony. Certain
clans join together not only several families but also several
already constituted sub-clans. The ancestor of the clan or sub-
clan is worshiped at an annual ceremony, when, standing before
the group assembled at the cemetery, the "notables" recall the
memory of the revered personage and give advice to the young
members of the group; the ceremony then concludes with a
communal meal. The clan, the fundamental unit, has its own
common treasury, its assembly house, its council made up of
all the adults who assemble to deal with affairs of common
interest (the adoption of orphans, the inflicting of punishment
or censure, decisions as to collective labor and allotment of
tasks, preparations of family ceremonies, etc.). The "great" men
(or "notables"), renowned for their piety, their virtue and their
wisdom, actually direct and know the "secrets" of the group's
business; they sometimes form a restricted assembly which meets
in the presence of one of the members of the *halqa*. Clan ties,
which remain very strong even among the emigrants to the

cities, have become even stronger with the reduction in the power of the *çoffs* (of the east and west), which used to quarrel violently at the slightest pretext. The division into *çoffs* is now a thing of the past, as witness the fact that intermarriages between *çoffs* have become more and more frequent.

Each clan designates its own chief and selects several elders from different families to represent it, and these men, together with the magistrates, form the *djemâa;* the latter formerly would meet at the *haouita,* an elliptical area marked out by twenty-six stones which had been borrowed from certain tombs and laid out on the market square, as if judicial deliberations and political debates affecting decisions on temporal matters sought the scene of commercial activity and secular dealings but were, at the same time, invoking the protection of the dead.

Just as the secular city is dominated by the mosque, all secular or political activity and the body through which it finds expression, the council of laymen, is dominated by the priests. The latter generally live in close proximity to the mosque and are divided into two groups, the major clergy, animated by a profound religious rigorism, and the minor clergy. The council of laymen has legislative and judicial power as it does in Kabylia and the Aurès. However, in the Mzab, it has no authority or effective power itself and is often limited merely to ensuring that decisions are carried out. For all questions of importance it assembles in the mosque in the presence of the "circle," a council composed of twelve representatives of the major clergy under the presidency of a *cheikh* or *sheik,* chosen by the clergy to be the local leader in religious affairs. These meetings are also sometimes held in the cemeteries, as if to strengthen the authority of the clergy, who are the custodians of ancestral tradition and final arbiters in any matter that depends on the observance of principles contained in the Koran or in the works of Abadhite doctrine. Among the members of the lay *djemâa,* only the "notables" are allowed to speak, and the role of the elders consists merely of attending the meetings and giving their assent. It is also from among the major clergy that the Mozabite cadi is elected. This magistrate judges cases both in accordance with the law of the Koran and according to the *ittifâqât,* the written compilation of Mozabite customs. These *ittifâqât,* which can be modified at any time to settle current problems, but which are always interpreted by reference to religious jurisprudence, govern political life as well as private morals and provide for archaic but very formidable punishments—bastinado, fines, banishment and excommunication, the latter being the supremely dreaded punishment which excludes the guilty person from the religious and social community and entails the loss of all his rights. Generally speaking, no important decision, no civil regulation, no new prohibition, no sanction against a serious crime, is taken without the intervention of the "circle." The chapter of priests, which also supplies the dignitaries of the mosque, the iman, the muezzin, the masters of the Koranic schools, and above all the five "priests who wash the dead" and who are at the same time "censors of morals" endowed with an immense moral authority, possesses considerable power. Since all Mozabites are equal with one exception—unless the rather hazy distinction between the *acils,* the descendants of the first inhabitants of the city and the *nazils,* the more recent arrivals, can also be counted as an exception—and since the exception lies in the superiority of the clergy over the laity, one can safely call this form of government a theocracy. No doubt the clergy holds itself apart from daily affairs and leaves to the assembly of laymen the care of temporal matters, authorizing it to draw up the *ittifâqât* concerning the organization of the city. Doubtless, too, laymen have a voice in the government of the city through their representatives on the assemblies who must always be consulted (before giving sentence of excommunication, for example); but, in case of conflict, the clergy always has the last word, because it possesses formidable weapons—excommunication against individuals and against the community, the suspension of all religious activities.[3]

Thus the consistory which rules the cities is at once an assembly of the elders and a moral authority. The *ittifâqât,* in which is expressed the scrupulously detailed realism already

[3] The authority of the clergy has been steadily weakened in the past twenty years. The lay *djemâa* is tending to free itself from the control of the priests and to dispute their right to judicial and legislative powers, although the sheik of the *halqa* (the circle) still has the duty of verifying whether decisions have been made in conformity with Abadhite doctrine.

noted in the Kabyle or Shawia customary laws—the constant and
meticulous intervention of the group being grounded in this case
in the religious doctrine—illustrate the whole coherent complexity of the Mozabite moral order, the basis for one of the
most astonishing of social successes, and the key to this miracle
of combining a completely successful adaptation to modern innovations with a total fidelity to an extremely strict tradition.

The opposition between clergy and laity, between the sacred
and the profane worlds, is echoed by the contrast between the
more or less extended political group and the fundamental social
unit of the agnatic type, between the wider and therefore less
substantial solidarities and the narrow particularisms which
find their strength in family sentiment. No doubt all the Mozabites are conscious of belonging to a larger unit that one may,
for lack of a better word, call a confederation, a unit created (like
its Kabyle homologue) by circumstance. All the reasons favorable to a development beyond the particularism of the agnatic
groups seem here to be combined: an insular situation in a
hostile natural and human environment, the memory of a common past, the feeling of belonging to a religious community
distinguished by its excessive rigor and intransigence, "the
family of God," the chosen people. Although this religious faith,
established in opposition to the orthodox Mohammedan faith,
possesses an acute awareness of its uniqueness, its way of assert-
ing this fact consists primarily of emphasizing its essential differences. Attempts at political union by the cities appear to have
been made only from temporary motives, either political or
juridical in nature (for example, at the time of the submission
of the Mzab to French rule). The representatives of the Mozabite
cities would meet on neutral ground to deal with questions concerning the general interests of the Mozabite confederation. But
these attempts at synœcism, constantly compromised by a spirit
of particularism, would vanish with the situation that had
prompted them. Thus (as in Kabylia and Aurès), once the great
disturbances which led to a revival of the wider political organization had died down, a balance was re-established that was
based on the narrow social units of the agnatic type, since the
ties joining the cities had been created rather through their

combined opposition to external forces than through internal
cohesion.

Puritanism and Capitalism

When one becomes aware of the power of the forces of
dispersion, however, one realizes how great must be the forces
of integration: indeed, it seems that nothing can make the Mozabite break with his community—neither the hardness and severity
of the work on the ancestral land nor the attraction of the easier
way of life that he encounters in the cities of the Tell, neither the
charm of acquired riches (for it seems, as if in the fairy tale, the
gold becomes only sand outside the confines of the Mzab), nor
the long sojourns far from his family and the life of the community, neither banishment because of a murder committed
during a fight between the *çoffs*, nor the conflicts of interest
between cities, groups or individuals. All these disintegrating
influences are opposed by the extremely vigorous pressure that
the group exercises over all its members through the intermediary
of its religious doctrine, through the cohesion caused by its
intensely active religious life, through the constant presence of
religious law in every act of life and in the hearts of all men,
a religious law which is felt both as a rule of life imposed from
without and as an inner guide to conduct. Consequently, the
least concession or the slightest relaxation of the rule would
suffice to bring about the ruin of this society which has been
artificially constructed in an artificially created world (for example, the island of Djerba). It is only, then, through a purposeful rigorism and an exclusivism based on a high awareness of its
own originality and excellence, only by virtue of an affirmed
particularism conscious of its own identity, that Mozabite society
is able to resist disintegration. Even when engaged in the most
secular activities of modern economic life, even when long separated from the center of his religious and social life, the Mozabite maintains unimpaired his attachment to the soil, to the
society and to the religion of the cities which remain for him
"the Ark of the Covenant, the closed cell in which the soul of

new generations is formed and developed in the rigid discipline
of the inviolate families and the theological atmosphere of the
seminaries" (E. F. Gautier).

The charm and the attractions of Tell lands cannot hold the
emigrants, because every device is used to impress upon them
—particularly those customs which require them to make periodic
returns to the Mzab both in order to maintain the permanence
of the group and to expose the emigrants once again to the
religious atmosphere—that the end of emigration is not emigration in itself, nor even what it can procure, but the conservation
of the group, the necessary condition for the survival of the
religious community. The fact is that by comparison with this
absolute imperative all else is relative. The religious doctrine
and the way of life that it inspires is the key to the Mozabite paradox. An attempt could no doubt be made to explain the
spirit and the success of this civilization by ecological determina-
tions; it might be claimed that, by reason of the poverty of their
land, the Mozabites could do nothing but emigrate and engage
in commercial pursuits, and this type of activity would, in any
case, have required them to display certain of the virtues that
their religious dogma imposes on them. But would it not be more
accurate to say that the doctrine and the rules for living that
it prescribes prepared the Mozabites for their success in the
world of business and for their adaptation to the modern economic system?

Since the unfathomable judgments of God are final and the
destiny of men, their election or their damnation, is fixed for all
eternity, faith is not sufficient in itself to assure salvation if it is
not made manifest by moral behavior and good works. The true
believer must maintain a happy medium between fear and hope;
he must neither rely entirely upon God for his salvation nor
abandon himself to his fate; neither despair absolutely of God
nor have absolute hope of salvation. By insisting on the absolute
transcendence and unity of Allah, the Abadhites refuse to recognize any mediation or intercession between man and God. Thus
they condemn the worship of saints. Intercession can only raise
the elect to a higher rank; it cannot open the gates of Paradise
to the sinner. Salvation can only be won through prayer, pious

living and hard work. Understood as a form of asceticism and as a discipline, work becomes a religious act and duty, while idleness is considered as one of the most serious vices. It often happens that the council will compel certain members of the group to go and work in the Tell and will undertake to find them a job. The lazy man often has much trouble in finding a wife. Worldly success can be based only on hard work, piety and respect for the precepts of the Koran; it is therefore regarded as a sign of election, especially when the accumulated wealth is devoted to praiseworthy ends (legal almsgiving, charity). Fierce defenders of the purity of public morals, desirous of returning to the very origins of their faith by a strict and literal interpretation of the sacred texts, the Abadhites condemn luxury as a sin, just as they condemn all human passions. In keeping with this, they reject celibacy, the use of tobacco, alcohol and perfumes, and disapprove highly of music and dancing. An activity is of no value unless it is intended to be pleasing to God and to provide a means of gaining Paradise, the seat of the infinite, intangible and invisible Divinity (who will remain so even in the hereafter). In such a society the ideal man is distinguished particularly by his moral qualities: the *taleb* must be wise, virtuous, detached from any desire for the goods of this world, pious and simple-hearted, devoid of all passion; he must conduct himself as a "living rule," do what he preaches and preach what he does. The religious doctrine also prescribes the virtues of honesty, exalts willpower and self-discipline, recommends an attitude of detachment in regard to the things of this world and strictly forbids prodigality. Any infraction of these principles is condemned by the *ittifâqât*. While they include articles resembling those of Berber customary law in their condemnation of murders, assaults and woundings, thefts, breaches in solidarity or in the respect due to women, these *ittifâqât* always include a good number of sumptuary regulations. Indeed, in the code of the city of Melika may be found a whole series of articles fixing the maximum value of the presents and gifts authorized for family festivals; other articles forbid any form of amusement. Thus, since he cannot spend on luxuries the money he has amassed, the Mozabite has no other recourse but to reinvest it.

Because this imposed asceticism in everyday life excludes any enjoyment of wealth, the accumulation of capital becomes an end in itself. Moreover, the religious doctrine holds as invalid those prayers whose meaning is not perfectly understood by those who recite them; the believer must know how to read and write the language of the Koran, and thus public education is the prime task of the clergy. As a matter of tradition there has always been much interest in education, even among the common people. The cultural associations and the Koranic schools receive very large subsidies. Having been provided with this minimum of learning demanded by religion, the Mozabite is equipped to engage in business pursuits. When reinterpreted, a number of precepts of the religious and social tradition take on a new meaning and function in the context of a modern economic system. Thus the mutual aid characteristic of the solidarity existing between members of the same faith, city or clan, is converted into a "commercial agreement," a buying cooperative, a limited partnership, and sometimes into a joint stock company. Generally speaking, the business establishments of the Tell are the property of the family group and, while the active partners control the finances, the profits are all returned to the family living back in the Mzab. Often the father employs his own sons or the uncle, his nephews; in most cases the employees are members of the owner's family or else come from the same clan or city. This "family" organization of the business enterprise allows the Mozabite merchants to sell at competitive prices; thanks to their very limited general expenses (expenditures being reduced to a minimum and labor costs not even being taken into account) they can be satisfied with a very small profit. With their early initiation into selling and accounting techniques, the Mozabites are highly efficient traders. Mutual aid is practiced on every possible occasion; the Mozabites exchange information (during their meetings at the mosque, for example) concerning prices and products, they grant each other loans and help newcomers to set up in business. In this way fidelity to the precepts of tradition, far from being an obstacle to their adaptation to the world of a competitive, capitalistic economic system, rather favors it and makes it easier.

The extremely strong cohesion of the family, combined with the sentiment of belonging to a unique religious community and the desire to remain faithful to this community, prevents the dispersion of this society while it makes possible the emigration of its members (cf. Kabylia). It is through the Mozabite woman, the real safeguard of the group, that the society of emigrants remains firmly attached to their homeland, as may be seen from the fundamental regulation, a true "law of public safety," which forbids any woman to leave the Mzab and by which is asserted the firm desire to preserve the community by preventing any permanent exodus. It is reported that in 1928 the whole population of Berriane combined to prevent a woman from leaving for Algiers.[4] This was done because it is felt that the women anchor the Mozabites to the land of their fathers, to their past and to their traditions, of which they, the women, are the guardians; under the surveillance of the elders, who watch over their conduct, they teach the children the fundamental virtues and strict respect for the laws.

Just as they do in the whole of North Africa, the Mozabite women form a society separate from the men. They have a special form of worship which includes many superstitions not recognized by the official religion, which is the concern of the men: they have their own magic, their own songs, their own special tasks or special methods of performing communal tasks, their own language that is original in its phonetics, vocabulary and phraseology. The separation of the masculine and feminine societies is almost complete (the veil which reveals only one eye, the reserved area in the mosque, etc.), and this helps to confer a certain autonomy on feminine society as is attested by the role of the women who wash the dead. These women exercise over the other women an authority analogous to that held by the twelve priests over the men. They are granted the power of excommunication, and their main task is to teach the other women the principles of religion and to watch over their conduct.

[4] The reformists have been endeavoring since 1953 to make it permissible for women to leave for the Tell. A certain number of Mozabites have taken their wives with them. Others have married the daughters of Mozabites already settled in the Tell.

The Interaction Between Permanence and Change

In order to understand a culture as coherent as that of the Mozabites, one must abandon the attempt to attribute everything to one particular cause. While it cannot be doubted that the challenge issued by an extremely hostile natural environment and their status as a minority group have made it imperative to react by this purposeful conduct, this incessant mobilization of all their energies, this tense, obstinate and stubborn effort to assure the survival of the group, in other words, by the very virtues demanded by their religion, it is nonetheless certain that by holding up work and mutual aid as sacred duties, by prescribing the giving up of luxuries and by inspiring in all the members of the religious community a strong sense of their distinctiveness and a firm resolve to defend their special way of life, the rigid, puritanical doctrine they profess has not only supplied them with weapons that were indispensable in overcoming natural obstacles but has given them the means and the will to succeed in the modern business world and, at the same time, has preserved them from the disintegration with which their society was threatened through contact with Western civilization. Everything is inseparably joined and connected, and consequently everything is at the same time cause and effect, and this holds true for dogma, for the natural and economic environment, and for the social and family structure. In each of these domains is manifest the whole spirit of this civilization, a building in which each stone may be considered a keystone. If we begin with any one of these cultural traits as the center of our investigations, it will be possible to recreate the entire culture, since there is no one trait that is not connected with all the others; thus the desolation and hostility of the natural environment refers us, on the one hand, to the irredentism and exclusivism of the religious doctrine which led to the choice of this environment and, on the other hand, to the system of emigration which permits this survival in the desert. But emigration itself presupposes, on the one hand, the religious doctrine, the guarantee of cohesion, which incites its followers to make a rational adaptation to their environment and which is regarded as the supreme value to be safeguarded by maintaining its economic foundations at all costs; and, on the other hand, emigration presupposes the strong cohesion of the family, the foundation of social equilibrium and the secure base for the emigrant. The stability and solidity of the family are themselves brought about by the religious doctrine, by the moral order established under the priestly government, and by the whole political organization; but the latter, in return, owes a great part of its coherence to the education given to the children by the family group, which is charged with teaching in accordance with precise, strictly defined methods, the respect for principles and the practice of virtues which are the basis for the society's existence.

It is not surprising, then, that a society so strongly conscious of its values, particularly those values that cannot be rejected without the loss of group identity, has been able to maintain its original character. After the annexation of the Mzab, certain observers debated the outcome of the clash between the traditionalist pentapolis and the rational and technical forces of the modern world, and predicted the rapid decadence of these cities of the desert. But in actual fact, while they have become businessmen and very astute financiers, the Mozabites maintain the custom of leaving behind their families and their homes in the desert, and continue to arrange to be buried in the soil of their own valley.

The resistance of a traditional group to the pressure of Western civilization cannot be based on willpower alone and must have at its disposal considerable material, spiritual and intellectual resources. The Mozabites are protected against disintegration by their wealth and by their admirable urban government. Thanks to their education they have been able to master modern commercial techniques and capitalistic practices sufficiently well to invest their assets in a highly competitive economy. Furthermore, their cities have never been in direct

Fig. 6. Simplified Plan of the City of Ghardaïa

Ghardaïa, the principal city of the Mzab, is built around its mosque which is situated at the highest point of the city (1,780 feet). Dominated by a minaret seventy-two feet high in the form of a pyramid which, in cross-section, measures twenty feet at the base and six feet at the top, the mosque is both a place for prayer and a fortress (the minaret serving as a watchtower), where the reserve provisions were formerly stored. Around this religious center the houses are laid out in concentric circles, as if to reduce as much as possible the distance they are separated from this center of religious life and also to reduce the length of the ramparts. The result is that the city presents the form of a pyramid made up of a series of ellipses laid out in tiers. Continuous streets surround the groups of houses (formerly occupied by distinct social units), while the houses themselves are serviced by dead-end streets. From the districts in the lower town a whole network of roads converge on the mosque. At first wide and gentle in gradient, they become steep and winding on reaching the upper level. Two streets only give access to the mosque: one leads to the main door, the other, which is entirely covered over, is reserved for the women.

The Malekite Moslems live in separate districts; the district of the M'dabih, in the northwest part of the city, and the district of the Beni Marzug, in the east. The Israelites also live in separate districts isolated beyond the ramparts in the southeast portion of the city. The Mozabites occupy the ancient district near the mosque, a district which is the most tranquil, the cleanest, and also the most austere. Any form of business is forbidden within its confines.

The commercial center is situated to the south of the city; the market square alone harbors 15 per cent of the businesses and to these there must be added the 45 per cent which are set up in streets adjacent to the square. This market square, almost rectangular in form and bordered on four sides by irregularly shaped arcades, is, then, situated in an outlying part of the city quite close to the ramparts (the latter are closed off by two massive gates, the Gate of the Shepherds and the Gate of the Blacksmiths). In the southern section of the market is the *mçalla* of Sidi el Hadj Bouafs, a block of masonry approximately sixteen feet by thirteen feet, projecting about three feet above the ground which is regularly white-washed and to which merchants and customers come to carry out their ablutions and make their prayers away from the business world and its blemishes. Beside this are twenty-four rough-cast stones of unequal sizes, half buried in the ground, in the form of an ellipse, the *haouita*. These stones were deemed to confer upon anyone who sat upon them the wisdom and the grace of those ancestors who were considered to be the protectors of the cemeteries from which the stones had been taken. The *haouita* was formerly the site of the city assembly.

Three hundred and fifty business enterprises may be counted in Ghardaïa (out of a total of 482 for the whole of the Mzab), that is to say, approximately one for every fifty inhabitants. A great part of the business transactions are carried out in the market place in makeshift stalls or sometimes even on the ground. Formerly a focal point of the

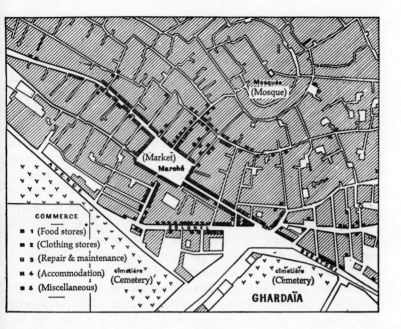

COMMERCE
- 1 (Food stores)
- 2 (Clothing stores)
- 3 (Repair & maintenance)
- 4 (Accommodation)
- 5 (Miscellaneous)

(Market) Marché

Mosquée (Mosque)

AVENUE

COLONEL

cimetière (Cemetery)

cimetière (Cemetery)

GHARDAÏA

great caravan routes, Ghardaïa is still today a redistribution and transit center. The Mozabites have been able to adapt themselves to the modern methods of transport and commercial techniques; they own the bulk of the trucking companies which serve the Sahara (fifteen such companies may be counted in the whole of the Mzab). With their 1,489 businesses (occupying 5,000 heads of families), among which are 729 textile businesses, 662 grocery stores and 98 miscellaneous establishments, they have maintained a preponderant place in the commerce of the Sahara. Moreover, one can estimate at approximatly 4,000 the number of commercial establishments (employing about 16,000 persons) which are owned by Mozabites in the whole of Algeria.

Although the new trends in business development are difficult to evaluate, there is still no doubt that even today the maintenance of the populations of the Mzab is almost entirely provided for by the profits realized from doing business in the Tell, since the production of the palm groves is not at all sufficient to support an over-all population of 58,000 inhabitants (made up of 39,000 Abadhites, 18,000 Malekites and 1,000 Israelites). The 130,000 palm trees, which cover approximately 1,500 acres, produce an average of 35,000 quintals of dates a year. Since the production of vegetables and fruit is low there is, then, scarcely a hundred market gardeners who can live exclusively on the results of their labor. If one takes into account the fact that to cultivate one hectare (2.5 acres) requires an outlay of $2,000 a year, according to the farmers, one gets some idea of the huge sums which must be invested each year to maintain these oases.

53

and continuous contact with Europeans.[5] But all this would be of little avail were it not for the spiritual force which animates this community. Moreover, their world of values is organized around two opposite poles: the domain of the secular, the economic life, and the domain of the sacred, the religious life. A real consciousness of this distinction on the part of the Mozabites can alone explain the fact that fierce resistance, obstinate and scrupulous particularism, and a touchy self-loyalty can coexist with a cautious desire for evolution, an attempt at compromise and planned development; never perhaps has the interaction between permanence and change been presented so clearly and distinctly. The maintenance of stability, far from excluding change, presupposes the capacity to modify oneself to adapt to new situations. But these adjustments (for which theological justification is found in the concepts of *takiya,* prudence, and of *kitmân,* the act of veiling, which authorize the Mozabite to dispense with the prescriptions of religion in cases when threatened with damages) must be accompanied either by a clear or an obscurely felt awareness of the values and norms whose permanence must be maintained at all costs, as opposed to those which can be modified or reinterpreted in order to assure the stability of the really important values. It is in this context that the material success of the Mozabites and their almost miraculous adaptation to forms of economic activity that are foreign to their strict tradition take on their full significance. This change in their way of life has been consciously adopted in order to guarantee the continued existence of those unalterable values on which their spiritual community is founded.

Just as the city develops around two distinct centers—the profane world of the market place, which is open to the great currents of modern life, and the religious acropolis with its mosque, a secret world only to be reached through a labyrinth of tortuous, narrow streets which seem intended to protect this most intimate and precious domain from any outside intrusion—so the soul and the life of the Mozabites are organized around two distinct centers which stand in the same opposition as the

[5] The Mzab, like most of the Saharan oases, is now experiencing the after-effects of the upheavals caused by the discovery of oil.

sacred and the profane. Thus it is that the modernistic adaptation to the world of finance and business does not contradict the rigid traditionalism of the religious life but, on the contrary, preserves it and makes it possible.

4. The Arabic-Speaking Peoples

Perhaps it is somewhat arbitrary to group together in the same cultural ensemble individuals and groups who have a common language and religion, and a common way of life imposed by this religion, but who, nevertheless, differ in their origins, in their mode of living and in their traditions. The regions presently inhabited by Arabic-speaking peoples have been the scene of an extraordinary intermingling of populations. The valley of the Chéliff, a great, natural highway, provides a characteristic example: in addition to the fact that it has always known immigration by the mountain peoples of the north and south (Berbers), it has been the path followed by the great Pre-Hillalian and Hillalian Arab invasions, the battleground for the clashes that occurred when migrating peoples from the east and west came face to face, and for the conflicts between these peoples and the tribes of the Dahra and the Ouarsenis. Even before the Hillalian invasions, the society of the Chéliff plain, peopled by Berber tribes, had already been converted to Islam as a result of Arab infiltrations. This constant coming and going of tribes in giddy succession did not give rise to a simple substitution of Arabs for Berbers, since those converted to Arab ways remained more numerous than the Arabs themselves. The same situation has prevailed to a greater or less degree in all the regions inhabited by Arabic-speaking peoples. The result is that it is almost impossible to divide the Arab element from the Berber element with any degree of certainty.

In this infinitely complex society several criteria, particularly those of a linguistic nature, permit a distinction to be drawn between different cultural units: the cities in which Pre-Hillalian dialects are spoken (called city dialects in opposition to the village dialects spoken, for example, in Little Kabylia); the zone of the Bedouin dialects which comprises, on the one hand, the coastal region and the region of the plains and hills (the High

Plains about Constantine, Mitidja, Chéliff, the hills bordering Ouarsenis and Dahra, the plains of Oranie), at present inhabited by new sedentary peoples (originally "semi-sedentaries") who live in a dispersed habitat and, on the other hand, the High Plains, the area in which Bedouin dialects are most prevalent, inhabited by nomads, by semi-nomads in the process of becoming sedentary, or by populations that have recently become sedentary.

According to the way of life, a distinction can also be made between the nomads and semi-nomads, the inhabitants of the desert and of the steppes, and the city dwellers, who have long been accustomed to a sedentary life. Between the two, however, there is a whole series of gradations both in space and, if one may say so, in time. The distance covered by the moves of the nomads is determined by the aridity of the country, by the quality of the pasture lands and by the degree of importance attached to stock raising, these different factors themselves being correlated to one another. Thus the moves become longer and longer as the nomads move closer to the desert. But the various modes of living are in constant evolution, and a general tendency to become sedentary is evident. Among the new sedentary peoples both of the plains and hills, and in the area of the High Plains, certain peoples have led a settled existence for more than a century, others for some forty or fifty years, still others have only very recently become attached to the soil.

The zone inhabited by Arabic-speaking peoples, of which the area of Bedouin influence forms the largest part, is in all Algeria the zone that has felt most strongly the direct shock of colonization, and the one in which the weakening of the old social structures has been most severe. European colonists have taken over nearly all the best land. This land includes the well-watered plains in the temperate zone (the inland plains in the Oran district, the valley of the Chéliff, Mitidja, the plain of Bône) and a good part of the High Plains near Constantine, which are relatively well watered and for this reason suitable for the extensive cultivation of cereal crops. Most of the original inhabitants of these regions have become the hired hands of the colonists. The native farmers and stockbreeders have been progressively driven back to the margins of the good farm land, to the regions of the

mountain forests of the Tell and to the regions of the South.
With their rudimentary agricultural implements they have here
managed to eke out a living on land that the Europeans consider
too poor for profitable farming. Having thus been driven out,
these people were compelled to bring new lands into cultivation,
particularly since population was increasing rapidly while the
land under cultivation was being reduced in size. Because the
land was poorer and was not allowed to remain fallow for sufficiently long periods, it necessarily gave a poorer yield and deteri-
orated more rapidly. Moreover, on becoming "sedentarized," a
good many of the semi-sedentary peoples and semi-nomads were
no longer able to engage in the occupation of stock raising which,
together with the growing of cereal crops, had been the basis of
economic equilibrium in the traditional society. Finally, the
extension of cultivated lands into the dry regions reduced the
size of pasture lands and at the same time placed restrictions on
the free movement of the nomads into the Tell. The *Senatus
Consulte* of 1863, as a result of their investigations, gave the
tribes the outright ownership of a definitely fixed territory. By
so doing they made it possible for the tribes to sell their best
land to the European colonists and at the same time hastened the
disintegration of the tribal structure.

We are here examining a society that is undergoing a radical
transformation. The ancient social structures, which have been
shaken or altered to a degree varying with their inherent power
of resistance and the violence of the shock they have received,
belong, truthfully speaking, neither to the present nor to the
past; consequently the reader must refrain from regarding the
following analyses either as a mere reconstruction of a bygone
society or as a strictly accurate description of the existing state of
affairs. Indeed, even when they seem to be utterly destroyed, these
structures continue to have an effect on the present; at least, if
one may say so, they have an effect through the very fact that
they no longer exist. This explains, then, the anguish of individuals who are adrift between the ancient structures, which would
be cruelly missed if abolished but if maintained intact would
prove an obstacle to much needed innovations, and the modern

structures, which can be adopted only at the price of a thorough transformation and a complete restructuring of society.[6]

The City Dwellers

The Algeria of 1830, a country of tribes and villages, had a very small urban population. As the scene of conflict and bargaining between the rural and the urban societies, the great cities were defined mainly by their functions: trading markets and religious centers, their vital core was the principal mosque and, close beside it, the highly animated business district. Thus, in Algiers, the lower town with its great commercial street running from the Bab-el-Oued gate to the Bab-Azoun gate was the site of several fine residences and of the largest mosques.[7] The upper town, a labyrinth of narrow, winding streets, often terminating in a blind alley, which were constructed for the use of pack animals, was the residential district of private homes.[8]

Exercising a magnetic attraction for the nomad and his caravans laden with merchandise as well as for the farmer of the small surrounding *douars,* who comes to sell the produce of his land and to buy the objects fabricated by the urban worker, the city is the center of commercial exchanges and is filled with great social animation because of the fact that it groups together people with very different social backgrounds. Religious worship is celebrated in close proximity to the market place, and the calendar of great commercial events coincides exactly with the calendar

[6] This remark is more or less true for all the regions of Algeria, although in varying degree, and is also true for all the societies discussed in this book.

[7] In 1817 the dey abandoned his palace in the lower town, which was situated beside the great mosque and the *souq,* to take up residence in the fort of the Casbah, which overlooks the city.

[8] Certain hypotheses shed some light on the apparently incoherent plan of the traditional city (Algiers, for example). The great streets of the lower town that follow the contour lines were probably former Roman roads; the roads running along the summit were probably paths. Finally, the narrow streets and alleyways that wind down the side of the hill probably follow the course of the little ravines that were hollowed out by the run-off and that were utilized in early times as sewers.

of the great religious festivals. By reason of their commercial
roles the cities are the intersecting points of many channels of
trade, and their economic prosperity is closely linked with that
of the surrounding countryside. Tlemcen, for example, which
was situated at the crossing of two important trade routes (Fez-
Oran, desert-coast) had become the great warehouse for caravans
from Morocco or the Sahara. In addition to its decaying manufacturing activity, this great commercial city assumed the role
of intellectual center, with its fifty Koranic schools and two
médersas, institutions for secondary education and higher learning. Thus, although it is distinguished from rural society by
its social structure, by quite a different form of collective existence, and by an entirely different way of life (language, culture,
manners, clothing, food, etc.), the city nevertheless lives in sym-
biotic relationship with the surrounding countryside from which
it draws its supplies and which, in turn, furnishes a market for
its manufactured products; as a result, any crisis in agriculture
leads to a drop in sales and unemployment for the shopkeepers
and manual workers in the city.

As a place of residence and as an industrial center, the city
is divided into districts provided with amenities considered indispensable for the life of the community—the mosque, the public
bath, the oven for baking bread and the shops. These districts
tend to form relatively autonomous and self-contained units. The
divisions into ethnic groups often coincide with divisions into
trade guilds because certain professions are traditionally followed
by certain groups. The particularism of the districts thereby
becomes even stronger. The corporation, placed under the patronage of a saint whose day is celebrated by communal re-
joicings, constitutes a kind of "great family" that is patterned
on the model of the regular family unit, even when its members
are not joined by real ties of consanguinity. This social body,
which is wider than the family but does not include the whole
city, is for the city dweller (along with his district) what the clan
or the tribe is for the country dweller; the feeling of corporative
solidarity, whose strength varies according to the particular city
and trade, is revealed by the mutual aid and assistance that the
members give to one another, by the reciprocal invitations that

are extended on the occasion of family ceremonies and by all the forms of communal festivities. The corporation is subject to a strict economic moral code which tends to exclude competition, which insists on the maintenance of just wages and fair prices, and which guarantees professional honesty.

There are almost no important business associations; the central bazaar groups together a wide variety of articles, but each article is sold by a different merchant. The largest manufacturing concerns include only about twenty workers and apprentices; the owner, who earns very little more than his workers, works among them and shares their troubles; any advantages that he may draw from his position are mainly those of honor and prestige. In short, although the urban society is constructed on the hierarchical system, and although a few men of wealth, particularly the great merchants, stand out above the mass of small craftsmen, shopkeepers, modest scholars and small landowners, who are half citizens and half peasants, there is no real class rivalry any more than there is in rural society. By reason of the spirit which animates the whole of this society, and also because of the small size and relative unimportance of the business concerns, the relationships between owner and worker, between rich and poor, are familiar, equalitarian and fraternal.

The spirit of the urban economy is not greatly different from that of the rural economy. The concern for productivity is unknown, and the main purpose of all commercial activity is the satisfaction of needs. Competition remains in a latent state. The rhythm of the working day is irregular and working hours vary. Religious ceremonies and family festivals considerably reduce the time devoted to work. Expenditures on luxuries eat up a great portion of the profits. For lack of capital, no new methods can be introduced. Techniques are transmitted by rule of thumb and, like the plant and equipment, are never renewed. The spirit of traditionalism, reinforced by the corporative system, stifles the spirit of free enterprise. The systems of measurement vary from one city to another, and often they may vary within the same city, depending on what is being measured. Commercial practice is based not on rational calculation but on speculation and chance; industry and trade are almost completely divorced; concern for the proper investment of funds is unknown. In short, economic relationships are never comprehended in all their brutal reality; they are always hidden behind the veil of prestige relationships and are tempered by the sentiment of fraternity. The fascination for social relations relegates the pursuit of profit to a position of secondary importance.

The city, where reside moralists, ascetics and jurists who rebel against the ritualism of the rural religion, is the bastion of religious orthodoxy and at the same time a center of intellectual activity because of its many schools and scholars. As centers of expansion for Islam and for Eastern civilization, the cities are animated by a refined mode of life that revolves around the mosque as its religious and cultural hub. The *souq* (market), the *hammam* (public bath) and the cafe are meeting places in which is developed the art of urbane conversation, and in which the different social classes may intermingle. On the one hand is the home, situated at the end of the quiet, winding street, withdrawn into itself, a private retreat, a closed world reserved for the women; in contrast to this is the open society, the men's world, the *souq*, the public square or the cafe, the domain of public life, of strictly controlled and codified social relationships, of lengthy conversations full of "witty slander and accepted platitudes" (W. Marçais). Between these two poles is enacted the life of these cultivated and refined city dwellers, of this society that is profoundly Moslem in character and is intimately attached to a way of life whose center may perhaps be said to be the art and the cult of social relations.

Turks, Kouloughlis (descendants of Turks and of native women), Andalusian Moors driven out of Spain (who formerly made up three-quarters of the population of Algiers and who were very numerous in Nedroma, Tlemcen, Médéa and Miliana), and new-rich "Arabs" and "Berbers" formerly made up the middle class of the cities. Excluded from all employment under the Turkish regime, the Andalusians controlled all local industry and engaged in commerce. To these were added whole communities of half-urbanized city dwellers, who preserved their relationships with their homeland, safeguarded their customs and their language, and, being grouped together in families, generally fol-

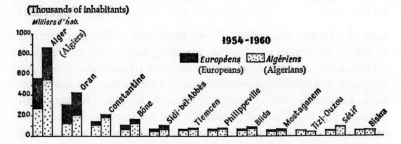

Fig. 7. Growth of the Principal Cities between 1954 and 1960

The trend to urbanization has not been limited to the large cities. Most of the towns and cities have had a large-scale increase. To gain an accurate idea of the size and form of these internal shifts in population, the data supplied by this diagram should be compared with that in Figure 14. The over-all population of the towns and cities has increased by 67.5 per cent in the region of Algiers, by 63 per cent in the Constantine region, and by 48 per cent in the region about Oran, a fact that illustrates that the war has been a decisive factor in speeding up the movement to the cities (see Fig. 16). Since the European population of the cities has remained almost constant, the increase in size of the principal cities (52 per cent for Algiers, 53 per cent for Constantine, 47 per cent for Bône, 38 per cent for Blida, 37 per cent for Oran) is due mainly to the influx of the native Algerians. Thus the Algerian population of Algiers has risen from 295,000 in 1954 to 558,000 in 1960, that of Constantine from 103,000 to 181,000, that of Oran from 131,000 to 218,000.

lowed the same trade: Kabyles, who came to hire out their services or to sell oil, figs and charcoal; Negroes, who sold lime and worked as masons; Ouargli and Biskri, water-bearers, porters and servants; Mozabites, operators of public baths, grocers and butchers; Jews, who were driven back to the perimeter and made to live in a special district; finally, a whole floating mass of country dwellers who had come to do temporary labor and who lived close to the city gates or in lean-to *gourbis* erected against the city walls.

The constantly increasing inpouring of rural masses attracted by the wages to be earned in the cities;[9] the creation and expan-

[9] The proportion of urban population to the total population increased quite regularly (at the rate of 0.16 per cent per annum on the average), going from 13.9 per cent in 1886 to 24.9 per cent in 1954. In 1959 it went up to 26.6 per cent, the average annual increase having tripled (0.42 per cent). Between 1936 and 1954 the urban population increased by 943,000 inhabitants (including 119,000 Europeans), and between 1954 and 1959 it increased by 550,000, including 50,000 Europeans.

sion of a capitalistic system of free enterprise which is concerned primarily with mass production, planning and profit; the development of the modern city, audacious and triumphant, built for purposes of commerce, speculation and administration; the influx of a European society which, although in close contact, still remains aloof and which incarnates and imposes the adoption of an entirely different mode of life—all these factors have brought about a profound transformation in the way of life and the art of living that were peculiar to the city of the past. The urban bourgeoisie, whose prosperity and influence were formerly based on business, handicrafts, and the practice of law and scholarly pursuits, has been able to resist the competition from an industrial economy and the influx of new techniques and values only at the cost of a complete transformation. New social classes have appeared: a new bourgeoisie, created by trade and industry, which has for several years been intermarrying with the old city families; intellectuals trained in European universities; a new proletariat, too, made up of mountain dwellers from Kabylia, shepherds from the High Plains, gardeners from the oases of the Sahara. The members of this new proletariat have streamed toward the cities as the economic and social equilibrium of their country districts has been shattered and, although they group themselves in districts according to their origin and preserve close contacts with their home territory, nevertheless they are now detached from the rural society without being truly integrated into the urban society. Driven from their country districts by poverty rather than attracted by the city, they are thrown with no training into a city that, owing to the nature of its occupations and its structure, is incapable of ensuring them employment and housing.[10] Thus placed amid material conditions that

[10] In 1954 the part-time workers and the unemployed made up about 30 per cent of the urban male population of working age. Algiers and Oran attract rural workers from those regions of which they are the administrative centers. In the area around Constantine the rural workers who do not leave for Algiers proceed to several different centers, particularly Constantine, Bône, Sétif and now Bougie. Generally speaking, the influx of country dwellers bears no relation to the possibilities of employment, and this is particularly true in the Constantine area. Thus Sétif, a rural market place, an administrative and military center, has had an increase which cannot be justified from an economic point of view (1,000 inhabitants in 1881, 51,000

are often catastrophically bad, this population of destitute small wage-earners[11] that encamps itself on the periphery of the European city, may also be considered to be living on the fringe of the modern economic system and of modern society. The city usually can offer to these disenfranchised citizens only its worst conditions and a life of utter poverty.

Nomads and Semi-Nomads

Nomadism makes its appearance when the resources of the natural environment are no longer sufficient for the permanent maintenance of the group—that is to say, in a line running approximately below the isohyet indicating over 157 inches of annual rainfall, the northern limit of the steppe—and has a function that is both pastoral and commercial in nature. The vegetation, although scanty,[12] still permits the large-scale breeding of sheep, goats and camels to be carried on, provided that the entire group can migrate between the south (rainy season) and the north (dry season) so that the shepherds may move their flocks according to the variations in vegetal resources. On the routes that were followed by their ancestors but which are now

---

for the whole of the commune in 1954), because of the influx of rural workers from the northwest and from the east who, at the beginning of the twentieth century, were driven out by the concentration of the great European land-holdings and who in recent times have been driven out by the introduction of mechanized methods of cultivation. The percentage of the population that had some form of employment was found to be very low in Sétif (about 25 per cent).

[11] One of the characteristic features of the Algerian cities is the hypertrophic development of the tertiary sector, a considerable number of intermediaries who are engaged in petty commerce and who speculate on the individual resale of such things as a bunch of bananas or a package of cigarettes.

[12] The contrast between the well-watered east and the drier west may be noted both in the High Plains and in the Tell. The High Plains around Constantine, which receive more rainfall, are suitable for the culture of cereals. Those around Oran and Algiers, in which the predominant crop is esparto grass, are more favorable to stock raising. Among the sheep-raising nomads of the west, densities of population vary between 5 to 15 inhabitants to the square kilometer (in the *arrondissement* of Aflou, 5; of Telagh, 7; of Frenda, 11, of Saïda, 12). Among the cereal growers of the east, the densities are somewhat heavier (in the *arrondissement* of Tebessa, 13; of M'Sila, 20).

strictly controlled, the tribes of the Arbâa and the Saïd Atba move by clans from the regions of Laghouat and Ouargla and conclude their northward migration by spending the summer at the approaches to the western Tell in the Sersou and Tiaret regions. Several tribes from around Touggourt and Biskra return to the High Plains of the Constantine area for the summer. Other groups may summer in the interior plains of the Saharan Atlas. While the nomads, who obtain most of their requirements from their flocks (their food consists largely of milk products, their clothing of wool, their tents of hide) and who generally own some palm groves and gardens in the oases, sow only a few acres of barley or wheat, the semi-nomads devote a much greater share of their activity to the culture of cereal crops and only leave their fixed residence for a five-month period, the period from the end of harvest to the spring plowing. In short, the life of the nomad, the man of the desert, is distinguished from that of the semi-nomad, the man of the steppes, only by the relative importance given to agriculture and by the amount of time devoted to sedentary activities during the year.

The nomadic migrations presupposed the making of agreements with the tribes whose territories had to be crossed and the payment of tolls to these tribes. Conflicts rarely developed, and relations were particularly friendly during the final period of the grazing cycle, which occurred at the end of spring and coincided with the sedentary tribes' harvest; the nomads would then take part in the work of bringing in the crops and would hire out their animals for the moving of the harvest. Moreover, they brought with them the products of the south, principally dates, and the products of their flocks, which they would exchange for cereals in accordance with fixed values set by custom. This type of association has been maintained more or less intact in the Constantine region, but has led to conflict in the districts surrounding Oran and Algiers.

The distinctiveness of the nomad lies mainly—and perhaps exclusively—in his way of life, which is inseparably linked to his own special attitude of life. Thus one must be careful not to regard him as radically different from the sedentary peoples. On the contrary, the thing that strikes one most is the *continuity of the social structure* amid the different ways of life of the Algerian peoples. For the nomad, as for the sedentary peoples, the consanguineous clan is the fundamental social unit; the nomad clan travels over a familiar, community-owned grazing territory, whereas the sedentary clan is restricted to the precisely defined limits of a village district, since each large family treats its land as private property. While the demarcation of boundaries is more precise between the fields of the sedentary clans, it is also true that in nomad territory the theoretical or real ties of kinship have been, as it were, projected onto the land to such an extent that one can distinguish all the grazing lands belonging to a particular tribe and, within them, the area belonging to each clan. The same uniformity may be noted in matters concerning the techniques of production. When they cultivate areas irrigated by the overflow of the wadis or low-lying lands (*djelf* lands), the nomads use a swing plow similar to that of the peasants. In the Sahara the nomad is the man of the plow who cultivates great, unirrigated expanses in contrast to the *ksourien*, the man of the hoe, the gardener of the small plots in the oases. The nomad differs from the *ksourien* in many ways;[13] on the one hand, the villages, with their houses of clay or unmortared stone, huddle together in the shelter of the walls for protection against the raids of the nomads, who are their protectors' rivals; on the other hand, the wandering tent and the great open spaces; here, the desperately hard and exacting work of the soil, all the virtues and tenacity of the peasant; there, the dawdling gait of the shepherd following along behind his flocks, the disdain for the agricultural techniques considered fit only for farmers, and the fatalism of a people subjected to the hazards of climate.[14] However, the fact

[13] The *medina* differs from the *ksar* (plural, *ksour*), which is mainly agricultural (palm groves and gardens), in its appearance (minarets of the mosques, larger and better constructed dwellings) and in its function as a manufacturing and commercial center. But there, too, all gradations may be found.

[14] According to an investigation carried out by M. Capot-Rey in the southern territories, the percentage of nomads, semi-nomads and sedentary peoples in 1938 was 58 per cent, 17.6 per cent and 24.3 per cent in the Plains and the Saharan Atlas, 30.3 per cent, 12.8 per cent and 56.8 per cent in the pre-Saharan zone, and 27.7 per cent, 8.8 per cent and 63.4 per cent in the Sahara proper. Since then the proportion of sedentary peoples, and semi-nomads has greatly increased.

that their interests were complementary necessarily led to agreements and cooperation between the two types of people. The great markets of the Sahara (Ghardaïa, Laghouat, etc.) are proof of the economic symbiosis that unites the nomads and the sedentary peoples. The city, with its armorers, blacksmiths, shoemakers, and weavers, welcomes the nomad who, during the periods of the great markets, comes to sell his meat, wool and leather, the products of his flocks; furthermore, the nomad formerly provided these cities with the greater part of their external trade, bringing them the grain from the Tell for which he had exchanged his dates and fruit. Moreover, the *ksourien* could not do without the help of the nomad, who would offer him or force upon him protection against pillage by other nomads. In return the pastoral nomad would leave to the sedentary dweller, his tenant farmer, the task of irrigating his palm trees and gardens, and would entrust him with a portion of his reserves. So the bond uniting them cannot be interpreted as being based solely on self-interest.

The pastoral economy and the way of life it implies are inseparably linked with a special attitude of mind. The permanence of the nomadic society, confronted with an extremely unproductive land and a pitiless climate, demands a proud adherence to this way of life. The nomad is aware of the fact that the temptation to lead a sedentary existence is for him a sure promise of moral decline and that his very existence depends upon retaining that profound and innate wisdom which is made up of haughty pessimism and resignation, of ascetic patience and gentilitial pride. The absolute authority of the leaders of the family, the group or the tribe, is a guarantee both of the continuance of the social order and of economic survival.[15] While the nomadic life did not rule out the acquisition of riches, its sole source of wealth lay in the flock which was subject to the hazards inherent in the alternation of good and lean years.[16] The desert world puts the nomad on guard against excess and extremes and at the same time reminds him of the need for collective discipline. The community, a kind of circle whose center

[15] See para., *The social structures,* ff.
[16] As a consequence of a year of drought (1945) the sheep population fell from 5,832,000 (1944) to 2,808,000 (1946).

is everywhere and yet nowhere, is indeed the foundation and necessary condition for all life in the desert.

This society has fallen into a great decline. The widespread, vigorous nomadism of the period prior to 1830 has been replaced by a limited, controlled and weakened form of nomadism. During the past fifty years stock raising has steadily declined, while farming has increased until it now extends as far south as the steppes. The pasture lands have been reduced in size by the advance of colonization, particularly in the area of Tiaret and Sersou. Moreover, the years of drought, the absence of any efficient methods of protecting and improving the flocks, the failure to set a firm value on the products of stock raising, explain the decrease in size of the flocks of sheep, which were reduced from ten to twelve million head at the beginning of the century to little more than six million in 1954. Other influences have aggravated this crisis of the nomadic way of life: the appearance of new methods of transportation (railway and truck) and the increase in the money supply (eliminating the need for barter) have brought about the decline in the caravan trade, which was the monopoly of the nomads; the establishment of law and order has permitted small groups to move freely from place to place and has stripped the nomad of the prestige attached to his role as "protector" of the *ksourien*; "the suzerainty of the nomad has ceased to be a form of insurance and has become a burden" (Capot-Rey); the discovery of oil and the creation of the oil industry have speeded up the overthrow of the former hierarchies—workers in the oil fields, often liberated slaves formerly employed as farm hands, sometimes earn wages much higher than the income of the tribal chiefs; the rapid increase in population related to (and perhaps dependent on) becoming sedentary; the crisis that oases farming is undergoing combined with the crisis in the sharecropping system have disrupted the balance of the Saharan economy. A great number of ruined nomads, semi-nomads, and sedentary peoples have been compelled to look for new sources of income, either by farming poor lands, or by gathering esparto grass, or by emigrating to the cities of the Tell. The nomadism of the shepherds, moving in great caravans made up of an entire tribe or of clans led by their sheik, has very frequently given way to the nomadism of the work-hungry, a nomadism which brings to the cities wretched persons who have been torn from their accustomed way of life and cut off from their now completely disintegrated community.

The New Sedentary Peoples

Economic equilibrium and human relationships.—Former nomads whose main occupation was stock raising and who lived in tents for part of the year, but who have been made sedentary for a fairly long period, make their living by the cultivation of cereal crops combined with stock raising.[17] Less attached to the soil than the settled village folk, such as the Kabyles, they often retain the scorn of the herdsman for agricultural pursuits, and form a less strongly integrated society. Existing conditions are the end result of a process that may be outlined in the following way: In the beginning, stock raising is favored. The flock is the private property of the extended family, but the pasture lands are owned in common by the whole clan or tribe. Each year, at the first autumn rains, the tribal *djemâa* and the *djemâa* of the clans allot the lands that are to be cultivated in accordance with the capacities and needs of each family, that is to say, in accordance with the number of men and the number of teams of plow animals (cf. in Kabylia, the distribution of lands by lot). The family has full use of the land for one or two years, at the end of which time a new allotment is made. Among all the tribes great expanses are set aside for pasture lands or left fallow by common accord, but they may also be used for farming if need arises. The fencing-in of the fields would be useless, since, even when owned as private property, they become communal pasture land every other year; thus their boundaries are very poorly marked, irregular, and sometimes even zigzag in outline. Distributed here and there over the countryside, they enclose small islands of shrubs,

[17] The limits of the area in which this type of people has settled are rather vague. It may be said to occupy all zones that are not inhabited either by the old established sedentary people or by semi-nomadic or nomadic shepherds, that is, principally in those areas of the plains in which the rainfall is over 138 inches, and in the wooded massifs.

mastic trees or jujube trees. This whole system obviously leads to a rather disorganized rural landscape. The group moves about over the areas of which they are the virtual owners. Each group and each family farms according to its needs and its means; by so doing, it establishes the size of its own area within the common territory, its force of expansion finding within itself its own principle of limitation. The winter encampment is the more stable, since it lasts from November to March. Here the group puts down its roots; here it has its underground granary (*matmoura*) and its cemetery, the tangible symbol of its attachment to the soil and to its ancestors. Around the winter *mechta* some farming is done on small fields which were first roughly cleared by fire; in spite of the system of letting part of the land lie fallow, the soil is quickly exhausted and the fields have only a relative stability. During the winter the flock is pastured in the immediate area of the *mechta*. In the spring the whole or part of the group leaves the winter *mechta*, and, since the flocks must be removed from the lands under cultivation, they are put to graze on the lands that will be sown in autumn, an original method of ensuring that the fields will be properly fertilized. The animals are shut in at night within the circle of tents (*douar*) or within an enclosure of jujube trees. When summer comes, the group returns to harvest the crop, the flocks feed on the stubble fields, and the winter encampment is again set up. Different causes (particularly the reduction of the flocks resulting from bad years) make the stock raisers decide to increase the size of the seeded areas; this in turn leads to the progressive abandonment of the system of annual distribution of land as each family now begins permanently to cultivate the same fields; it also results in the group's becoming permanently settled in the winter camp, while the nomadic system of grazing flocks over limited pasture lands is replaced by a system of regular transhumance in charge of the shepherds. With the institution of family property, there finally appears within the tribe the distinction between those who own the land and those who cultivate it.

Extensive farming, devoted particularly to cereals, is thus combined with extensive sheep raising; this type of farming is based on the alternation of growing and leaving the fields to

lie fallow, thereby permitting the soil to rest and at the same
time providing food for the flock. In this subsistence-level economy the combination of agriculture and sheep breeding ensures
the satisfaction of essential needs. The staple diet consists of the
barley and wheat which (mixed with salt water, with meat and
vegetables often added) are used to make the couscous. The flock
provides meat, the main course for the meals that are held during
family or religious festivals,[18] and milk, which is drunk fresh or
in the form of whey. The wool of the sheep and the skin of the
goat are used in making clothing and tents. Thus the markets
provide only a small extra source of income to the family economy. Agricultural yields are low and vary greatly with the climate (four to five hundredweight per hectare for wheat and
barley and sometimes, if rainfall is abundant and well distributed
during the year, 15, 20 or 25 hundredweight). However, balance is
maintained between the resources and the relatively small population. A balance has also been achieved between the techniques
employed and the natural conditions. Land is not cleared by
grubbing and uprooting but is merely cleaned off by burning.
The fellah first sows the seeds, then buries them by merely scratch-
ing the ground; the swing-plow is also well adapted to the soil
conditions;[19] and furthermore it spares the living plants which
preserve the soil from erosion and which will provide food for the
flock when the cultivated land is left to lie fallow again. A heavier
and hence more expensive plow would demand a long and difficult preparation of the ground, would risk bringing about the
rapid exhaustion of a soil that is not enriched by fertilizers, and
would probably be too heavy for undernourished animals to pull.
One could show in a similar way that the most archaic features
(harvesting with the sickle, lack of shelters for the animals,
absence of reserves of hay, etc.) all have a functional significance
when referred to the over-all system. This type of farming
requires only a small capital—the land, the seed, the plow, and,

[18] The poorest of the poor would be dishonored if he did not have his
quarter of mutton on the day of the Aïd. If the worker is too poor to buy it,
tradition demands that the master give him a supply of mutton on the occasion of the great festivals. This is often stipulated in the contracts.

[19] According to the latest farm census (1951), those engaged in traditional
farming were still using swing-plows on 300,000 of the 630,000 farms.

above all, the team to pull the plow. The rudimentary techniques produce only a very low yield, but at the lowest possible cost. Thus balance appears to have been attained at the highest possible level within the limits imposed by the lack of advanced methods and techniques and by the lack of capital. It would therefore appear to be impossible, given equal means, to achieve any greater success. The attainment of any higher level of adaptation would presuppose the acquiring of better technical methods and devices, and the possession of extensive capital, and would involve a complete transformation of the social, economic and psychological structures.

This insecure and constantly threatened equilibrium conceals considerable tension. The reason for this is that agriculture and stock raising are complementary but at the same time competitive. Heavy rainfall leads to an extension of the area under cultivation at the expense, and to the detriment, of the share of the land given over to the flock; a favorable lambing season, a good cereal crop which will enable him to buy livestock—the fellah's pride, the tangible display of his wealth and the only way in which he can accumulate capital [20]—and the flock will increase far beyond the possibility of providing it with water and pasture lands, both of which are subject to the hazards of climate. The animals being now less well fed are more vulnerable, and a severe winter, a period of drought or an epidemic kills off great numbers; the following year, for lack of draft animals and the necessary cash to buy seed, the size of the areas under cultivation is restricted. In short, the balance between the size of the flock and the farm value of the pasture land is established not so much by the will of man as by the forces of nature working to produce the alternation of abundance and famine which has so profoundly marked the life and vision of the world of the North African fellah.

While it is true that as the group becomes more sedentary

[20] This attitude in regard to the flock is widespread even among the sedentary farmers. Wealth is measured by the size of the flock as much as by the extent of the land under cultivation. Since land is held in joint possession, the continuance of which is ensured by various protective measures, it cannot be easily assigned a commercial value. Hence the function of the flock.

each family tends to retain as its own property the lands used for farming, the common ownership of pasture lands and uncleared sections (*ârch* lands) maintains the cohesion of the tribal community. However, the territorial unit does not always coincide with the social unit (tribe or clan). It frequently happens as a result of land sales that the patrimony is farmed by several families of different origins. Thus there is much criss-crossing of the lands under cultivation, since a certain social unit may own fields that are hemmed in by the lands of one or of several other groups, and vice versa. The patrimony, which generally bears the name of its founder, remains the joint property of the extended family, that is, of all the descendants of the same ancestor down to the third and fourth generations, the share of each of these virtual heirs being fixed by vernacular tradition. In most cases the land is farmed in common by the members of the same extended family or by several families issuing from the same stock. It is not the property of a collective entity, but of individuals who have been ascribed rights that may differ greatly but are always well defined, and these individuals are free (at least theoretically) to withdraw their share of the jointly held property. The shares due to each of them are expressed in fractions whose denominators have sometimes seven or eight figures; the situation is complicated, moreover, by the fact that the right of full ownership is here granted to the surviving husband or wife, so that a marriage always offers an outside family the possibility of acquiring rights to a jointly held property. To avoid having it go out of the possession of the family, a property is frequently set up as a private *habous* and so becomes inalienable. Examples have been cited of acts of partition (*freda*) which have allotted a beneficiary two or three square centimeters from one hectare held by several hundred joint owners. Were it not for the system of joint possession, the patrimony would frequently become worthless as a result of being divided into extremely small plots through the strict enforcement of Moslem law. Thus legalism, carried to extremes, ends by thwarting its original intent and demands, as it were, its own negation.

The institution of joint possession is, then, a guarantee of equilibrium. Looked at from the standpoint of the modern eco-

nomic system, it may, no doubt, merely appear as an absurd
archaism because it chains the peasant to a strict routine by for-
bidding the introduction of new methods and the exercise of
individual initiative. In reality, however, it protects the integrity
of the patrimony and, therefore, of the family group, against
excessive division, against the intrusion of outsiders, and against
the absorption of small lots by large-scale farming developments.
The same purpose is served by the legal right to pre-empt property (chefâa). Furthermore, by bringing about a union of all the
means and all the forces available to the group, joint possession
permits a realization of the best possible adaptation to the
natural surroundings and guarantees subsistence to those individuals who would generally be unable to survive on the tiny
plot of ground they would be awarded were the property to be
divided by the court.[21] Because of the scarcity of capital and the
prevailing high interest rates, and because of the high cost of
plow animals, community farming becomes the only feasible
course of action. Moreover, through this institution (as through
the private habous), the community protects itself against im-
providence, indifference or wastefulness on the part of its individual members, since it can strictly control both methods of
production and of consumption. Finally, this type of association
affords the best form of protection in an economy characterized
by the alternation of good and bad years. Thus joint possession
performs the same function, although in a different setting, as
the mutual aid characteristic of rural society; indeed, only by
combining their efforts can these people more or less compensate
for the unreliability of the techniques at their disposal.

In this mobile society with its vaguely defined "nominal
property," a society in which real property is in fact only the
land that is under cultivation, so that the most important fact
is the particular relationship existing between man and the soil,
and in which the exploitation of the natural pasture lands requires great expanses to be set aside for grazing purposes, the
quest for equilibrium between man and man brings into play
mechanisms that are no less complex than those involved in the

---

[21] The number of peasants ruined by selling off their property by auction
to speculators is proof of this.

pursuit of equilibrium between man and the soil. Hence the exuberant flowering of pacts and agreements, which time and again are jeopardized by the temptation to indulge in pilfering and strife.

Everything combines to bring about a dynamic balance, the result of various tensions, the internal tensions that have already been analyzed and the external tensions caused by the fact that the efforts of expansion of the group are limited by the expansions of rival groups. "One of the permanent causes of agitation and division among the Arabs," wrote Captain Richard, "is the vagueness of the boundaries separating the various parts of the territory. The old caïd of the Beni Merzoug, when questioned as to how it came about that a vast piece of land situated between his tribe and that of the Beni Menna had always remained uncultivated, answered that from time immemorial this field of fatal memory had never been seeded by anything but the corpses of their tribes." In other words, the domain of the tribe is defined by opposition to the land of the neighboring tribes. On this tribal territory each group or each family has joint ownership of the portion that it brings into cultivation. Thus, under an appearance of disordered and anarchical distribution, of a wasteful use of land, there is a whole network of contracts, each of which represents a conflict that is either being resolved or is latent. Nowhere is there illustrated more clearly the essential nature of the pact (cf. the agreements between the nomads of the Sahara and the tribes of the Tell), which creates a precarious and constantly threatened reciprocity between groups that may form associations while continuing, nevertheless, to remain hostile to one another.

Equilibrium is born of tension—the rivalries between groups compensate for one another. Such a situation favored the de-

Fig. 8. Plan of a Part of the Domain (*haouch*) of the Ben Chaoua

This part of the domain of the Ben Chaoua is situated north of the main road running from Blida to Algiers. The shaded areas represent: (1) uncleared land; (2) cultivated land; (3) pasture land; (4) dwellings. (After Isnard, *La réorganisation de la propriété rurale dans la Mitidja,* Algiers, 1948.)

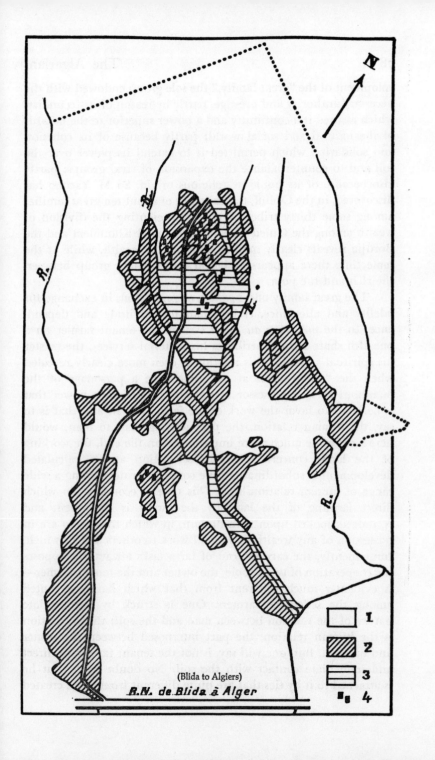

(Blida to Algiers)

R.N. de Blida à Alger

1
2
3
4

velopment of the "great family," the sole group endowed with the
necessary authority and prestige, partly by reason of its fecundity,
which assured it a continuity and a power superior to the hazards
of the natural and social world; partly because of its cohesion
and solidarity, which permitted it to extend its power over the
soil and to counterbalance the expansion of rival groups; partly
also because of its noble or religious origin. So M. Yacono has
discovered, in the Chéliff, the existence of about ten great families
among some thirty tribes. A chart representing the division of
wealth among the Ouled Khelouf, the Ouled Khouidem and the
Bordjia reveals clearly marked contrasts in wealth, while at the
same time there appears to be no intermediary group between
the rich and the poor.

The great family offers *çohba,* or protection, in exchange for
fidelity and allegiance, rather than for servitude and dependence. In the *métayage au quint* system, the tenant farmer on a
one-fifth share basis contributes his material services, the master
his spiritual services. This relation is even more clearly revealed
when the "seigneur" is at the same time a personage of the
marabout class, a possessor of the magical religious power that
is believed to favor the work of the farm. The means, that is to
say, the human relation, the pact uniting man to man, would
here seem to be much more important than the end, the working
of the land; concern for technical action and a calculated
development is subordinate to the concern for developing a wide
range of human relationships. This type of economy—in which
direct farming of the land by the owner is infrequent and
is, indeed, looked upon with disdain, in which those who are in
possession of any wealth leave field work to others and in which,
consequently, the carrying out of farm tasks always presupposes
the cooperation of two people, the owner and the tenant farmer—
is evidently much different from that which has been noted
among the sedentary farmers. One is struck by the mediate
nature of the relation between man and the soil; this mediation
is the human relation, the pact interposed between the owner
and his land. But, one will say, is not the tenant farmer in direct
and immediate contact with the soil? No doubt he is, but he
is attached to it by ties that are quite different from those created

by ownership, and perhaps it is not exaggerating to say that the tie between the worker and the soil involves the master.

If such is indeed the nature of the sharecropping system, it is evident that the tenant farmer benefits from this institution and that the change to the status of wage earner which, according to our way of thinking, may appear as a promotion, is, in this context, to be considered as a demotion.[22] Judged according to our criteria, this contract is very much like servitude: the sharecropper is bound to the master, who dictates the clauses of the contract and is apparently the only one ensured against risk; the former gives up his liberty and initiative and receives in return only a very small share of the crop (generally one-fifth, with local variations). It may even happen that he is chained to his master by a debt which compels him to renew his contract indefinitely so that sometimes, when reduced to extreme poverty, he has no recourse other than flight.

However, the above description overlooks the essential features of a pact which reveals a unique view of economic relations. Hired by verbal contract at the beginning of the farming year, in the months of October or November, the sharecropper merely contributes his physical labor while the master provides him with the land, the seed, the implements, and the team to do the plowing. Since the contract comes into effect in autumn and the harvest is not reaped until May or June, the master must advance the necessary supplies to tide the sharecropper and his family over this period. At the festival of the *Achoura* he must give the tenant a *gandoura* of cotton and a pair of shoes; at the time of the great Moslem festivals he must provide him with a supply of mutton. The pact is a man-to-man arrangement, and one would seek in vain to find any guarantee other than that of the "fidelity" demanded by honor. Its one-sided nature is tempered by the pressure of a public opinion that is quick to censure any abuses on the part of the master. There are no abstract regulations, no

[22] Estimates as to the number of sharecroppers vary from 60,000 to 150,000. The discrepancy may be explained by the fact that a number of farmers and temporary or permanent agricultural workers are at the same time tenant farmers. From being approximately one-third of the active rural population in 1914, the number of sharecroppers has been reduced to less than one-tenth at the present time.

definite sanctions. The pact is vitalized and maintained by a
sense of honor and the fear of public disapproval. Because he
would be breaking his word if he failed to live up to the contract,
the tenant remains faithful to the master. For the same reason,
if he judges himself to be oppressed or exploited, he can denounce
him publicly, and the pressure of public opinion is generally able
to force the landowning class to live up to its rank, to behave in
a way that commands respect, and to protect the poor. Magna-
nimity and generosity are not only attributes of greatness but are
virtues with which greatness is naturally endowed, so that to be
lacking in these virtues would be an act of self-repudiation and
self-denial. Moreover, far from considering himself as a slave
or proletarian, the worker participates intimately in the life of
the family group whose cares, troubles, and sometimes poverty,
he shares, whose interests he regards as his own, since he considers
himself to be "an associate" and not a mere hired hand. For these
reasons the contract appears to have been patterned on a deeper
relationship, that of father and son, since, in fact, the master
pledges himself to ensure the livelihood of the tenant and to
free him from all worry concerning the future. Consequently,
the latter is generally assured against the uncertainties of the
future, against unemployment and total destitution. The tenants
generally farm the areas that are suitable for cereal crops, and it
is only because of this institution of sharecropping that the
poor worker is assured of his supply of semolina, his basic diet.
Thus it is not surprising that, as has been noted recently, paid
workers should at times demand the advantages of sharecropping
(payment in kind, advances), for example, at the time of the
heaviest farm work. In an economic system that is continually
overshadowed by the threat of famine, does not this institution
of sharecropping afford the best form of protection and insurance?
Protected against extreme poverty, the sharecropper is also protected against isolation from his fellows, an inestimable advantage in a society in which the individual exists only in and
through the group, is conscious of his own identity only through
the group, and has a legal and social existence only to the
extent that the group will consent to be responsible for him
and to defend him.

It is very easy to show the advantages the master obtains under this system. The institution of sharecropping facilitates the management of his property, and requires him to use only the resources provided by his estate, a considerable advantage in an economy in which money is scarce. Furthermore, the master is assured of diligent and conscientious work on the part of the tenant, who is also interested in obtaining a good crop. But is the profit he derives from this association really of an economic order? One may doubt this when one thinks of his obligation to support the sharecropper, even in years of scarcity and without any hope of repayment. In reality, riches are valued less for themselves or for the material satisfactions they provide than for the enhancement in prestige, influence, and ascendancy that is procured by the possession of a "clientele," that group of dependents which is, as it were, a projection of the power of its protector. If the proprietor does gain by this system (although he would appear to lose by it if one considered only economic factors) it is because the pact is primarily a relation based on honor and prestige, even though it may be undermined by the more or less hidden temptation to exploitation on the one hand and to parasitism on the other.

Furthermore, since there is no monetary exchange or circulation of currency in the modern sense, sharecropping and the other types of agricultural association provide the only possible solution both for the owner and the worker. Indeed, money in this society does not play the role of universal medium for dealings among men as it does in a capitalistic economy; thus moneylending, while an integral part of the system, is the business of specialized minorities; and even then interest-bearing transactions are generally carried out only with allogeneous groups, the nomads of the desert and particularly the mountain dwellers, whose economy is of a complementary nature. Thus it is that the honor-ruled exchange of gift and countergift, of protection and homage, is the predominant form of exchange. Consequently, wage earning cannot really exist in a system of this nature, and sharecropping appears to be the only form of association possible between the man who owns the land and the means of production and the man who has nothing to offer but his arms for the working of this land.

The preceding analyses will have shown to what extent the social and the economic structures are closely interlocked. The clan and the tribe may be defined primarily as the group in possession of a particular domain, pasture lands, forests and farm lands. It has also been shown that the jointly held patrimony is the basis of unity for the extended family. Thus the aim of customs and laws throughout all Algeria, and especially among the Berber-speaking peoples, is to protect the integrity of this patrimony. The sale of land is, in point of fact, impossible, since it demands the consent of all the heirs. Moreover, should it happen that one of the owners could be induced to sell, the other members of the family always have the right (and to a certain extent the duty) to pre-empt the land, *chefâa*, according to an order established by custom. For the same reasons the mortgage loan, which may lead to the dispossession of the debtor, is almost unknown, whereas the pledging of real estate as security for a debt, the non-payment of which only allows the creditor to enjoy the use of the land, is quite common. The daughter, through whom the patrimony might pass out of the ownership of the agnatic group, is often in actual fact disinherited; the father can dedicate his property to some pious foundation (private *habous*), thereby making it inalienable. If this society surrounds the property of the agnatic group with such a great number of protective laws, it is because the integrity of the patrimony, the unity of the extended family and the authority of the head of the family are intimately connected. If one or another of these were weakened, the very existence of the family, the keystone of the whole social edifice, would be threatened. The *Senatus Consulte* of 1863, by facilitating the division and commercialization of the *ârch* lands, shook the tribal structure to its very foundation. In a different way, the breaches in the system of joint possession, which have become more and more frequent during the last twenty years, have coincided (without its being possible to determine cause and effect) with the challenge to the authority of the head of the family, with the disruption of the normal chain of matrimonial exchanges, and with the disintegration of the family unit.

The social structures.—The preceding analyses may have given the reader a better understanding of the various social structures, particularly the structure of the tribe, the most complex of all social units. It appears, in fact, that all the different interpretations that have been made as to the nature of the tribe must be placed in question, whether they explain it by consanguinity, or by the initial expansion of mother stocks projecting their shoots in all directions, or by the dissemination of wandering groups. Before dealing with the intricacies of concrete cases, it would perhaps be useful to give a rough definition of the "ideal type" of tribe, although it is rarely met with in reality.

The extended family, the basic social unit, groups together several conjugal families founded by the direct male descendants of a common ancestor. The patrilinear structure and the patriarchal system imply both the role of the "father" and the absolute preponderance granted to the men, women's rights being subordinate to those of the agnates. The "fraction" (*ferqa*), or clan, is also founded on male consanguinity and is comprised mainly of the agnates. It includes several extended families of which the male members consider themselves to be "sons of the paternal uncle," without defining their precise degree of relationship. The members of the same clan do not seek blood vengeance on one another. The clan has its own leader, the sheik, who decides on the moves of the group, and its own name, which distinguishes it from the other units that make up the tribe. Usually it honors with a special cult its eponymous founder. It has rights to a fixed portion of the tribal territory, and all its flocks (bearing the same brand) move out as one flock to the pasture lands, although each family in the group has outright ownership of its animals, its grain, and its implements. The tribe is a federation of clans whose members claim to have descended from a common ancestor, an ancestor who is likewise honored with a cult. It is led by a sheik, generally the leader of one of the more important clans. Finally, there are the confederations, vague and ill-defined organizations that usually stem from war, when a coalition may bring together two or more tribes threatened by a common danger. A weaker tribe may then seek the protection of powerful strangers at the price of its own submission, or groups of equal power may join together to oppose a common enemy or make new conquests. It sometimes happens that a vast confederation will be formed around a particular great family which holds the weaker tribes in a state of loose vassalage. Thus on the eve of the French occupation eastern Algeria was dominated by the sheik of the Hanencha of the Harar family in the east, the sheik el Arab of the Bou Okkaz family in the south, and the sheik of the Medjana of the Ouled Mokran family in the west.

The real state of affairs is, however, infinitely more complex than this simplified outline. In the first place, the extreme variety of family origins that is concealed under the apparent unity created by the common name, a consequence of the fiction of the common ancestor, forces one to abandon the hypothesis of consanguinity. The tribe is a patchwork agglomeration formed by the joining together of various elements; a single example will illustrate this (Despois, *Hodna,* p. 119): the tribe of the Ouled Madhi not only includes some descendants of the Athbedj, but, even more important, a large foreign element (Moroccans, the Ouled Naïl, mountain people, etc.). Secondly, how much credit should be given to the hypothesis of dissemination from mother stocks that have projected their branches in all directions? Groups which swarm over the transhumance routes, social units which break up into segments, "colonies" of nomads settled in the Tell, individual migrations and collective expansion as the result of commercial activities, all these phenomena of the past are supposed to explain, for example, the fact that the same name can be found in groups that are a considerable distance apart. In point of fact, the genealogical system is only an attempt at an imaginary reconstruction (see that shown in Fig. 9). The attempt to produce a historical explanation is scarcely any better substantiated. This, however, raises a number of questions: by granting that the explanation lies partly in the swarming of peoples and partly in migrations, will one thereby have taken all the factors into account? Why does this recourse to the fiction of the eponymous father keep on recurring? Why do certain tribes attract others to them? It is necessary to reply to these questions before examining the problem—which seems to be at the core of all these difficulties—of the relation between the name and the tribal reality.

In the first place, social or political relations are formed on the model of family relations. The result is that the pattern of social organization is merely the projection of the family organization: several families make up the clan and several clans constitute the tribe, envisaged as an association of clans united by a bond analogous to that existing between members of the same family. Within this framework the genealogical fiction is allowed to come into play in order to establish a family relationship (filiation or cousinship) between individuals who have been joined together in accordance with quite different mechanisms. "This social organism may split up, or it may increase in size by the adoption of foreign elements, or it may even fuse together with other organisms . . . that have been fortuitously brought in contact. But with the passage of time an entirely theoretical explanation covers over and hides this utilitarian grouping; most of the great tribes are really only disguised confederations. The important thing is that its members should be ignorant of this fact or should have wilfully forgotten it, and that they should attribute to the bonds that unite them the same value that they do to the natural ties of blood relationship" (G. Marçais). In short, once it is admitted that the pattern of genealogical affiliation constitutes the structural model, then the constant recourse to the fiction of the eponymous ancestor as the foundation of every social unit—even when, in reality, this unit is merely a cluster —obviously becomes the only possible form of rationalization that can explain the real lack of cohesion that exists. This accounts, then, for the sort of desperate eagerness to establish a bond of fictitious kinship when real kinship is lacking; it explains why the tribe, too, claims to be of one name and one blood, and descended from a common ancestor, whereas in reality tribal ties are not based on a natural but on a conventional kinship.

Again, it is the homogeneity of the social and family structures which helps us realize that this society is organized around

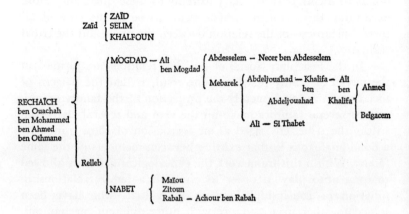

Fig. 9. Family Tree and Social Organization of the Tribe of the Ouled Rechaïch

According to the oral traditions, a certain Rechaïch ben Ouachah ben Mohammed, ben Ahmed ben Othmane is supposed to have come and settled in the country that is still occupied today by the tribe of the Ouled Rechaïch, which takes its name from him. The Ouled Zaïd and Ouled Selim consider their ancestors to have been Zaïd and Selim, the sons of a Zaïd who was the son of Rechaich. Mogdad is said to be the common ancestor of the four present-day groups that are joined together under the name of Megadda and to which four of his descendants, related to him by varying degrees of kinship—Necer ben Abdesselem, Ahmed ben Ali, Belgacem ben Ali, and Si Thabet ben Ali ben Mebarek—have given their name. Nabet is said to be the ancestor of

the clan. Beyond the clan the bond of unity becomes a fictitious one, so that the feeling of fraternity which spontaneously unites the members of this great family must be replaced by other principles of cohesion, and, lacking these, the larger unit will be disrupted. Consequently, because of the fragile foundations on which its unity is based—the cult of a common eponymous ancestor, "fictitious" kinship between its members, etc.—the tribe is aware of itself as a distinct entity only when it comes into opposition with other similar groups. Thus M. Despois notes that the cohesion of the Ouled Madhi was forged during the course of the struggles which opposed this tribe to several clans of the Ouled Naïl. Similarly the tribal patrimony is defined by oppo-

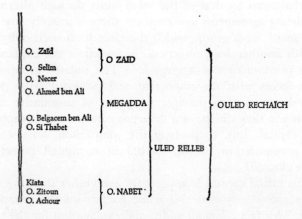

the three groups called the Ouled Nabet. His son Zitoun and grand-son Achour, the son of his son Rabah, have given their names to the Ouled Zitoun and the Ouled Achour, while the Kiata are supposed to be descended from a certain Maïou, an adopted son of Nabet.

More or less imaginary, in any case surrounded by legends like that of Maïou, this genealogy really appears to be that of a few great families who have imposed their authority on the other groups that go to make up the tribe. This may be seen, for example, in the fact that the family tree of the Megadda, the dominant group, is given in much more detail than that of the other groups, the Ouled Zaïd and Ouled Nabet. Similarly, it may be assumed that Relleb was introduced into the genealogical pattern to establish the social tie that links the Megadda to the Ouled Nabet and the Ouled Zaïd.

sition to that of other tribes. "A group that is much more ex-tensive than the clan, the tribe has a less developed personality; its functions relate particularly to what one might call 'external affairs,' relations with other tribes, questions of alliances, de-cisions as to the *h'orma* of the tribe, and its limits, and matters concerning weapons and war" (Doutté). Whereas the clan finds within itself its own principle of internal limitation, the tribe is essentially defined through its opposition to other tribes.

Why should a certain tribe be endowed with a magnetic power which attracts to it isolated, scattered and vulnerable groups? No doubt in a society in which equilibrium is achieved only through tension, the power of each social unit being counterbalanced by that of the other units through alternating or coexisting agreements and conflicts, there is scarcely any place for the small, weak group, which therefore finds itself obliged to join with another for protection. But what is the explanation for this phenomenon of aggregation? The isolated group tends to join forces with the important and powerful tribe, which thereby becomes even stronger by a sort of cumulative action analogous to that which, in a different context, causes capital to attract capital. But, to prolong the comparison, how was the initial accumulation of this capital of combined power and prestige effected?

This initial capital is apparently none other than *the name* and the ascendancy that this name confers on the group that bears it. This fact offers an additional explanation for the prevalence of the genealogical phenomenon. "Today particularly, when the exploits of the first conquerors, magnified by the passing of time, have been popularized by the rhapsodists, in a country in which almost every feature of the ground recalls these deeds to mind, there is not a shepherd who does not openly boast and actually believe that he is a descendant of the Hillalian warriors" (Vaissière). We are in a land in which certain names resound like the *chansons de geste*. In the eyes of the farmers, the nomads are endowed with an immense prestige: they speak the language of the Koran, move about on horseback, own flocks and do not work the land. The peasants seek out their protection, strive to speak their language and to become members of their tribe. They then adopt the patronymic name of the clan or tribe, and, as time passes, they end up believing themselves related to it. From then on they wish to be called Arabs, because they speak Arabic and have an Arab name. It is doubtless in this manner that onomastic changes have occurred in the course of time. One must take care not to conclude that onomastic identity means ethnic identity; the group may profess both its link with the tribal ancestor and the different ancestry traditionally assigned to its clan or family, and may call upon one or the other as occasion offers. Thus certain names are conserved, while the social aggregate is entirely altered, and certain groups remain identical, while their name may change—a complex interplay of permanence and change that is centered on the name.

The name is a power in itself. In the formation of the tribe of the Ouled Madhi the main role appears to have been played by the Athbedj of the Riyah confederation, the advance-guard of the Hillalian Arabs. In other tribes it was the moral and religious ascendancy of the marabouts that served as a cementing bond. Within the vicinity of the most venerated *zaouïa*, "maraboutic" tribes have been formed whose members consider themselves to be descendants of the saint and who, in addition to adopting the name of the marabout, have considered themselves as belonging to a religious nobility. In all these cases it is not at all surprising to find that the names conserved by tradition are those of the victorious clans or of the principal families whose protection was sought by the other different groups. Nor is it surprising to find that the names vary from one period to the next. Sometimes, from a previously constituted group, an influential family will emerge which imposes its name and authority upon the tribe. The result is that quite often the various elements which make up the tribe have nothing in common but a name and the history of this name. "Sometimes, even, there is no dominant group. The tribe, properly speaking, is only a confederation, an assemblage of heterogeneous elements joined together under a collective appellation and under an illustrious name to which one of the member families has the sole right" (G. Marçais).

In order to understand the importance of the name and the fact that it takes precedence over historical or social reality, one must look on it from the standpoint of honor and prestige. A certain group or family may place itself either under the protection of a family with a great name that has been made illustrious by legendary ancestors, or of a proud chief marked by divine favor, or even of an influential marabout. In return for tribute the family or group is allowed to develop under the wing of its defender, whose protection is at first granted as a temporary measure but in the course of time comes to be extended to its descendants. All those who bear the same name are united by a fundamental solidarity and by what might be called an identity

of being. The dependent group may be allowed to assume their
protector's name, which they then bear like a sort of emblem
that is both respected and feared. It would seem that a magic
bond unites the name to the thing named; to borrow the name is
to share in the virtues of its owner and particularly in his *baraka*
or vital force, that mysterious and beneficent power that favors
outstanding men. Thus we see the power attached to the name,
which is both a symbol and a guarantee of protection, a symbol
and guarantee of honor and prestige, or, better, a guarantee of
protection because it is a symbol of honor and prestige.

The actual mechanism is, however, much less simple than
the preceding analyses might lead one to believe. In point of fact
the phenomena of assimilation are always accompanied by phenomena of dissimilation. As Ferdinand de Saussure has remarked:
"In every mass of people, two opposing forces are simultaneously
at work: on the one hand the particularist spirit, the 'parochial
spirit'; on the other hand the desire to have mutual dealings
with other peoples, to have communication with other men"
(*Cours de linguistique générale*, p. 281). This law is operating
with full force in North African society; we have seen other
examples of it. The temptation to identify oneself with others
and lose one's individuality is being constantly counterbalanced
by the desire to oppose others, to assert oneself as being different,
to be oneself. The name, just as it constitutes the best symbol
and bond of unity, may also be employed as the best means of
developing the distinguishing feature on which the group will
seek to base its special identity. The result is a tendency to
classify groups according to name only, and the dispersal of
tribal names appears to reflect this tendency.

The principle of equilibrium between the forces of assimilation and dissimilation may also perhaps provide the key to those
strange organizations, the *çoffs*. Here the mechanism is possibly
even more in evidence; what is the unity of a *çoff* based on if it
is not on a name? The use of the name as the only basis for clas-
sifying groups here becomes the purest kind of formalism, since
the different "classes" have no real distinction, and the antithesis
between classes is either purely onomastic or is expressed by simple symbols (e.g., the opposition between the Ouled Madhi and

the Ouled Naïl is shown by black as opposed to red tents). The fact that the phenomena resulting from the operation of this law should hold such an important place in Algerian society can, moreover, be explained: indeed, if one admits, as M. Lévi-Strauss suggests, that human societies are defined "by a certain *optimum* of diversity beyond which they cannot go, but *below which they likewise cannot go without being endangered*" (*Race et histoire*, p. 9) it would appear that the existence of a common fund of culture of such a size and extent that it seemed liable to bring about a monotonous uniformity, made it necessary for the principle of dissimilation to come into operation.[23] This is no doubt why, when we consider the reality of Algeria, we are in turn struck by its unity and by its diversity.

[23] The fact that only those groups that are kept in equilibrium by another form of tension should escape this division into two opposing factions (for example, the opposition between the nomads and the gardeners of the oases, or between the nobles and vassals among the Touaregs) seems to constitute a proof *a contrario*.

5. The Common Cultural Heritage

Continuity and contrast, assimilation and dissimilation—in fact, beneath these appearances runs a single theme allowing infinite variations. But just as one must take care not to confuse diversification, that is, the conscious creation of differences, with diversity, so one must oppose identity to identification, which is a product of the contact and interaction between two cultural groups.

Cultural Interpenetration and Kaleidoscopic Mechanism

Exchanges have been so intense and so prolonged that opposed terms such as "Arabism" and "Berberism" now can scarcely be distinguished except by an artifice of the mind; one must see in them *ideal types* that are born of a merely historical reconstruction—with all the uncertainties that this implies—and that are necessary for the understanding of that original synthesis resulting from the dialectical confrontation which has always placed the local culture in opposition to eastern cultural importations. An example of this is Kabyle law, in which it is impossible to distinguish the borrowings that have been reinterpreted in terms of the receiving context from the vernacular institutions and from the dissimilating reconstructions protecting against invasion by Koranic law. Inversely, everywhere the Berber rock may be seen just beneath the surface of Moslem legislation. A mass of local institutions have been absorbed by Moslem law in the name of the principle of "necessity" and of "necessity making law." It has been noted by G. Marcy that the most typical Moslem institutions are marked by the spirit of Berber law, for example, the agricultural and stock-breeding associations, and the accessory stipulations of marriage contracts. An additional example may be noted in quite a different domain: while the nomadic Bedouins have spread values peculiar to a pastoral civilization, among which may be included a scorn for the techniques of the farm worker or artisan and a dislike for field work, on the other hand the sedentary mountain dwellers, as they have come down into the plains, have brought with them their way of life and, above all, their attachment to the land and to the stubborn toil required to make it fertile and their desire to make it their permanent possession. One must be careful not to think only in terms of the phenomena due to Arab influence simply because they are the more obvious. The Bedouin groups become Berberized as they become "sedentarized"; they are constantly absorbing Berbers into their groups and with them foreign techniques and traditions (political ones, for example). In the dialogue that brings the different groups of Algeria face to face, there is being worked out an original form of civilization, a cultural *koinè*. As a final example, it may be noted that the way of life peculiar to the Israelites[1] indicates that they were very closely related to the other Algerian "cultures"; a few characteristics will suffice: intensity of community feeling, patriarchal structure of the family, whose head is revered as much as any overlord, simultaneous or successive polygamy, a cult of saints resembling the cult of marabouts, superstitions and magic beliefs, Arab language, etc. Thus no group escapes this intense cultural interpenetration, and there is no group which does not seek to give itself a distinctive personality by stressing certain aspects of the common cultural heritage; the result is that while certain motifs stand out against this tapestry of interweaving lines, they always do so as shade upon shade. No doubt the principle of dissimilation is coming into play, but it operates within well-defined limits: shiftings of accent, partial reinterpretations, a different combination of elements, all are capable of bringing forth entirely new entities. If indeed it is a fact that Algerian

---

[1] The Israelites, about 150,000 in number, are divided according to origin into two groups, the "Spaniards," driven from Spain in 1492, and the autochthons, who are very similar in manners and civilization to the other natives of Algeria. While conserving a number of their traditions, they are for the most part engaged in the Moslem business sector and follow the European mode of life. They are particularly numerous in the cities.

society is organized in accordance with this kaleidoscopic mechanism, then it becomes clear why it presents these contradictory aspects of diversity and uniformity, of unity and multiplicity.[2]

This society has always looked to the past for its ideal way of life, so that, while change does take place, it has come about slowly. "Follow in the path of your father and your grandfather," says a Kabyle proverb. The general respect for the past becomes, in the Bedouin, a worship of the past. The latter is continually measuring his present position by reference to a golden age, an epic of conquering nobles that is sung by the *meddah* and that delights his soul; this inner migration toward the past, encouraged by myth and by the retrospective illusion, is an effort to obscure the harsh picture of present-day reality through evocations of ancient nobility and greatness which also seem to give promise of an imaginary kingdom to come. Thus it is that even the future is conceived of in the light of the past and that criticism or refusal of the present arises not so much from the vision of a better order or from the condemnation of the present and the past, but from the stirring memory of the ancient order, the basis of pride and the supreme defense against self-doubt.[3]

Fidelity to ancestral tradition, the highest of all values, dominates all the principal acts of social existence. It controls first of all the cultural apprenticeship of the young, both by determining the ends to be pursued and the means to be employed to achieve these ends. Tradition is communicated by the elders mainly by means of oral traditions, stories, legends, poems and songs, through which is transmitted that tight network of values which hems in the individual and inspires his every act. These teachings seem to have a double purpose: on the one hand, to impart the learning of the ancients and, on the other, to pass on the group's ideal image of itself. Hence these gnomic

[2] Since the principle of dissimilation operates mainly against the Europeans, the colonial situation and the war have aided in breaking down particularisms and have fostered the development of a national consciousness.

[3] A distinction must be made between traditional traditionalism and colonial traditionalism. In the first case there is fidelity to oneself, in the second, opposition to others. In one, there is inner adherence to the values offered by a sacred tradition, in the other, a passive resistance opposed to the intrusion of values that are being imposed from without.

poems, so numerous in Kabylia for example, these epitomes of wisdom and experience which provide a solution to the most distressing problems of existence and allow for the avoidance of errors by the repetition of behavior that has been tested in the past. "More than just a rule of life, the *mos majorum, lâada imezwura,* is a guarantee against bad luck, sometimes a vital necessity" (Mouloud Mammeri); in short, a shelter from the anguish of improvisation and from "catastrophic reactions." Women play an essential role in ensuring the permanence of tradition; the little girls learn from their elders the virtues that the wife should possess (absolute submission and discretion) and the magic and ritual practices (the cult of the "genii," local pilgrimages, rites, etc.) so that they may in turn play the role of guardians of tradition. This type of education tends to mold the child on the pattern of his ancestors and to forge for him a future which will be a living image of the past, so much so that this past is not experienced as such, that is as something left behind and situated some distance back in the temporal series, but as being lived again in the eternal present of the collective memory (cf. proper names: Ali the son of Ali).

Within his family the child also learns the rules of politeness and, to be more exact, the words he must say in each circumstance. The code of politeness supplies ready-made formulas for all the situations of existence, a genuine devotion to the cliche. A conversation can be carried on almost indefinitely without anything being left to improvisation. In short, the cultural apprenticeship tends to produce true psychological sets or prepared attitudes, the purpose of which is apparently to guard against, or even to forbid, any improvisation, or at least to impose an impersonal form on thought or personal feeling. In these formulas is expressed a whole philosophy of dignity, resignation and self-control, a philosophy which, from being constantly repeated and acted upon, pervades all thought and behavior. If it is realized that most of these expressions are confessions of faith and that in them is affirmed a wisdom in conformity with the Moslem vision of the world, then it will perhaps be better understood why the religious imprint on this society should be so marked. Indeed "politeness" is not only good manners but

an art of living; for example, *hachouma,* which is both dignity
and reserve, forbids the display of the self and its inmost feelings;
it is as though relationships with others—even within the family
—must necessarily be mediated by the culture, as though the person, in his unique oneness, had to efface himself behind the
mask of convention, which, being identical for all, suppresses
individuality in the interests of uniformity and conformity.

The concrete attitude of this society towards language is
revealed in the following conformity: whereas our civilization
uses language excessively and even thoughtlessly, North African
civilization makes a parsimonious and controlled use of it, forbids
people to talk indiscriminately on any subject, while verbal
manifestations of feeling are limited to certain occasions and
then can be repeated only in the form prescribed by the social
culture. Here, then, takes shape a way of life that is based on
a modesty which hides from others one's true nature and character and which prizes the pleasure of the formal word and the
measured gesture above the search for novel expressions and
effective action.

This preference for the artificial, this desire to reveal to
others not one's inmost being but a semblance of oneself, a stage
personage, appears to be characteristic of a personality which
envisages itself primarily as a "being who exists for others" (*être
pour autrui*), who is constantly before the eyes of others and who
is controlled by the overwhelming force of public opinion. While
the group controls behavior very carefully, particularly in the
realm of social relations, it is satisfied with this semblance of
himself offered by the individual and counts on ensuring from
without an outer conformity of behavior. Hence it becomes evident how the sentiment of honor, like its reverse, the fear of
shame and group censure, can affect so deeply the most trivial
actions of daily life and can dominate all relations with other
people.

A being who exists for others, the individual is also "a being
who exists through others" (*être par autrui*), who is, as it were,
the point of intersection of many relationships, and who has
much difficulty in thinking of himself as an autonomous personality. It is almost impossible for him to dissociate his own and

his children's destiny from the common destiny of the family group. In the rural communities, closed microcosms in which everyone knows everyone else, social pressure is very strong, and the individual is highly dependent on the group. Social life stifles any real personal life. The individual is narrowly confined within the extended family, whose choices and decisions rule his actions as they do his thoughts. But he does not consider this pressure to be a form of compulsion, since his greatest fear is to lose the vital solidarity which unites him to the group; and since he feels that he exists only as a member of the totality, that he has being only in relation to the group, that he is immersed in the "unanimous" group, that is to say, that he is engaged in a relationship that is prior in fact and in value to the terms which constitute it.

The family is the alpha and omega of the whole system: the primary group and structural model for any possible grouping, it is the indissociable atom of society which assigns and assures to each of its members his place, his function, his very reason for existence and, to a certain degree, his existence itself; the center of a way of life and a tradition which provide it with a firm foundation and which it is therefore resolutely determined to maintain; last but by no means least, it is a coherent and stable unit situated in a network of common interests whose permanence and security must be assured above all else, even, if necessary, to the detriment of individual aspirations and interests.

The preponderance within the extended family of the agnatic group implies, among other things, the superiority of rights of descent over the rights of marriage and the complete subjection of the wife, a fact which leads to the custom of either simultaneous or successive polygamy.[4] This custom is facilitated by the power of repudiation conferred on the husband and by the separation of the sexes. A paradoxical consequence of male

[4] Polygamy is steadily becoming less frequent (89,000 polygamists in 1886 as opposed to 29,571 in 1954). The ratio of polygamists to the total male population was reduced from 64 per 1,000 in 1911 to 30 per 1,000 in 1948. The proportion is higher in the territories of the south (47.2 per 1,000 compared to 23 per 1,000 in the *département* of Algiers in 1948). It is very low in the mountainous regions.

superiority is the existence of a female society that is subordinate but at the same time relatively autonomous. This society of women who live in a closed world, who are not permitted
to assume any important responsibilities and who, for the most
part, receive no religious education, exerts a great influence over
the masculine society, both because it gives the children their
earliest training and passes on to them the magic beliefs in
ritual practices and because it opposes an effective, secret and
underground resistance to any modification of a traditional order
of which, at first sight, it would appear to be the victim.

The outstanding fact, however, is *the invariability of the
social structures,* which remain constant in spite of the great
diversity of ways and conditions of life. In all cases family
descent is defined in terms of the patrilinear relationship; the
social units are based on the existence of a common ancestor who
is often revered and worshiped. Everywhere the social system is
patterned on the model of the genealogical system, thereby permitting—in theory at least—dispersed and ramified groups to
discover common ancestors. Although it constitutes the best system around which to organize social units and their interconnect-
ing relations, the real or mythical genealogy supporting the
onomastic logic is really only the social structure projected into
the past and thereby rationalized and legitimized (see Fig. 10).
In each village (or clan) of Kabylia, one family belonging, in
certain cases, to the oldest branch and for this reason deemed
to have sacred powers, was given the privileges of officiating at
the solemn spring-plowing ceremonies and of leading the group
into war. In the southern Aurès, in addition to performing these
functions, this family was called upon to march at the head of
the group when it was time for it to move with the flocks. This
custom was the same as that prevailing among the nomads and
semi-nomads. Everywhere is found the same lack of precision in
political nomenclature. There are several reasons for this: (1)
there are few occasions when the use of proper names to designate social units will not suffice, if exception is made of the great
tribal gatherings which formerly met for war, for the allotment
of specific territories, and for decisions as to flock movements;
(2) the definition of the social unit varies with the unit in terms

of which it is being defined; (3) apart from those restricted groups that are united by ties of real consanguinity, the political organization may be on occasion redefined to meet the needs of the moment, with the result that, in case of conflict between groups of different lineages, different political units are formed; and most important, (4) both the narrowest and the widest social units have been organized in accordance with the same structural pattern, so that there exist a great number of almost equivalent potential points of segmentation, although it remains true that the most stable and coherent group is the clan in which the tie of kinship is effectively felt by its members. If one is to believe popular interpretations, the different groups are supposed to be the result of a process of subdividing which began with the original stock and proceeded in accordance with the logic of kinship through the male descendants. It is claimed that the tribe, originally only one great family, broke up into several groups which were formed by the descendants of each of the sons of the common ancestor and which took their name from these sons. Through successive dividings and subdividings operating in accordance with the same principle, it is claimed that these groups have in turn given rise to the present multiplicity. Thus there is said to be no difference between the most extended and the narrowest group except for differences in size and in remoteness from the founding ancestor, the latter distinction determining the degrees of alliance and the types of allegiance. Although this spontaneous theory is usually only a rationalization, it brings out the fact that the whole system is dominated by the tension between the tendency to fusion and the tendency to fission, the basic group tending to dissociate itself from its counterparts as it becomes more self-contained and strengthens its own unity. The ambiguity of the whole system may again be found in the basic unit on which it is modeled, namely the family, the scene of rivalry between two types of relationship, that of authority, modeled on the relation between father and son, and that of brotherhood. Each brother is the potential breaking point of the family continuum and of opposition between the segments of the same line of descent (cf. the Kabyle proverb: "I hate my brother, but I hate whoever hates him"); the rupture remains in

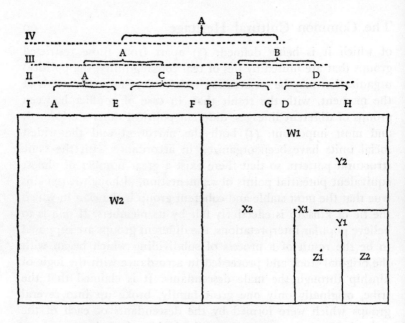

Fig. 10. Dynamics of the Social Groups in Kabylia

This simplified family tree illustrates clearly the logic involved in conflicts between patrilinear branches. When individual A is opposed to individual E, with the two belonging to generation I, only their respective groups enter into the quarrel. When A (or E) is opposed to C (or F), the group of A joins the group of E, that is to say all the descendants of A (II) are opposed to groups C and F, the descendants of C (II). When A (or E, or C or F) is opposed to B (or G, or D, or H), the groups of A, C, E and F, namely the descendants of A (III) are opposed to groups B, G, D, and H, the descendants of B (III). When A (or E, or C, etc.) is opposed to N or P, descendants of a different ancestor, the groups of A, E, C, F, B, G, D, H, that is to say all the descendants of A (IV) are opposed to N or P. Thus each family connection, even at the lowest level, constitutes a virtual social unit. The political organization is redefined in each case in accordance with the relative position in the family tree of the individuals who are in conflict with one another. Consequently the same logical process can bring together greatly extended groups, that is to say, all the descendants to the fourth or fifth generation of a known or a mythical ancestor, as well as very restricted groups such as the extended family or even the single family.

The same process comes into operation whether dealing with conflicts between individuals or conflicts between groups, the question of membership in a certain group being settled by reference to the nature of the opposing group. When Z_1 is opposed to Z_2 (or else when A considers himself to be a member of Z_1 in relation to E and considers the latter to be a member of Z_2 because he is his opponent), no other group intervenes. When Y_1 is fighting against Y_2 (or else when A considers himself to be a member of Y_1 through his opposition to C who is considered to be a member of Y_2), then Z_1 and Z_2 unite to form Y_1. When X_1 is opposing X_2 (or when A, member of X_1, is opposing B, member of X_2), Y_1 and Y_2 unite to form X_1. When W_1 is opposing W_2 (or when A, member of W_1, is opposing N or P, member of W_2), then X_1 and X_2 join to form W_1, and so on.

The existence of possible oppositions between the agnatic branches of different generations, even the existence of oppositions within the same family, must not be allowed to hide the fact that society is organized at all levels in accordance with the same principle. Paradoxically, it is because the principle of unification—the opposition mechanism—is the same for the widest as for the most restricted groups that cohesion between branches or within the agnatic sections is not permanent but is dependent on circumstance. The single organizing principle does not prevent groups from being united in a great many different ways.

Moreover, although it plays a decisive role, it would be quite wrong to regard this method of attaining solidarity through opposition to similar groups as being the only principle of unification for the social groups. The Kabyles make a distinction between *taymat,* meaning both "fraternity" and the group of brothers, and *tadjadit,* consanguinity and lineage, the entire group of descendants of the same real or mythical ancestor. The point being raised here is that there are two ways of integrating an individual into the group. The *taymat* is invoked when it is a question of opposing oneself to another group; for example, if the clan is attacked, the individual considers himself to be a member of the clan *tagmat.* This is a real and active solidarity between individuals joined by true ties of kinship which possibly go back to the third and fourth generation. Membership in the *tadjadit* is determined not by circumstances but by the position of the individual in the genealogical tree, a position which determines his bonds of solidarity with a specific group of individuals. The *tadjadit* is much wider in scope than the *taymat* which is but one branch, whose importance varies with circumstances, of the total unit of solidarity that is based on genealogical ties. The Kabyles resort to the concept of *tadjadit* to establish solidarities that are widely extended but are more or less consciously understood as being mythical in origin. If someone, for example, is rejected by the group, he can plead that he belongs to the *tadjadit.* In such a context, a clearer understanding may be gained of the function of a system based on genealogy which allows present-day groups to lay claim to having roots in a more or less imaginary past.

Thus the cohesion of the group can be established in two very different ways, either by opposition and in relation to another group, or in an absolute manner and by reference to itself. Undoubtedly "fraternity," or *taymat,* the integrating principle for social units which are only defined through their opposition to other similar units, actually plays a much greater role than does the consciousness of a common heritage, *tadjadit.* For do they not say: *"Taymat* is today, *tadjadit* belongs to yesterday"?

These analyses also allow one to understand certain characteristic features of North African societies: the lack of precision in political terminology resulting from the fact that the social units and their generic name are always defined in relation to special and varying frames of reference; the function of marriage with the parallel female cousin in order thereby to tighten the bonds within the smallest social unit, which is itself constantly threatened with being split (in this case, for example, A and E), and to isolate it from the other units at the same level (C and F, B and G, D and H); and finally the authority of the father or grandfather (*djeddi*) who alone can maintain real cohesion within the group of agnates.

a potential state as long as the *authority of the father* is fully exercised, such authority being founded mainly on the institution of joint property, on the sentiment of honor, and on the power of disinheriting. It is from the point of view of this logic that marriage with the parallel cousin, the closest female relation in the family line outside the limits of incest, may be understood; this union, which presupposes the authority of the head of the family, tends in point of fact to strengthen the cohesion of the minimal agnatic unit, and at the same time tends to dissociate it from homologous segments by tying marriage bonds within the group rather than outside it. Thus light is shed on the function of the genealogical model, which allows, if need be, for the setting up of the most extensive types of social units in spite of the real division that may exist among the associated groups and in spite of their diversity of origin.

The Economy and Attitude Toward Life

This distinctive form of interhuman relationships can be understood only by reference to the specific mode of relationship existing between man and the soil. Indeed, if this civilization is inseparable from a particular type of economy (which even in the present day affects three-quarters of the indigenous population), the economy itself can be understood only in terms of this civilization, because of the fact that it is closely tied to the social structures whose cohesion more or less guarantees a balance between man and his natural environment. This economy is dominated by a lack of technological resources, which leads to various consequences: in the first place, an almost total dependence on physical surroundings and on climatic conditions, the balance between resources and needs being infinitely more sensitive to the rain cycle than to fluctuations in the world market; secondly, the immense disproportion between production on the one hand and the expenditure of time and effort and the number of workers employed on the other; and, finally, the excessive growth of human relationships which have been developed partly by way of compensation.

In such a system, work aims only at satisfying primary needs and at ensuring the group's subsistence. Each unit seeks to be self-sufficient, consuming its own produce. Most of the trade is done by barter. Money, together with certain articles of consumption, is used to provide a common denominator of value, but is not employed in speculation. Thus this society is almost totally ignorant of capital and capitalistic mechanisms. While there exists an accumulation of transferable property and assets (particularly in the form of jewels), there is no amassing of capital in the true sense. Both in production and in trading exchanges relations are personal, direct and specific; hence the importance of the exchange based on honor and prestige, of those protective agreements and cooperative associations which, in the absence of capital and a labor market, ensure the circulation of goods and services.

The bond which unites the fellah to his land is mystical rather than utilitarian. He belongs to his fields much more than his fields belong to him. He is attached to his land by deeply affective ties, as witness the agrarian rites in which is expressed a sentiment of dependency in regard to this land, which cannot be treated as a mere raw material but rather as a foster-mother whose authority must be obeyed, since, in the final analysis, it is on her benevolence or ill-will, much more than on human effort, that wealth or poverty depend. Should not this fatalism that has been associated with Islam be rather considered to be the fatalism of the peasant conscious of his powerlessness when confronted with the caprices of nature?

The work of the individual, which is prescribed and determined by the head of the family and carried out in a familiar setting in collaboration with the family group, is felt to be both creation and communion. The land is an end in itself and not a mere means of existence, and work is not a way of earning a living but a way of life. With this in mind, the following often noted characteristic of the precapitalist spirit may perhaps be better understood: an increase in wages brings about a reduction in the amount of work performed. In other words, for the traditionalist mind, the prospect of earning more money is less attractive than that of doing less work. The worker does not ask himself how much he could earn in a day by working his hardest, but, indifferent to the extra money to be gained, how hard he will have to work to earn his previous wage, which was adequate to supply his needs. As Max Weber has said, "Man does not have a natural desire to keep on earning more money, but simply wishes to lead his accustomed life and to earn just enough money to maintain this mode of living."

This conception of work is inseparable from another characteristic feature of this traditionalist spirit, namely the absence of rational economic planning. For the peasant living in a natural environment, time does not have the same significance that it does in a technical environment in which working time is closely calculated; since the concern for productivity which leads to the quantitative evaluation of time is completely unknown, it is the work to be done which prescribes the time schedule, and not the time schedule which limits the amount of work that is done. Proof of this attitude is seen in the fact that land is evaluated in terms of plowing-days. The rhythm of work on the farm is closely linked to biological, animal and vegetable cycles; life is given a rhythm by the divisions of the ritual calendar, the actualization of a mythology; the peasant spirit traditionally implies a submissiveness to time, since rural life is one long wait for the natural cycles to revolve. Nothing is more foreign to it than an attempt to gain power over the future. This does not mean that there is a total absence of that economic calculation which consists, by definition, of making a choice from among different possibilities that cannot be simultaneously satisfied. The existence of reserves (the *guelâa*) is a proof of this. But is this really an example of a rational economic calculation? Economists distinguish between direct wealth, which offers or may offer an immediate satisfaction, and indirect wealth, which aids in the production of direct wealth but which in itself affords no satisfaction. The building up of reserves, which consists of setting aside a portion of the direct wealth as a reserve for future use, and which presupposes *forethought* acting to impose abstention from consumption, must be distinguished from the hoarding and accumulation of indirect wealth for capitalistic purposes (investment), this "creative saving" being based upon a calculated, rational *forecast*. Thus the economic calculation to be found in an agricultural economy, in which the whole production cycle can be taken in at a single glance, in which the peasant does not separate his labor from its economic result, and in which the setting aside of reserves is simply a deferred form of consumption, presupposes the idea of a concrete and almost tangible future. So it is, for example, that the expenditures for investment in new stock are decided not in terms of the anticipated profit, but in terms of the revenue from the preceding year's harvest. The modern economic system, in which the production process is extremely long and can be set up only after precise calculations, presupposes on the contrary the existence of an abstract objective. In short, the conception of an abstract and symbolic future is the condition that makes possible the commonest and most fundamental economic institutions and activities of our society: fiduciary currency derived from exchange through a process of symbolization, conceptualization and projection into the future; wage earning and the rational timing of wage distribution, which implies a rational economic calculation; industrial operations and commercialization which imply planning, etc.

Nothing is farther removed from this rational speculation dealing with an abstract future than the life of the fellah. If the institution of credit is as difficult for him to understand as the cruel hold of usury and *rahnia* would seem to indicate, it is because it is associated with a completely different way of thinking (cf. P. Bourdieu, "The Attitude of the Algerian Peasant," in *Mediterranean Countrymen,* Julian Pitt-Rivers, ed., pp. 45-62).

The credit to which he resorts is a kind of emergency credit intended only to relieve consumers' needs, but, in this society, credit is normally replaced by a solidarity and mutual aid or by the honorable exchange of which the *taousa* affords an example. The modern institution of credit, like the *taousa*, presupposes trust—a trust, to be sure, that is not unmixed with distrust, since, because the repayment or countergift is deferred, the future intervenes as a factor and with it the element of risk. But while each takes on analogous functions in its own system, these institutions differ greatly. Whereas in the exchange based on honor the duty of returning and of returning more than one has received is imposed by personal honesty, the guarantees being provided by the man rather than by the wealth at his disposal, in the modern credit system the lender takes care to guarantee his loan by demanding securities (solvency of the debtor, etc.); moreover, credit implies the idea of interest and presupposes that the value of time can be reckoned as an object of rational calculation. Such a calculation, as well as exact methods of accounting, is absent from the traditional economy, whether due to the logic of overgenerosity in repayment or because the prices of goods have been set by tradition so that the seller restricts his efforts to disposing of as much as he can at these fixed prices. Finally, the gift establishes a supra-economic bond between two *persons,* since the idea of the countergift is already implied in the interhuman relation created by the original gift and to which it lends an added solemnity; modern credit presupposes, on the other hand, completely impersonal relationships and the taking into account of a purely abstract future. Thus we see contrasted two radically different conceptions of business dealings and of the most fundamental human and economic values, the one based on honor and prestige, the other on self-interest and calculation.

As a final characteristic of this civilization, in which economic relations are always personal and direct, we have the absence of class antagonisms: to be sure, considerable differences in wealth and status separate the owner from the worker or the landed proprietor from the sharecropper, but the pact which unites them is interpreted according to a logic of honor, so that the major conflict is not, as in our society, between wage earners and employers, but between borrowers and usurers.

It is as if this society refused to face economic reality and to understand that an economy is governed by its own laws—laws different from those which regulate interpersonal and, more particularly, family relationships. This has resulted in a permanent ambiguity: the system of exchanges is played in the double register of unavowed self-interest and loudly proclaimed generosity, and this may explain why the true economic motives (from our point of view) are always hidden under the veil of fraternity, loyalty or prestige. Is not the logic of the gift, of mutual aid or of the pact of honor a way of surmounting or of concealing the calculations of self-interest? While the bestowing of the gift, like the extending of credit, demands in return the duty of repaying more than one has received, this honorable obligation, however imperative it may be, is only implied. Since the countergift is postponed, one might think that the generous exchange, contrary to the brutal cash-down or charge, tends by means of this time lag to conceal the self-interest that would be manifest in a simultaneous transaction. It is as if this society were contriving to deprive economic dealings and relations of their strict economic meaning by accentuating their symbolic significance and function.

Islam and North African Society

Everywhere in the Maghreb may be seen the imprint and the ascendancy of Islam; no matter how restricted a social unit may be, it examines, elaborates or reinterprets itself by reference to Koranic dogma. The set phrases of polite speech or the social gestures which are all so many affirmations of Islamic values, the daily conversation punctuated by eulogies of, and invocations to, the Prophet and many other traits illustrate the tight control that religion exercises over daily life. The whole of life from birth to death is marked by a series of Islamic, or Islamized, ceremonies, rites, customs and prescriptions. There are the obligations and the interdictions, the distinction between the kinds of meats that may or may not be eaten, the prohibitions against fermented drinks, against gambling, and against charging interest on loans. There is the custom of circumcision or the wearing of the veil. There are the law courts, whose judgments are based on the jurisprudence of the Koran, and the cadis, whose function is both religious and social. There are the rites performed at birth and at death, and those which mark all life's activities—meals, illnesses and marriages. There are the religious festivals, which give a rhythm to social and family life; the call to prayer uttered by the muezzin five times a day from the top of the minarets, marking the passing of time. There are the conjugal ties, the testamentary laws, the domestic customs, and the institutions of a combined legal, religious and social character. There is the feeling of belonging to a community of believers, of belonging to the "House of Islam." In short, it is the atmosphere of Islam which permeates all of life, not only religious or intellectual life, but private, social and professional life.

However, to consider Islam as the determining or predominant *cause* of all cultural phenomena would be no less fallacious than to consider contemporary religion as being merely a *reflection* of the economic and social structures. Indeed Islam, considered as a religious message, is not connected with any particular economic or social system; and justification could very well be found for radically different political orders or economic systems in the name of the same religious doctrine. In the second place, there exist obvious analogies between historical Islam and the religion of civilizations not yet subjected to industrial revolution, particularly in their attitude to economic facts. Certain writers consider that the total, absolute control of religion over daily life, the failure to distinguish between dogma and law, between law and ethics, between the spiritual and the temporal, are all characteristic of Islam; but have they not made the error of attributing solely to the Islamic spirit an attitude to religion that is not peculiar to the Moslem only and that must be understood as one aspect of the Algerians' more general attitude toward the world? Could it not be that they have confused the "age of theology" (as Comte would have put it) of the Moslem society with the theology of the Islamic religion?

Let us consider, for example, the traditionalist attitude that has so often been imputed to Moslem "fatalism." Doubtless, in the old Algeria, traditionalism assumed its particular form because all the acts of existence were tinged with religiosity; marabouts, religious brotherhoods, and the *khouan* constituted the framework of rural life; the cult of patron saints, connected with the seasonal cycle of farm tasks and with the calendar specifying social and ritual events, conferred upon the driest aspects of religious dogma a vivid, eloquent form; the innumerable set phrases with which everyday conversation is interspersed and in which are expressed resignation to the hazards of existence, abandonment to the Divine Will and submission to the *mektoub,* helped to strengthen this inner attitude by giving it a means of expression, a language, by providing justifications and rationalizations. It is no less true that the fundamental traits of the traditionalist spirit peculiar to the native of Algeria, namely, the attitude of submission to nature and to the passage of time, can also be observed in most civilizations which have not yet had an industrial revolution, and hence these characteristics must not be considered as the consequences of an adherence to the Islamic religion.

Moreover, theologians have noted that the Koran hesitates between the doctrine of predestination and the affirmation of free will. That the doctrine of predestination, which could very well have remained a belief reserved for learned theologians, should have become a popular belief that is profoundly felt and is reaffirmed at every opportunity, that the believers should particularly have retained the fatalistic aspect of the Koranic message and should have found in it the justification for a traditional way of life (whereas predestination does not necessarily signify predetermination and belief in predestination can actuate an entirely different way of behavior)—these are the facts that create a problem. If we explain the fatalistic attitude of the believer as being caused by religion alone, would we not be putting forward as an explanation the very thing that needs to be explained? [5]

The religious message combines both allusion and ellipsis; it suggests more than it defines. It is characterized by a superabundance of meanings and by a great number of possible interpretations. Consequently it offers only glimpses of its true meaning, and no one image conveys the entire message. It has often been remarked that what seem to theologians to be the crudest and most superficial aspects of the Koranic message are often those to which the greatest importance is attached in social life. Inversely, the most strictly prescribed ways of conduct are not the ones that are most rigorously obeyed. There are few Moslem Algerians, for example, who say their five prayers daily, particularly in the urban environment, whereas prescriptions that are secondary from the point of view of dogma (taboos concerning food, circumcision, the wearing of the veil, etc.) are scrupulously observed and play an important role in the life of the religious community. We also know that historical Islam is quite the opposite of a monolithic reality and that in it there may be distinguished profoundly different and even contradictory tendencies (modernist, traditionalist, secularist, reformist). Thus it would seem as if the actual religion of a civilization were the result of a selection, a selection which would illustrate the totality of choices (conscious or unconscious) that this civilization is making by the very fact of its existence. Without denying that each religious message has its own structure and presents an original system of meanings and values which are offered as "objective potentialities," without denying that among these potentialities there are some which offer themselves with greater urgency and which seem to

[5] One could make a similar analysis concerning the social character of the religious duties. The fact that the fundamental religious practices (prayer, fasting, almsgiving, pilgrimage) should often assume the form of social demonstrations, the fact that the observance of the religious imperatives may often be attributed primarily to group pressure, all these features and many others besides are by no means special features of the Moslem religion, but must be understood by reference to the type of social attitude favored by Algerian society: the relationship to others takes precedence over the relationship to oneself, and consequently the feeling of the fault as shame in the eyes of others takes precedence over the feeling of sin as shame in one's own eyes or in the eyes of God.

have a greater claim to existence, one must nevertheless admit
that everything seems to indicate that every civilization, at each
period of its development, "was making a choice," by reference
to the system of its fundamental choices (a culture *being* a system
of choices which no one *makes*), of those aspects of the religious
message which were to be turned into reality while the others
would be discarded.

Thus it is that all the choices that the culture has turned
into reality in such spheres as religion, economics, politics, etc.,
appear to have been organized around the same fundamental
intention. The strength of Islam in Algeria is due, indeed, to
the fact that it is in harmony with the spirit of the Algerian
civilization. The Koranic message contains prescriptions that are
in conformity with the traditionalist way of life, and the system
of standards that it proposes is in agreement with the underlying
structures of Algerian society. But are we not merely illustrating
the miracle of the pre-established harmony between the two by
making an arbitrary distinction between the implicit patterns
of behavior and the explicit standards set by religion? Are not
the patterns of behavior in reality the norms that are imposed
by religion, even when they are not understood as such? Let
us take, for example, the prohibition against lending money at
interest. Does this not illustrate the influence of the religious
doctrine, and should we not then conclude that the Islamic ethi-
cal system determines the economic ethos of Algeria? In reality,
the control of religion over daily life and particularly over economic behavior is due to the fact that it is "preaching to the
converted," so to speak, to the fact that the standards and the
values which it proposes are in full agreement with established
patterns of behavior. Since the form of credit they employ is a
credit devised to meet the needs of consumption and not of
production, popular conscience is strongly aroused against
excessive usury. In the original Algerian society, speculative practices were left to the members of heterodox sects, such as the
Mozabites, or of different faiths such as the Israelites.[6] The system
of values that is implicitly affirmed in the economic life does not

---

[6] In the cities, lending at usurious rates of interest has always been
practiced by certain Moslems, although in a disguised form.

permit material values to be recognized. Moreover, is not the prohibition against loaning money at interest merely the negative aspect of a positive demand for a morality based on honor, as exemplified in the obligation to extend fraternal aid? In short, the economic ethos of this civilization finds a perfect expression in the moral philosophy of Islam. The exaltation of the attitude of contemplation over that of action, the sense of the futility of all earthly things, the condemnation of cupidity and of the love of wealth, the censure of those who look down upon the poor and the unfortunate, the encouragement given to the virtues of hospitality, mutual aid and politeness (*adab*), the feeling of belonging to a religious fraternity that is free of any economic or social basis, are all prescriptions of the Koranic doctrine that are in close agreement with the spirit of the Algerian culture. Historical Islam has codified the conception of property that is characteristic of Algerian society (joint possession, the right of pre-emption, etc.), and has sanctioned the essential structures of this society. The Koran makes the agnatic family the base of the *umma* and recognizes the agnatic group to be the main concern of law: hence all the regulations concerning marriage, repudiation or inheritance; hence the primacy of the group and the inferior status of woman. Finally, while working to create a universal community founded on ties other than those of kinship, Islam has nevertheless allowed social communities such as the clan or the tribe to continue to exist, so that ties of blood have long continued to prevail, at least in rural society, over the ties created by belonging to the Moslem community.

It is, then, because of the acknowledged fact that there exists a structural affinity between the way of life favored by the Moslem religion and the way of life peculiar to the Algerian society that the Koranic message has been able to penetrate so deeply into this society. But, in addition, one has the feeling that having called upon the religious message to provide solutions to the problems created by its existence, Algerian society has retained mainly those answers which consecrate, that is to say corroborate and ratify, sanction and sanctify, the answer that it had already provided through the very fact of its existence. Thus the link between Algerian society and the Moslem religion is not that of cause and effect, but rather that of the implicit to the explicit, or, we could equally say, of the experienced to the formulated. The Moslem religion provides an unexcelled means of expression whereby the tacit rules of conduct may be enunciated. Algerian society avows and proclaims itself to be Moslem, and the nature of this confession is such that it brings into being what is being confessed by the mere fact of expressing it in words.

The product of an involved interaction between the underlying structures of the culture and the standards proposed by the religious message, orthodox religion is one of the forms of self-awareness acquired by the community. According to Wilhelm von Humboldt, "Man apprehends objects mainly . . . as language presents them to him. In accordance with the same process by which he unravels language out of his own being, he also becomes inextricably entangled in this language; and each language forms a magic circle around the people to which it belongs, a circle from which one can escape only by taking a leap into a different circle." Historical religion, as a language, is not a simple reproduction of reality, but indeed the symbolic form through which the reality itself is revealed. Religion unveils reality, but at the same time it veils it, since this reality is unveiled only by way of religion. These ritual words, the vows, the reflections concerning existence, the prohibitions and prescriptions, the innumerable formal phrases of daily language, do not merely describe the world and actual experience, but, by expressing them in words, they are actually creating them; by saying them aloud, they shape them to the spoken word.

The religious life of Algeria bears witness to this reciprocal adjustment of the standards set up by religion and the cultural structures. Among the fundamental religious prescriptions, those which are unanimously observed are the ones whose social character is most clearly marked; thus the fast of Ramadan, which is controlled by the pressure of public opinion, is almost unanimously practiced, whereas prayer is often neglected. Islam is felt as a pressure rather than as a call, and the religion of the masses tends to ensure that a minimum of exterior conformity of behavior will be observed. This type of religiosity, expressed principally by ways of conduct that are regulated by ritual prescription and controlled by custom, results from the way of life peculiar to the masses rather than from the Moslem religion itself. As Max

Weber has written, "A religion fit for a 'hero' or a 'virtuoso' has always opposed a religiosity of the masses"; in this respect one must not take the word "mass" to mean those who occupy a socially inferior position in the secular hierarchy, but rather those who, from the religious point of view, are not "virtuosos." And how could they be? The great majority of the Moslems of Algeria do not have access to the religious texts, and generally know the message of Mohammed only through oral traditions which have deformed and caricaturized it; they possess only fragments of Moslem law, which have been often reinterpreted and confused with popular beliefs. The teaching of the Koran, which formerly flourished even in the country districts, has lost its vitality and its dynamism. Moreover, because of the absence of any properly constituted clergy, the religious education of the masses remains in a very rudimentary state. Ritual phrases and ways of behavior are transmitted much more easily than are the doctrinal writings, which are generally reserved for scholars. So it is not surprising that religious fervor and the uplift of the heart are often replaced by the automatisms of custom and the illusions of superstition.[7]

In the traditional society the religion of the city dwellers, that of the often cultivated and refined bourgeois who are conscious of belonging to a universal religion and who seek to define their form of religion by contrasting it with the ritualism of the country dwellers—the cities have always been the favorite site of the reformist movement—has been opposed by the religion of the rural dwellers, a religion completely permeated with survivals from the past, profoundly rooted in the soil, and generally unaware of the subtleties of dogma or theology. But each of these forms of religion was defined by comparison with the other: the religion of the country districts, however far removed it was in

[7] The observance of the Moslem religion, particularly the prescriptions whose social aspect is evident (fasting, etc.) is also, in the colonial context, a way of defending the personal identity, and it has now taken on the function of a symbol, a symbol which expresses both an alliance and an exclusion. Hence may be explained, at least in part, the revival of Islam following the conquest (e.g., the erection of the mosques in Kabylia between 1925 and 1945) and the renewed devotion to religious practices which has been noted since 1955.

spirit and in practice from the authentic Moslem religion, never-theless remained attached to Islam because of the fact that it never ceased judging and interpreting itself by reference to the standards prescribed by Islam; as for the religion of the city dwellers, it was certainly not unaffected by the naturistic beliefs, the fear of the "genii" or the cult of saints that were character-istic of the rural religion.[8]

The Islam of the rural communities is closely linked to the cultural reality; it is correlated with the social structures and the economic activities. Indeed, this form of religiosity is basically appropriate to the community-minded, to the man whose reli-gious experience springs from his awareness of collective ties. The veneration for the head of the family (the symbol of the community and the priest of the domestic religion) and the ances-tor-worship (which was formerly the focal point of all rites and ceremonies) illustrate the fact that the extended family, the keystone of the cultural system, is also a religious unit. The cult of nature, of grottoes and springs, trees and rocks; the belief that the world is peopled with "genii," mysterious beings everywhere present and imbued with a sort of diffused and impersonal holiness, the *baraka,* this mysterious and beneficent power which favors elite beings and can be transmitted by heredity, by initiation or by the borrowing of the name; the magic practices designed to conjure up the powers of nature and to make the land fertile and wives prolific—all these are typical of the reli-gion of the peasant, a man who feels greatly dependent on the natural world and who, by placing the accent on ritual, makes life become a kind of long-drawn-out liturgy.

The God of Koranic dogma remains remote, inaccessible and impenetrable; the common man feels the need to be in closer contact with this Divinity, and attempts to draw near Him by calling on mediators and intercessors. The fellah and the woman of the people, who quite often are completely ignorant of the true religion, beg favors of those saints who are both familiar and prestigious, human and superhuman, whose miracles have been recorded by the ancients, whose names are attached to particular

[8] One could also make a distinction between the religion of the men and that of the women.

sites, regions or tribes, and to whom are attributed specific powers. Since the saints have been endowed with *baraka,* they can cure illnesses, foresee the future or bestow the blessing of fertility. So it is that the belief in *baraka* has become the essential tenet underlying the organization of the religious brotherhoods and the *zaouia,* both of whom claim to be invested with the authority of some particularly revered and powerful saint. The marabouts and the dignitaries of the brotherhoods offer a form of religion which speaks to the heart and to the imagination; by their material and moral power they exercise an immense influence over the life of the country districts. On the whole, Islam has acquired its strength among the rural population and taken on its present form because it has been able to accommodate itself to the aspirations of these country folk at the same time as it was assimilating them and because they were shaping it while it was shaping them. The popular religion is the scene and the result of a continuous, complex interaction between the local forces and the universal message. The attitude of the orthodox religion with respect to this marginal religion has always been one both of intransigence and of tolerance. The tendency to consider the local laws, such as the Berber customs, or the beliefs in magic and the naturistic cults as survivals or deviations has always been counterbalanced by the more or less methodical attempt to absorb these forms of religion or these laws without granting them open recognition. In the same way a great number of local customs have been incorporated into the penal and civil law, although they were not officially recognized as legal obligations. Against this background, because the "marginal" folk religion, for its part, is at all times referring to the universal religion for guidance, there is an inextricable mingling of reciprocal attitudes: certain animistic or magical practices are translated into the language of the universal religion: for example, it is frequently the case that sacred springs, grottoes and rocks are placed under the protection of a holy personage; precepts of the universal religion are redefined in terms of local customs; thus there is both an obstinate defense of the rural religion's individuality and a unanimously felt recognition of the fact that it is a part of Islam. The secret feeling of shame inspired by contact with the orthodox religion is always counteracted by the sometimes exaggerated assertion of irreducible uniqueness. The interaction of reinterpretations, oppositions, and compromises has made Algerian Islam into a singularly complex whole, in which no distinction can be made, except arbitrarily, between what is peculiar to Islam and what has been contributed by the local stock, and in which agrarian beliefs cannot be distinguished from the strictly religious beliefs. Islam in North Africa presents itself as a stratified system in which different levels can be isolated by analysis: animistic devotion, naturistic cults, agrarian rites; the cult of saints and marabouts; the control of practical affairs by religion; applied law; dogma and esoteric mysticism. A differential analysis would no doubt reveal a diversity of "religious profiles." These would indicate the hierarchical integration in each individual of the different levels, the relative importance of which would vary with his way of life, his education, and his aspirations.

Historical religion, joined by a thousand ties to the cultural reality, was bound to feel the repercussion from the upheavals to which Algerian society was subjected as a result of the clash between civilizations caused by European colonization. The result is that there can now be discerned, in addition to the traditional Islam of the rural communities or of the cities, a religiosity of the masses. The disintegration of the organic communities and the process of urbanization have given birth to the man of the masses, bereft of roots and traditions, of aspirations and convictions, of social ties and of laws. Torn from his family surroundings and the social setting in which his entire life, and particularly his religious life, was spent, removed from the religious atmosphere of his former communal existence, placed in extremely trying material circumstances and confronted with radically new problems, the man of the masses has no choice other than indifference or superstition, although his inclination to indifference is checked by the historical situation, which has made of Islam a social and political *signum*. The superstition that constitutes his alternate choice is a sort of institutionalized piety, a series of gestures, devoid of meaning, that are passively and mechanically carried out, a whole group of observances determined by the apathetic submission to a changing tradition. The rupture with tradition brought about by emigration, the contact with a technical civilization that is completely directed towards secular ends, the passing over from the clan, whose members are united by sacred bonds, to the workshop and the factory, or to the political party and the trade union, in which solidarity is based on material interest or political choice—all these are influences which have led to a veritable transmutation of values and are destroying the very soil in which traditional religion was rooted.

Must this decline of community religion, which is linked to the disintegration of the social structures, be considered an irresistible and irreversible movement which can have no conclusion other than a slow death by indifference, or a possible reprieve in the form of superstition? Or can one expect that a *personal* religion, founded on the conscious adherence and the elective will of individuals, may arise from the ruins of the community religion? Will the attempt at revival be made by the new elite, who have generally been educated in Western schools? In the case of the Algerian intellectual—a man standing between two civilizations, who has been deeply stricken by all the tragedies of his people, and who quite often is himself inclined to a lukewarm or an indifferent attitude in regard to religion—is it possible that he will have the ability, the knowledge or the desire to lead a movement for the revival of Islam which will offer the disorganized masses a new kind of personal religion, a religion that will be free of the ritualism and formalism which, in the past, have been imposed only by the force of public opinion, a religion that will be free at last from the spell and from the enchantments of magic? Will he consider this task to be the most urgent? What we can be sure of is that the only message that will make itself heard, whether it be religious or political, will be the one in which this deeply disrupted society will be able to recognize its true self and find justification for its existence.

6. Disintegration and Distress

This society, which has been successful in achieving the highest degree of equilibrium compatible with the limited techniques at its disposal, and whose integration seems to be in inverse ratio to its precarious and uncertain adjustment to the natural world, has been subjected to a radical challenge as a result of colonization and the influx of European civilization. This explains the occurrence of those phenomena relating to the destruction and reconstruction of the social structures whose principal laws may be defined as follows: the law of unequal rates of change, which applies when certain aspects of the cultural system are transformed more rapidly than others (for example, the population increase on the one hand, the economic system and production techniques on the other), with a resulting imbalance; the law of differential compatibility, which allows the limit of possible borrowings between two civilizations to be defined, a limit beyond which the borrowing can no longer be integrated except at the cost of a complete mutation of the society; the law of context, according to which the borrowing is reinterpreted in terms of the receiving context; the law of change in scale and of change in the frame of reference, according to which native cultural traits are significantly altered when placed in a new cultural setting: for example, when situated in the framework of an economic system based on monetary exchange the marriage payment tends to be interpreted as a purchase price and the bond of honor between master and sharecropper becomes a simple relationship between capital and labor; finally, the law of interconnection of cultural elements, according to which one change in detail may suffice, in certain cases, to bring about a complete and radical disruption of the whole culture.

* The dogmatic tone of this chapter (very schematically organized) is merely a result of a lack of space, which prevented the inclusion of corroborative analyses and examples.

The Colonial System

The colonial society is a system whose internal necessity and logic it is important to understand, because it is the context which gives meaning to all forms of behavior, particularly to the relations between the two ethnic communities. While the contact between a highly industrialized civilization, supported by a strong economic system, and a completely unmechanized civilization might have been sufficient to bring about a breakdown in the structures of the traditional society, it is nevertheless true that to these disturbances, which are the natural and inevitable consequences of the contact between two civilizations which are so very different from an economic and social point of view, there must be added the disruptions that were knowingly and methodically produced in order to ensure the control of the dominant power and to further the interests of its own nationals.

One of the main consequences of the colonial situation is that the exercise of the power of choice, which theoretically belongs to those societies that confront one another, has not been granted to the dominated society; the mere fact that the dominant power should have been able to impose its own judicial and administrative standards, in defiance of the social realities and in contempt of the resistance offered by the dominated society, was sufficient to bring about a breakdown in the social structures of the dominated society. Thus the important laws pertaining to landed property—the Cantonment of 1856-1857, the *Senatus Consulte* of 1863 and the Warnier law of 1873—were conceived, even by their originators, as measures which would lead to the destruction of the fundamental structures of the economy and of the traditional society. One of the advocates of the *Senatus Consulte* of 1863, A. de Broglie, declared that this measure had a double purpose: in the first place, "to cause a general liquidation of the land," so that one portion would remain in the hands of its former owners, not as a collective heritage of the tribe, but as "strictly defined, privately owned, personal property," and the remaining portion would be available "to attract and receive

emigration from Europe"; in the second place, "to disorganize
the tribe," the main obstacle to the "pacification" of the country.[1]
A true example of social vivisection that cannot be confused with
mere cultural contagion, this agrarian policy, which tended to
transform jointly owned lands into private property, facilitated
the concentration of the best properties in the hands of the
Europeans through the sale by auction to a single purchaser of
lands held in common, or through the ill-considered sale of farms
by individuals; at the same time it contributed to the disintegration of the traditional social units by disrupting an economic
balance whose best safeguard had been the joint ownership of
the land by the family or the tribe; finally the disintegration of
the tribe and the land evictions led to the creation of a rural proletariat, a mass of dispossessed, uprooted individuals, fit only to
provide a reserve of cheap labor.[2]

Captain Vaissière relates that when the Ouled Rechaïch
found out that the law of the *Senatus Consulte* was going to be
applied to their tribe they were thrown into consternation, so
clearly were they aware of the destructive power contained in
this measure. "The French defeated us in the plain of Sbikha,"
declared one old man. "They killed our young men; they forced
us to make a war contribution when they occupied our territories.
All that was nothing; wounds eventually heal. But the setting up
of private property and the authorization given to each individual to sell his share of the land, this means the death sentence
for the tribe, and twenty years after these measures have been
carried out the Ouled Rechaïch will have ceased to exist." [3] The
clearly reasoned resistance that the whole of the dominated
society offered to this law, which had been introduced like a
Trojan horse and was capable of striking at the very heart of its

[1] A. de Broglie, *Une Réforme administrative en Algérie*, Paris, 1860.

[2] By the end of 1961, two-fifths of the farm lands were under French
control, that is to say, subject to the regulations of French law (all European-
owned land plus an additional 5,607,500 acres); two-fifths of the non-French
lands were private property (*melk*); one-fifth of the non-French lands remained the property of the tribes (*ârch*). During the last twenty years
breaches in the family system of joint possession had become more and more
frequent.

[3] Captain Vaissière, *Les Ouled Rechaïch*, Algiers, 1863, p. 90.

cultural system, has remained ineffective, because it clashed with the interests and the powers of the dominant society. Whether it was openly and cynically confessed to be an "engine of war," [4] or whether it was supposed to be based on an assimilationist ideology that was more generous in intent but no less fatal in its result, the colonial policy with its aforementioned property laws, its sequestrations of land after the early revolts, its expropriations, its forestry laws, its regulations concerning pasture lands, and a host of other measures that were either forced upon the administration or inspired by its policy of giving preferential consideration to the interests of the Europeans, weakened the keystone supporting the whole of the traditional cultural system.

According to agricultural statistics, 22,037 European farm properties (of which 13,017, about 59 per cent, are less than 125 acres in size; 2,635 are from 125 to 250 acres; 2,588 from 250 to 500 acres; 3,797 or 17 per cent are more than 500 acres in size) occupy an area of 6,815,000 acres, whereas 630,732 native-owned farms (of which 438,483 or 69 per cent are less than 25 acres, 167,170 from 25 to 125 acres, 16,580 from 125 to 250, 8,499 or 1.3 per cent are over 250 acres) cover an area of 18,372,900 acres, the average size of each farm—European and native—being 300 as compared to 27 acres (see Fig. 11). Moreover, while the more fertile, usually irrigated European properties produce profitable crops (870,000 acres of vineyards, citrus fruits, early vegetables), at least half of the lands belonging to the Algerians are made up of pasture lands, and the other half consists mainly of soils which are suitable only for cereal crops and small orchards (fig and olive trees) and which produce very poor yields. But the state did not stop at merely facilitating the settlement of colonists by procuring them the necessary land. It constantly gave them aid in various forms: the creation of the substructures that are indispensable for agricultural development, such as drainage

[4] Captain Vaissière comments as follows on the above incident: "Such perspicacity is surprising on the part of simple, ignorant minds. The *Senatus Consulte* of 1863 is indeed the most efficient engine of war that could be devised against the native society and the most powerful and most useful tool that could be placed in the hands of our colonists." Here can be seen the combination of clear-sightedness as to the short-term results and inability to realize the long-term results.

and irrigation projects (three-quarters of the irrigated lands belong to Europeans; the result is that now one hectare, or approximately 2.5 acres, of irrigated land produces ten times more than one hectare of unirrigated land and, in the case of certain crops, twenty to thirty times more), financial and technical assistance, and commercial protection.

Between the years 1830 and 1880, the state sought to bring in colonists on lands that it had taken over, purchased or cleared for their use. It was a very small-scale attempt at colonization in which progress was slow and success uncertain. Short of capital, and wishing to obtain a crop during their first year of settlement, the early colonists devoted their efforts mainly to the growing of cereal crops. In 1880, however, the phylloxera disease that attacked the French vineyards brought about a sudden transformation in colonizing methods with the introduction of the winegrowing industry. The latter required heavy investments in farming equipment, storage facilities and processing plants; this, in turn, led to the development of cooperative associations and to the close connection which has existed since that time between the winegrowing industry and the Bank. It was in 1880 that the Bank of Algeria was authorized to extend credit to individuals. This capitalist form of agriculture has always produced for export (43 per cent of the total value of exports in 1907; 66 per cent in 1933; 39 per cent in 1956). It was in 1884 that a customs union was established. The railway network, built between 1879 and 1892, connected the great winegrowing regions. The ports were developed. The winegrowers' associations formed pressure groups who soon demonstrated their power in the political and economic domains. From 1900 to 1946, in accordance with the policy of granting the colony financial autonomy, the administration of the Algerian budget was handled by the Financial Delegations, which included 50 landed proprietors out of a total of 72 sitting members. The first industries to be created supplied the products required for the upkeep of the plantations and processed the by-products of fermentation. Parallel to this development, the European population increased from 410,000 in 1882 to 780,000 in 1911 and at the same time began to break up into social classes: the 11,500 vineyard proprietors were highly privileged persons

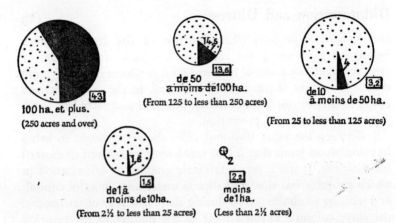

100 ha. et plus.
(250 acres and over)
43

de 50
a moins de 100 ha.
(From 125 to less than 250 acres)
14,5
13,6

de 10
à moins de 50 ha.
(From 25 to less than 125 acres)
4
3,2

de 1 à
moins de 10 ha..
(From 2½ to less than 25 acres)
1,6
1,5

moins
de 1 ha.
(Less than 2½ acres)
2
2,2

Fig. 11. Distribution of Farm Properties According to Size and Ethnic Category

The surface area of each circle is proportional to the total area covered by the farms in a particular category. The sector in black represents the percentage of the total area that is cultivated by Europeans (indicated by the figures inside the circle). The figure inside the square represents the percentage of farms owned by Europeans.

The average size of the European property is about 225 acres, whereas the average property owned by Algerians is only about 45 acres in size. The small or average-size European farm is rarely found, although such farms do exist in the Sahel of Algiers and in the wine-growing coastal region of Cherchel, both of which were settled as a result of the colonizing efforts of Marshal Bugeaud and the government of 1848. These small European farms, planted with vineyards and orange groves, may also be found in the coastal region of Mostaganem and of Oran, in the valley of the Issers, in the coastal region of Bougie, Bône and Philippeville, and in the winegrowing regions of Médéa and Miliana. On the High Plains, on the other hand, the large property (from 125 to more than 250 acres) predominates.

compared to the grain growers (160,000 francs gross income per hectare as opposed to 30,000). Property became concentrated in a few hands.[5] The contrast between the eastern and the western sections of the country became accentuated as winegrowing continued to expand in Oranie (67 per cent of the total in 1954) and to diminish in the areas around Algiers and Constantine. Winegrowing is essentially, however, a European form of enter-

[5] In 1930 some 26,153 Europeans owned 5,585,000 acres; in 1950, 22,037 owned 6,815,000 acres. The 6,385 properties that are more than 250 acres in size cover approximately 80 per cent of the total area.

Seventy per cent of the fellahs own farms of less than 25 acres, of which on an average only 12 acres can be farmed each year, a fact which tends to prevent any modernization of farming methods and techniques. The fellahs who farm more than 125 acres are few in number. The small Algerian property only exists in very small numbers in the rich zones of heavy European density, whereas it is in these zones that the small European property predominates. The High Plains, on the other hand, is the area in which are located the large European properties and in which the small Algerian farms have been pushed back to the less fertile land bordering the plains. At Saint Arnaud, for example, in the wheatgrowing plains of the Sétif region, the 13 European farms are all over 250 acres in size; alongside them, 157 fellahs are each farming less than 25 acres, 120 are farming from 25 to 125 acres, 30 from 125 to 250 acres, and 50 only have farms of over 250 acres. At Littré, in the Chéliff area, out of 14 Europeans, 13 are farming over 250 acres, whereas among the neighboring fellahs, 64 are each cultivating less than 25 acres and only four have properties greater than 250 acres in size.

Thus it is only in the coastal regions and in the zones producing lucrative crops (vineyards and particularly the vineyards planted on the hillsides) that the small European property has been able to establish itself. In the Sersou district, on the High Plateaus of Constantine, on the High Plains of Sétif, the small farms created by the official projects of colonization during the second half of the nineteenth century have been replaced by the immense modern farms, while in the same zones the small Algerian farm has continued to exist.

Whether he is farming a small property on which he raises lucrative crops, such as grapes, early vegetables or citrus fruits, or whether he is managing a large-scale farming development, the European colonist is always the head of a business enterprise or is a highly paid manager rather than a mere farmer. This fact explains to a considerable extent his behavior and psychological attitude. (Based on the Department of Agriculture census.)

prise. Thus the rapid development of this industry coincided with the appearance of a geographical form of segregation that is revealed by the regional structure of Algeria (see Fig. 12): on the one hand, the rich facade of the coastal plains and hills containing 75 per cent of the vineyards and 80 per cent of the European population (cities included); on the other hand, the High Plains devoted to the growing of cereal crops and to sheep raising.[6] Since winegrowing requires a plentiful supply of labor, the dispos-

[6] It is estimated that in the Mitidja more than 80 per cent of the lands belong to the colonists and in the Sahel of Algiers more than 90 per cent. Analogous percentages may be observed in the plains of Bône and of Philippeville as well as in certain regions around Oran.

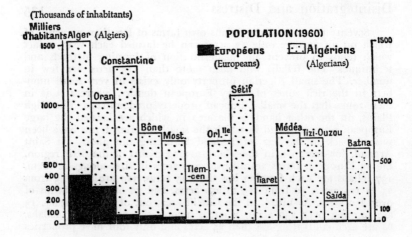

(Thousands of inhabitants)
Milliers
d'habitants Alger (Algiers)

POPULATION (1960)
Européens (Europeans)
Algériens (Algerians)

Constantine
Oran
Bône
Most.
Sétif
Orl.lle
Médéa
Tizi-Ouzou
Batna
Tlem-cen
Tiaret
Saïda

sessed fellahs and the former tenant farmers became the hired workers of the colonists. The gap widened between the colonists (who tended more and more to take up residence in the cities, leaving the working of their lands to their farm managers or foremen) and their very poorly paid Algerian workmen.

As a result of the regulations controlling the wine industry that were set up in 1929, the rapid growth of the vineyards was quickly checked and the maximum of 1 million acres was reached in 1935. The economic equilibrium that had been based on continuous expansion was broken. As M. Isnard has remarked, "An industry that was formerly one of risk now became one of privilege, winegrowing being a highly profitable undertaking. . . . The pioneers were replaced by the bourgeois, jealous of their legal advantages, keen to defend their class interests, continually making demands, and always ready, in case of disputes, to call on the state for aid and protection. After having been progressive and even revolutionary in character, winegrowing became a conservative branch of agriculture." However, the growing of citrus fruits, which also requires large capital investments, soon came to replace it and expanded rapidly as a result of the increase in irrigated areas (construction of the great dams) and the opening up of the metropolitan market (the civil war in Spain). The years 1940 to 1953 mark the end of the progress of colonization, for in

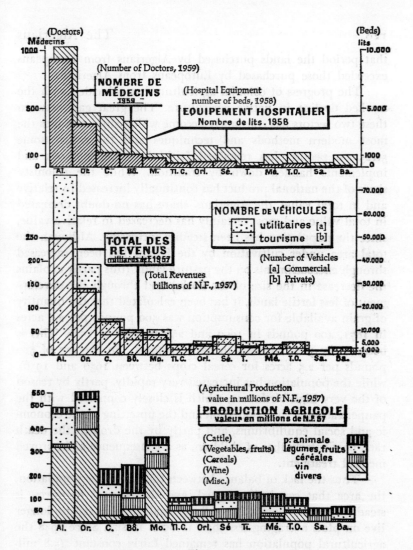

Fig. 12

Statistical Tables According to *Département*

The thirteen Algerian *départements* have been arranged in descending order according to the number of European inhabitants. It will be noted that the indices of economic development (equipment, resources and revenues) vary proportionately to the size of the European population. Value of the franc: 5 new francs to $1.00.

that period the lands purchased by Algerians from Europeans
exceeded those purchased by Europeans from Algerians.

The progress of colonial agriculture has coincided with the
marked decline in native agriculture. The great gap between
these two sectors has constantly become wider, since one uses the
most modern methods and techniques and the other (some
5,125,000 people) has remained faithful to the methods and
implements handed down by tradition. While the colonists'
share of the national product has continually increased in relative
and in total value, the Algerians' share has no doubt decreased
in total value and most certainly has decreased in relative value,
since the population has been steadily increasing. Although the
total area under cultivation by the fellahs has been increased
through encroachments on the pasture lands (this partly explains
the decrease in the size of the flocks) and through the development of less fertile lands, it has been calculated that the quantity
of grain available for consumption was 500 pounds per 2.5 acres
in 1871, 400 pounds in 1900 and 250 pounds in 1940. This is
because the yield appears to have dropped (an average of 500
pounds per 2.5 acres for cereal crops between 1950 and 1956),
while the population has increased very rapidly, partly by reason
of the very high birth rate, which is closely connected with the
pauperization of the population and the upsetting of the economic and social equilibriums, and partly by the drop in the death
rate, particularly that of children, as a consequence of improved
medical treatment.

Thus the lack of balance between the size of the population,
the area that can be cultivated, and the natural resources, is
steadily growing worse. The 438,483 small farmers can no longer
live on plots averaging less than 12 acres in size. Since 1948 the
agricultural population has remained fairly constant (5.8 million); it is estimated that, out of 2.7 million men of working age,
1.7 million are employed on the average for 100 days a year. For
all Algerians who live by means of agriculture, the average family
income was estimated in 1957 at about 175,000 francs ($350) a
year. In 1954 the Europeans produced 55 per cent of the total
gross revenue, the Algerians only 45 per cent (of which 20 per

cent came from stock raising). With respect to the total real
money income resulting from the sale of their products, the
Europeans have a 2 to 1 advantage, since the fellah consumes
more than 40 per cent of his own produce as opposed to 3 to 4
per cent for the colonist. A large part of the rural population has
great difficulty in eking out a bare subsistence. This explains the
abnormal urbanization of rural workers that has taken place, particularly after 1930, as a result of their being driven from their
farms by sheer poverty. Since 1954 there has been a great increase
in the number of government employees and minor officials, a
group that was relatively few in number up to that time. Commerce and the manual trades employ a good portion of the population. But, in 1957 workmen and unskilled laborers made up
the most important social group: the total unemployed or part-
time workers—some 900,000 persons, families included—probably
remained constant between 1954 and 1957 and decreased slightly
between 1957 and 1959.

Partly unintentional, partly methodical, depending on the
time and circumstance, this colonial policy of systematically
induced disintegration operated in the same direction as the laws
governing the contacts between civilizations and the laws of
intercultural exchanges and so hastened their action and increased their effectiveness, rather than having a tempering or
moderating effect upon them; thus it was to be expected that
Algerian society, thrown off balance and in a complete state of
disorder, should have been swept down a dizzy path leading to
the abyss.

The Colonial Society

It is in reference to the colonial situation, that one must attempt to achieve a comprehension of the way of life peculiar to
the Europeans, and to know their system of values and the type of
relationship they maintain with the indigenous society. Indeed, if
we merely consider this society as an empire within an empire,
as being cut off from any relations with the colonized society and

the metropolitan society,[7] if we note only its origins and present structure,[8] we should be overlooking the factors which give it its specific character.

The history of the settling of European society gives us a better understanding of its original characteristics. The first colonists, settled in large numbers on farms that were too small for efficient production, often ignorant of farming methods, confronted with a difficult and unhealthy climate, generally lacking in capital resources, were often the victims of speculators. As a result, the small colonial farms (in 1954, 8,000 accounted for only 1.5 per cent of the total land owned by colonists) have progressively been replaced by large-scale projects.

The spirit peculiar to the Europeans of Algeria was forged during the time of the expansion of the winegrowing industry, and it was also during this period that the rural landscape and the social and regional structure of the Algerian countryside began to assume their present form. The first colonists emigrated mainly in order to have a better life than they had had in France; with the success of the winegrowing venture, the pioneers, who had come to a new country as the heirs of a technical civilization but also as peasants who were desirous of acquiring a larger property, were replaced by the capitalistic speculators, who devoted all their profits and any money they could borrow to increasing the size of their domain and developing their means of production. Forced to work quickly in order to overcome the hazards of climate, and compelled as a result to use heavy technical

[7] The pioneer (or *pied noir*) portrays himself as the opposite of his definition of the Frenchman (whom he calls a "*francaoui*"): on the one hand generosity, virility, the cult of the body, that is, of the enjoyment of physical strength and beauty—a cult whose temple is the bathing beach; on the other hand pettiness, impotence, intellectualism, asceticism, etc. But then again, he describes himself as being the opposite of the "Arab," who in his eyes incarnates an instinctive way of life, a lack of culture, ignorance, routine, etc. Thus his description of himself is somewhat contradictory.

[8] According to the census of 1954, 79 per cent of the Europeans were born in Algeria, 11 per cent in France, 6 per cent are foreigners (59,000). It is estimated that half are of French origin and half of foreign origin (Spaniards, Italians, Maltese, etc.). The structure of the European society is analogous to that of France; the most important difference lies in the small percentage of farmers (6 per cent); on the other hand the tertiary sector is larger. The percentage of workers is practically the same as in France.

equipment requiring a large financial outlay, the colonists were necessarily obliged to resort to credit. This was true in the case of the grain growers and even more so in the case of the wine-growers. Thus, in 1914, the proportion owned by Algerians of the total value of stocks and bonds and the total value of chattels and personal fixed assets, particularly the value of real estate, was extremely low (32.5 and 73.7 per cent in France as opposed to 4.5 and 6 per cent in Algeria). If to this we add the fact that the colonists were, to a certain extent, persons who had been up-rooted from their homeland, had broken with their traditional world and, in their isolated condition, had been compelled to depend on themselves to create their own land and their own world, then it becomes clear why they developed a realistic atti-tude of mind, more attached to material values than to specula-tive thought. At the same time the face of the country was being changed: the accurately surveyed fields worked by machines and marked by regular furrows; the gigantic grain elevators; the fermentation plants; at the heart of the new domain, the house of the colonist. All these things indicated his complete appropri-ation of the land, his desire to introduce his own way of life and to enforce its adoption without making any concessions to the traditional order. This same attitude was evident in the colonial villages, which were laid out in perfectly straight lines, and in the great cities, which were then beginning to take on their present appearance. Thus the European gradually created an environment that reflected his own image and was a negation of the traditional order, a world in which he no longer felt himself to be a stranger and in which, by a natural reversal, the Algerian was finally considered to be the stranger.

The capitalistic speculators, the industrialists of agriculture, had been superseded by inheritors, who were born into this world already molded and fashioned by their fathers and whose attitude was often like that of parvenus determined to defend their new privileges.[9] All through colonial history the Arab seems to be receding into the background; the European has become

---

[9] While it is more particularly characteristic of those colonists among whom it developed, this attitude is more or less evident in the whole of the European population, which has long had the great landowners as its leaders.

more and more separated from him by the many walls and obstacles that have been erected between them; as proof of this
we have the evolution in the image of the Arab given to us by
literature and painting, an image varying from pure romanticism
and exoticism to sheer ignorance or caricature. The European's
knowledge of the autochthonous peoples has steadily diminished
with the development of a *de facto* segregation that is based
on differences in standards of living and on the economic isolation of the various regions. The "Arab" no longer receives any
notice apart from his economic relation to the European. Relations are becoming more and more tinged with paternalism or
racism. As the European moves in and becomes established, the
Algerian society becomes even more disintegrated, thereby giving
the European an additional excuse for avoiding it and for view-
ing it with contempt. Concentrated in the cities, or rather in the
European districts of the European cities,[10] the European population lives unto itself and finds in a complacent press sufficient
justification for the ignorance and indifference it displays towards the tragedies, the misery and the revolt of the Algerians.

As the Europeans draw farther apart from the Arabs, they
also draw farther apart from France, not only from the ideal
France, whose values all seem rather naive and in radical contrast to the logic of the colonial system, but from the "Frenchmen of France," who are always suspected of liberalism and who
are assigned the role of scapegoat whenever it is a question of
explaining a clash between the real world and the imaginary
world in which this whole society seeks to live.

Considered from a synchronistic point of view, the colonial
society makes one think of a caste system.[11] It is, in point of
fact, composed of two distinct, juxtaposed "communities" which

[10] Seven hundred and sixty thousand Europeans were living in the urban
communities in 1954.

[11] Although there are no racial laws in Algeria, although the Algerian
can travel in the same buses or in the same railway compartments, go to the
same hotels or send their children to the same schools as the Europeans, the
differences in cultural traditions (the role of the woman in society is a case
in point) and in economic standards as well as the frequent separation of
residential districts, tends to create a real form of segregation, since social
relations beyond those developed at work or in business are rarely entered
into.

have not united to form a larger group. Membership in each of these communities is determined by birth; the badge of membership is one's physical appearance or sometimes one's clothing or family name. The fact of being born within the superior caste automatically confers privilege, and this tends to develop a feeling of natural superiority in the person benefiting from these advantages. The separation between the castes is also illustrated by the few instances of intermarriage and by the rarity of any kind of mutual exchange between them in the form of such things as gifts, meals, etc. The two societies are placed in a relation of superior to inferior and are separated by a great many invisible barriers, set up by institutions or by spontaneous self-defense. As a result, relations between members of the two castes seem to have been reduced to an irreducible minimum by a sort of tacit agreement. The two "communities" are thus content to coexist without making any real attempt to communicate and, still less in fact, to cooperate with one another. Everything, then, will run smoothly, provided that each individual perform the role for which he is naturally fitted. Hence a *de facto* racial segregation has developed. The function of racism is none other than to provide a rationalization of the existing state of affairs so as to make it appear to be a lawfully instituted order. Similarly, paternalism is the privileged mode of behavior of the superior, so long as the system is not challenged and each person remains in his proper place. The European society, a minority exercising the rights of a majority in the social, economic and political spheres, is attempting, through racist ideology, to transform its privileges into law, in other words, to authorize each society to remain as it is, with the dominant continuing to dominate and the dominated continuing to be dominated. To be sure, the hierarchy ruling social status will not in fact be found to coincide exactly with the hierarchy system governing the two societies, since each caste is itself divided into classes. But while each caste has its own system of graded social positions, and each individual is permitted to climb the rungs of the social ladder of his caste, it is practically impossible to cross the abyss that separates the two ladders. Caste spirit stifles class consciousness, a fact that is clearly demonstrated by the attitude of the

European lower classes; political life and political conscience have become Manichean in form.

But the colonial system can function properly only if the dominated society is willing to assume the very negative nature or "essence" (the "Arab" cannot be educated, is improvident, etc.) that the dominating society holds up for it as its destiny. And thus the situation has developed whereby, as the system gains in logic, it loses reality; as it tends to become fully realized, it tends to prepare for its own disappearance.[12] The gap separating the dominant society from the dominated society steadily becomes wider, as much in the social and psychological as in the economic domain. The effect of the system is to produce persons whom the colonists scornfully call "natives," that is to say, individuals who have been detached from their community but who, even though they have been cast into a capitalistic economy marked by competition, have maintained a way of life and an attitude of mind which only had meaning in the context of their old community. The colonial situation thus creates the "contemptible" person at the same time that it creates the contemptuous attitude; but it creates in turn a spirit of revolt against this contempt; and so the tension that is tearing the whole society to pieces keeps on increasing.

The Total Disruption of a Society

The phenomena of disintegration can be observed in all aspects of Algerian existence and are all inseparably connected, although for greater clarity each must be dealt with in turn. The population explosion resulting from the coexistence of an extremely high birth rate that is linked to the conditions of extreme poverty and a death rate that has been appreciably reduced by improved sanitation is undoubtedly one of the main factors contributing to the present maladjustment, because the former highly precarious state of equilibrium was based in part on the

[12] Since the system tends to preserve itself intact, it would be easy to demonstrate that it ruins any attempts at reform, either by turning them to the advantage of the Europeans or by making them ineffectual.

small size of the population. The disparity between population
and resources is further increased by the fact that the soil, which
is now less fertile and more intensively cultivated,[13] is rapidly
becoming exhausted, with a resultant drop in yield, and above
all by the fact that a population that has increased enormously
in size (to the demographic factor has been added the mass
descent of the mountain dwellers into the plains) must live on
a much reduced patrimony. With the very foundations of the
agrarian order shaken and in certain regions completely destroyed, a rapid decline in the standard of living has become
evident. The closed and static traditionalist economy cannot
stand up to competition with a capitalistic economy which pro-
motes the growth of large commercial enterprises, is provided
with the most modern equipment, has its own credit corporations, and utilizes a method of farming that is designed to produce high yields and is aimed primarily at the export trade,
a method which, needless to say, has quickly brought about the
ruin of the rural craftsmen and of the way of life exemplified by
the nomads and semi-nomads, who have now been driven back
to the High Plains. The peasant, caught up in the machinery of
the modern financial system—whose regulating mechanisms (sale
at the lowest price immediately after the harvest, purchase at
the highest price in order to tide him over) bring about the
irrevocable ruin of the whole previous system of balances—soon
has no resort other than to borrow at usurious rates, to sell his
land or to emigrate and assume the status of a sub-proletarian;
as such, he will be "considered as good for anything and consequently as good for nothing by his employers" (Dresch), will be
placed in conditions of material and moral misery, will feel "de-
socialized" and dehumanized, and, with the undermining of his
fundamental values, will be a prey to a feeling of chronic frustration (see Fig. 13). With the changes in the property laws and
the introduction of the law requiring the registration of property
titles, which has made it easier for the small farmer to sell his
land, all the protections of the agrarian order, such as the institu-

---

[13] The fellah has had to clear and bring into cultivation new lands whose
soil is often rather poor; he has also been obliged to work more continuously
the lands which he formerly allowed to lie fallow.

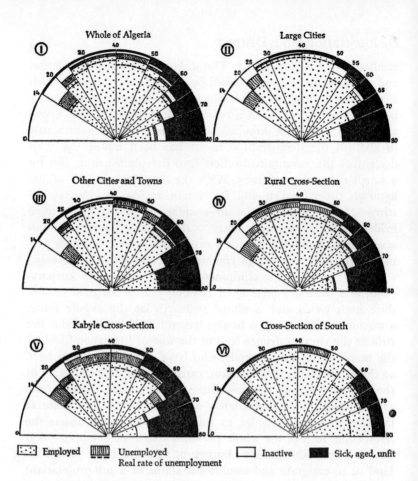

Fig. 13. Distribution of the Male Algerian Population According to Type of Activity and Age Group

(Based on an investigation carried out by sampling representative groups during the summer of 1961, the results of which are to be published under the title, *Travail et Travailleurs en Algérie*, Vol. I, Statistical Data, by A. Darbel, J. P. Rivet and Claude Seibel; Vol. II, Sociological Study, by P. Bourdieu.)

The real rate of employment (defined by the percentage of people who were working on the day the investigation was made) is in general very low (57.5 per cent) and particularly, if one considers the whole of Algeria, for the people in the fourteen- to twenty-year age group (36.7 per cent). Life histories indicate that the years of adolescence have been the most difficult years of existence for the great majority of Algerians. A good number of them have been compelled to look

136

for work very early, sometimes even at the age of ten. Before succeed-
ing in finding a stable employment, most of the workers and the minor
employees have engaged in several temporary trades. The percentage of
those employed increases quite rapidly from the age of fourteen to the
age of twenty-five, then remains remarkably constant until about the
age of fifty, after which there is a sudden drop. Nevertheless, the proportion of people over seventy years of age who declare that they are
still employed remains quite high. The main break in employment
takes place at the age of fifty in the large cities and is apparently quite
drastic. 89.2 per cent of the men from forty to forty-nine years of age
were employed the day of the investigation as compared to 59 per cent
of the men from fifty to fifty-four years of age; the same sharp break
occurs at fifty years of age in the other cities, but from then on there
is no perceptible drop until the age of sixty-five; the same situation
prevails in the rural cross-section; in the Kabyle strata, there is a very
sharp break which takes place at the age of sixty. Finally, in the
southern areas, the drop in the real rate of employment only shows up
at the age of seventy, and even then 80 per cent of the men over
seventy years of age declared themselves to be employed.

The percentage of the men who declare themselves to be employed
is always higher than the percentage of the men who are actually employed. The gap is particularly noticeable in the southern cross-sections,
since here, for example, the men from fifty to fifty-five years of age declared that they were 100 per cent employed. The reason for this is that
the ideas of employment or unemployment are relative to the whole of
the cultural system. Thus, in the case of real rates of employment
which are very much the same, the rural dwellers of the Kabyle cross-
sections quite readily state that they are unemployed if they judge
that their activities are insufficient to provide a living, whereas the
inhabitants of the South prefer to say that they are employed. This
may easily be understood because of the fact that the former, by reason
of a long tradition of emigration to France and to the Algerian cities,
have a direct or mediate experience of the modern economic system,
with which the latter have remained relatively unacquainted. In the
traditional rural environment, the lack of work is not understood as
being unemployment. Agriculture and stock raising have their rhythms,
the changes from periods of great activity to periods when work pro-
ceeds at a much reduced pace. All the members of the family, from
the old patriarch down to the young adolescent, take part in the farm
tasks in varying degrees and with divers functions. Thus they all feel
that they are fully occupied and permanently employed because, however little it may be, there is always something to do for everyone.
The man who declares himself to be unemployed, on the contrary,
understands and judges his condition in relation to a new system of
reference and brings in, either implicitly or explicitly. The idea of full
employment which he has derived from his experience of the modern
economy and from his work in the European environment. This is
also illustrated by the fact that the young men from fourteen to twenty-
five years of age who had no employment the day on which the
investigation was made almost all declared that they were unemployed
in contrast to the statements of the older individuals.

It may be seen, moreover, that the real chances of obtaining employment increase as one moves from the country to the city, the real rate of employment rising from 46.5 per cent in the Kabyle areas to 54.8 per cent in the non-Kabyle rural areas, 61 per cent in the cities of average size, and finally to 78.8 per cent in the large cities. It is also a known fact that industrial wages are higher in the large cities than they are in the smaller towns and cities and that, generally speaking, urban incomes are higher than rural incomes.

tion of joint property, have either been abolished or have lost a great deal of their effectiveness. In addition, the importance given to economic values, particularly monetary values, is disrupting an order that was formerly based on personal relations. Thus the former bond of patronage that united the landowner and the tenant farmer is now broken: either the advances to the tenant are considered as a loan which must be repaid, so that the latter, no longer finding the system to his advantage, prefers to become a wage earner, or else the former system is maintained; but here too, although the situation may appear identical to what it was before, the whole relationship has been altered.[14] The result has been the advent of wage-earning, which implies an impersonal relationship between capital and labor, and the appearance of the farm worker who has broken with his family or his tribe, a person unknown to the former society. Moreover the colonist, with his techniques, his different attitude to the land—his way of looking on it as a mere raw material—and the surveyor, with his introduction of the notion of property limits, have brought about a transmutation of values and the collapse of the former agencies which mediated the relationship between the peasant and his land. The very nature of this relationship is being modified; along with European agricultural methods and techniques, there is being introduced a "materialistic" view of the land, and the old methods of farming are losing their ritual significance.

This land, moreover, seems to shrink in size once its com-

[14] In 1956 the traditional tenant farming system was prohibited and replaced by the *métayage* system (sharecropping). Certain owners at that time demanded a sum of money or an acknowledgment of indebtedness covering the hiring out of animals, the provision of farm implements, and half the cost of the feed. In other cases the tenant (*khammès*) became a farm worker. Certain ones continued as in the past in spite of the new law.

mercial value is revealed. An impersonal and abstract monetary value is replacing the former values of prestige and honor. In this topsy-turvy world each one adapts himself as best he can or succumbs; there is a strong temptation to convert one's miserable little plot of ground into cash and buying power, and those who yield to this temptation end by joining the ranks of the uprooted and disoriented rural proletariat. The cleverest among them make use of legal techniques to accumulate a fortune or to acquire great domains; the great lords, loath to adapt themselves to these new conditions, preserve a mere facade of wealth by mortgaging their lands, a fact which has contributed to the relative overthrow of the traditional hierarchies; finally, there are those who remain faithful to the soil and continue to work it as in the past, but with a much keener awareness of their wretched condition.

By reason of their functional interconnection, the economic and the social structures were doomed to a similar, parallel disintegration: the emigration of the uprooted, poverty-stricken proletariat to the towns and cities, the destruction of the economic unity of the family, the weakening of the ancient solidarities and of the restraints which had been imposed by the group and which had protected the agrarian order, the rise of the individual and of economic individualism which shattered the community framework, were all so many breaches in the coherent fabric of the social structures. The administrative and political measures that were adopted merely increased the shock to the ancient order: the *Senatus Consulte* of 1863 created new social units, the *douars;* for the most part the new territories that were carved out at that time did not follow the natural divisions of the traditional society; the family group was often divided among several *douars,* whereas groups of different family origin would be joined together in the same *douar.* It even happened that, when a tribe was considered to be too small in numbers, it was incorporated into the *douars* of a neighboring tribe. Whereas in Arab territory the *Senatus Consulte* divided what had been united, in Kabylia they united what had been divided by grouping several villages into the same *douar.* If, in Kabylia and the Aurès, parallel institutions long continued to function (the council of the clan or group) while the *djemâa* of the *douar* remained an artificial and superimposed organization, the administrative unit in the Arabic-speaking territories gradually became a real social entity at the expense of the traditional units, because members of the same *douar* came to feel united by their common interests, preoccupations and administrative problems. The appointment of the caïds has also tended to hasten the disintegration of the ancient structures by substituting an administrative hierarchy for the traditional hierarchies.

The laws of acculturation have been operating in the same direction as the ill-considered policy of intervention on the part of the administration: new methods of transportation have led to a shifting of the main trade routes; thus, with the coming of the railroad, Tlemcen gradually lost its importance as a great commercial center; there has been a widening in the range of human contacts; a number of the small tribal markets have lost their importance and have disappeared, being replaced by the markets of the European cities, stocked with the industrial wares (kitchen utensils, toilet articles, fabrics, etc.) that have taken the place of the products formerly made by the family in rural communities; the once closed social units now have many outside contacts, and the range of matrimonial exchanges has greatly increased. The wider acquaintance with the world brought about by emigration, by urbanization and by increasing mobility, the impact of the new ideas and images introduced by the school, radio, cinema and newspaper, have favored the creation of new needs and of a rise in the aspiration level. Both of these have developed more quickly than the techniques and values required for adaptation to the Western economic system can be transmitted (saving, the rational utilization of money, credit, the sense of the importance of workmanship) and far more quickly than the production of the goods required to satisfy these needs and ambitions can be increased (see Fig. 14). At the same time there developed a growing awareness of the inequalities and barriers separating the two societies, the fundamental cause of the revolt against the dominant society. This new awareness is all the more acute, since it is developing both at a time when the Algerians are discovering, above and beyond the colonial

system, the image of the ideal France, a France that is the herald
of new ideals, and at a time when the dominated society is being
swept along in a great proletarianizing movement.

Various disruptive forces are breaking down the unity of
the family, whose functional significance has already been analyzed. We have seen those forces being exerted against the rural
family; in the cities the challenge is even more radical. The
disintegration of the agrarian order has led to an abnormal development of the cities. Life appears to have nothing stable or
durable to offer the urban populace, which has been completely
and irrevocably cut off from its former environment, lives
crammed together in incredible densities in the unsanitary dwellings of the old city districts or of the new shantytowns,[15] and is
generally filled with uncertainty as to the future. The misery
and insecurity have been made even worse by the distress resulting from the loss of the group ties on which the individual's
psychological and social stability was based in the old communities. One can imagine how precarious family unity must be in
such a context, undermined as it is by a great many factors: by
the frequent repudiation of wives; by the tension existing
between the traditional standards, which demand widely extended solidarities, and the imperatives of the individualistic
economic system, in which the single family household is the
basic unit; by the crisis in the moral education of the children,
who are now often left to roam the streets; by the disorientation
of the young people, who are gaining a political consciousness,
are haunted by the fear of unemployment, and are generally
being induced to challenge both the traditional standards and
paternal authority; by the conflict between the different generations, a conflict that is especially noticeable in matters concerning the concept of marriage and the role of the wife in society
(the law of matrimonial constraint, the wearing of the veil, the
question of equality in marriage, of employment for women,
etc.); by the dispersion of the single-family units, connected with
the new economic conditions and with the desire to attain the

---

[15] An effort has been made to resolve the problem of urban housing.
Thus there have been constructed during the last four years some 100,000
dwellings.

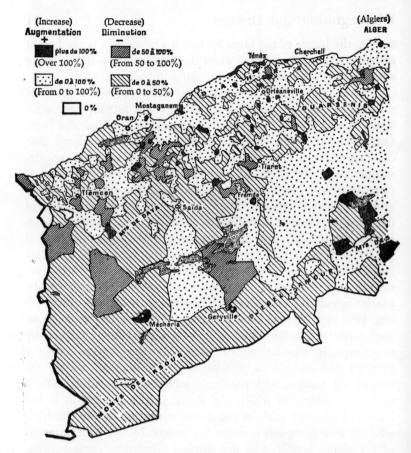

status of wage earner and thereby gain economic independence. Thus the extended family is being replaced by the single-family unit; the communities of the old society are disintegrating into a cloud of separate individuals at the same time that the traditions they maintained and on which they were based are also disappearing.

This radical upheaval of the economic, social and psychological world has led to a deep feeling of anguish, which finds expression in the French-language novel and in the oral literature of the common people. All these contradictions affect the inner nature of "the man between two worlds"—the intellectual, the man who formerly worked in France, the city dweller—is exposed

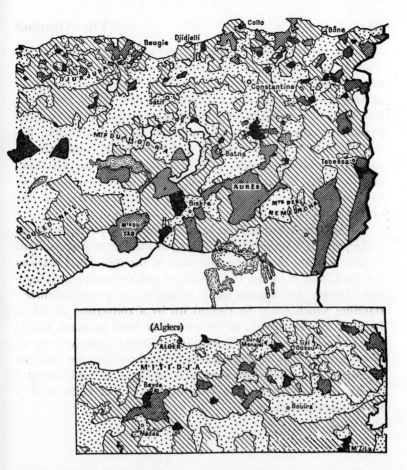

Fig. 14. Population Shifts Within Algeria Between 1954 and 1960

This map, which has been drawn up in accordance with the figures given for each commune or district as a result of the census of 1954 and of 1960, should be compared with the map showing the military situation in 1957 (Fig. 15) and a relief map. It can be observed, on the one hand, that the zones in which the population has decreased the most are those in which the army of national liberation has been most firmly entrenched from the beginning of the revolution and which, as a result, have been most affected by the war. On the other hand, it can be seen that, in addition to the frontier zones, the regions in which a great decrease has been recorded correspond to the mountain zones, whose inhabitants have departed for the cities or have been re-settled in the plains. The black spots, indicating an increase of over 100 per cent in population, correspond to the cities or to the areas in which the resettlement centers have been established.

to the conflicts created by the weakening of the traditional systems of sanctions and by the development of a double set of
moral standards. Constantly being faced with alternative ways
of behavior by reason of the intrusion of new values, and therefore compelled to make a conscious examination of the implicit
premises or the unconscious patterns of his own tradition, this
man, cast between two worlds and rejected by both, lives a
sort of double inner life, is a prey to frustration and inner
conflict, with the result that he is constantly being tempted
to adopt either an attitude of uneasy overidentification or one
of rebellious negativism.

While presented only in broad outline, the preceding pages
make possible a better understanding of the war in Algeria. This
conflict was not merely the sum total of the individual passions
involved, that is to say, the irrational and subjective manifestation of inner tensions, nor was it by any means a mere misunderstanding which could be cleared up by a conversion of minds
induced by propaganda or education or even by some simple
economic changes; but in reality it was based objectively on an
objective situation of which the individual tensions are only the
resultants. Its underlying causes may be found in a bitterly real
drama: the overthrow of a vital order and the collapse of a
whole world of values.

7. The Revolution Within the Revolution

The causes of the war in Algeria, the particular form it assumed and the consequences it has entailed are all aspects of a single phenomenon of which it is important to understand the over-all significance. If any one of these three aspects is disassociated from the whole of which it forms a part, it cannot be properly understood.

To deny that the revolutionary war had its basis in an objective situation is to refuse to admit its true character and to deny the real reason for its existence. To claim that the war was imposed upon the Algerian people by a handful of ringleaders who resorted to compulsion and trickery is to deny the fact that the struggle was able to draw on strong popular sentiment for its vital strength and purpose, a sentiment inspired by an objective situation. It is true that the war existed and continued only in relation to the situation within which and because of which it came into being; but at the same time it modified the original situation by the very fact of its existence and its persistence.

As we have already seen, the indigenous society had been shaken to its foundation on the eve of the revolution as a result of the colonial policy and the clash of opposing civilizations. Moreover, the whole of this society was being torn asunder by the hidden or open tensions that existed between the dominant European society and the dominated Algerian society. Now the evolution of the colonial system causes the gap (and the correlative tension) which separates the dominant and the dominated societies to keep on widening, and this occurs in all the spheres of existence—economic, social and psychological. The almost stationary state of equilibrium in which the colonial society was maintained is the resultant of two opposing forces whose strength is constantly increasing: on the one hand, the force that tends to bring about an increase in inequalities and in real discrimination, a consequence due in part to the pauperization of the people and to the disintegration of the original Algerian culture; on the other hand, the force constituted by the feelings of revolt and resentment aroused against this increase in social inequalities and discrimination. In short, when carried along by its own internal logic, the colonial system tends to develop all the consequences implied at the time of its founding—the complete separation of the social castes. Violent revolution and repression by force fit in perfectly with the logical coherence of the system; while the colonial society is as unintegrated as ever, the war now became completely integrated within the colonial system and allowed it to be recognized for what it really is.

Indeed, the war plainly revealed the true basis for the colonial order: the relation, backed by force, which allows the dominant caste to keep the dominated caste in a position of inferiority. Thus it becomes evident why the return of peace should in the eyes of certain members of the dominant caste seem the worst kind of menace. Without the exercise of force, there would be nothing to counterbalance the force directed at the very roots of the system—the rebellion against an inferior social position.

That only a revolution can abolish the colonial system, that any changes to be made must be subject to the law of all or nothing, are facts now consciously realized, even if only confusedly, just as much by the members of the dominant society as by the members of the dominated society. Those among the former who linked their very existence to their membership in the dominant caste were unable to conceive that any possible order could be substituted that would not entail their disappearance from the scene. The members of the dominated society, for their part, understood that they could expect no real result from reforms carried out from within the system and directed at changing it internally, because these measures tended in reality to strengthen or at least to conserve and protect the system under the pretext of an attempt to transform or abolish it. Thus it must be granted that the primary and indeed the sole radical challenge to the system was the one that the system itself engendered; the revolt against the principles on which it was founded.

Special Form and Meaning of the War

We must now define very roughly the special form and meaning that this war acquired because of its being waged in this unique situation. If, as is so often done, one adopts the standpoint of formal legality, and if one admits that in international relations violence may legitimately be resorted to by both sides, whereas within a single country it may be legitimately employed only by those who represent the power of the state, then one will apparently be justified in looking on the Algerian war as a rebellion against the established order and in regarding the repressive measures adopted as being a mere police operation in which the forces of law and order have the legal right to act against the criminals. It would be only too easy to show that the point of view of formal legality implies an ignorance of the sociological facts and a refusal to recognize the situation in which the revolution broke out and against which it was directed.

Once the false issues have been put aside, the thing that strikes one is that the "hostile intention" of this war had a certain abstract quality. Two texts from a great many that could be cited will suffice to illustrate this point: "The Algerian revolution is not a holy war but an attempt to regain our liberty. It is not a work of hate but a struggle against a system of oppression." [1] "The war in Algeria is not the war of Arabs against Europeans nor that of Moslems against Christians, nor is it the war of the Algerian people against the French people." [2] One will possibly look on these sentences as mere tricks of propaganda. However, they do seem to express one of the essential characteristics of this war, namely, that it was directed less (in its hostile intention, it must be repeated) against actual enemies than against a system, the colonial system.

[1] Letter from the Front de Libération Nationale to the French: quoted by Favrod: *La révolution algérienne* (Plon, 1959), p. 174.
[2] Ferhat Abbas: Speech of February 17, 1960.

The revolutionary radicalism of the Algerian rebels is a direct consequence of their conscious awareness that the colonial society constitutes a system and for this reason can not be only half-destroyed; that what must be changed are not attitudes of mind, economic structures or legal and political institutions, but the established system in its entirety. As Mohammed Dib has said: "No doubt racism was evident even in the looks directed our way—blank looks which seemed to relegate us to the background. But we used to think that even this was the result of a system; it is the system in its entirety that we wish to be rid of, not only these looks." [3] The colonial situation is the context in which all actions must be judged. Thus as long as there is a continuance of this system from which the European, whether willingly or unwillingly, knowingly or unknowingly, continues to derive advantages, the most generous actions from the point of view of strict intention, whether they be the acts of individuals or those of government, will turn out in practice to be either perfectly useless or, because they take on their meaning from the social context, actually harmful. The benevolent or generous acts that the members of the dominant society perform (more frequently than is commonly believed) in favor of the members of the dominated society are almost necessarily bound to be misunderstood, because they are interpreted in the light of the relationship based on domination which exists between the two societies; thus in answer to benevolent acts, which may be either subjectively or objectively tinged with paternalism, the usual response is an attitude of dependency. So intersubjective communication rarely fulfills its end. Would it not be easy to show, for example, that the unacknowledged purposes of many individual acts of generosity is to allow the benefactor himself to hide from himself the fact that injustice is consubstantial with the existing state of affairs and that, all things considered, they are really taking advantage of the injustice of the system in order to do good?

Even if the relations between two persons are perfectly happy and harmonious, there is always lurking in the background the

[3] Interview granted to the newspaper *El Pueblo* of Buenos Aires, March 16, 1958.

hostility which separates the two groups and which is constantly threatening to come forward to impair the good will. This may perhaps be an explanation of the fact that the ties between persons of the two societies are often exceptionally intense, when they do succeed in getting established. But the colonial situation never lets itself be forgotten, and sometimes it succeeds in coming between men who considered themselves to be face to face. Thus it would appear in this context as if the most generous intentions cannot help having a harmful effect. This is why, although it may be pure and sincere in its intentions and although it is a thousand times to be preferred to a passive or cynical adherence to the prevailing conditions, formal good will is perverted in its very essence by a situation which it seeks to overcome, because it tends to sanction an established order while appearing to be attempting to correct it. In the colonial context, no other form of good will is possible except that which works for the coming of an order in which good will some day will be the ruling force in determining human relations.[4]

Nothing would then be more erroneous than to see in the Algerian conflict a mere explosion of aggressiveness and hatred, an irrational and subjective manifestation of inner tensions born of frustration and insecurity. Although aggressiveness may have made this war take on a special form in proportion as individuals came to find in it an opportunity to resolve their personal conflicts, and although the role of individual passions and of subjective motivations may have continued to become more important as the conflict was prolonged, it is nevertheless a fact that the individual conflicts were based on an objective situation which conditioned all the dramas that went on in men's consciousness.

The real question concerns the kind of situation in which

[4] One example will suffice to provide a factual content for these analyses which may appear rather sophisticated. After the uprisings in May 1958 signs were posted bearing this text: "Each Moslem hand that you shake brings integration nearer." Is fraternity possible when "fraternization" is officially encouraged, particularly when this policy is linked to the policy of repression? Hence one can understand the difficult position in which the anti-colonialist Europeans, who have actual experience of all these contradictions, find themselves.

personal relations may be established in the future, since the nature and form of these relations are determined by the situation in which they are established. It would indeed be useless to hope to abolish racism without destroying the colonial system of which it is the product; it would be the height of pharisaism to condemn the racism and the racists spawned by the colonial situation without condemning the colonial system itself, that is to say, the oppression exercised by one group of men over another group of men.

The destruction of the colonial system cannot be the result of a conversion of minds which would induce the members of the dominant society solemnly and collectively to give up the privileges they hold in order, by a conscious choice, to "integrate themselves" willingly into the dominated caste or to "integrate it" into their caste, which would mean the same thing if we ascribe to the words their full meaning. This conversion can only be the act of a few "traitors to their caste." The whole rationale of the colonial system tends, on the contrary, to make this sort of collective suicide impossible, and it would be even more impossible in this war, which made the schism more marked. The "miracles of the thirteenth of May" must be regarded as mere attempts at mystification or as staged demonstrations.

The awareness of the fact that the colonial system can only be either maintained in its entirety or totally destroyed was equally acute among the members of both societies. If the idea of an Algerian state was inconceivable to the majority of Europeans, it was because they felt that it would involve a repudiation of all they stood for and their complete destruction. Hence is explained an extremist type of radicalism which is in perfect conformity with the logic of the colonial situation.

If the first demand of the members of the dominated society is that they be treated with respect and dignity, it is because the real nature of the colonial system and the caste division of the colonial society have been concretely experienced through humiliation or alienation. Even when they do not think of it in this manner on a rational level, the implicit and affective attitude of the masses towards the colonial society is to regard it as a system which can be replaced only by destroying it in its entirety. Thus it follows that the revolution directed against a distinctive social order has itself certain distinctive characteristics and cannot be considered as purely and simply a class struggle inspired by economic demands, although it is true that motivations of this sort are present, owing to the fact that differences in economic status are one of the most obvious indications of belonging to one or other of the castes, and although economic revolution appears to be a necessary step in the destruction of the colonial order. For the same reason the Algerian revolution can be considered neither an international nor a civil war, although it presented features reminiscent of both. If the struggle against the caste system assumed the form of a war of national liberation, it was because the creation of an autonomous nation together with the setting up of a government of the Algerians by the Algerians appeared to be the only decisive way of bringing about the radical change in situation that could cause the total and definitive collapse of the caste system.

The war unveiled the true face of the colonial system. All the masks and ambiguous expressions were removed; hence there became evident among a good number of the members of the dominant society a conscious or unconscious fear of peace, motivated by the realization that the war brought about an irreversible change which would become fully apparent with the return of peace; hence also the admitted or unadmitted desire among certain others for a total war that would end in absolute victory or, in other words, in the restoration of the caste system, unchanged and intact. For the members of the dominated caste, the disagreement and the contradiction between the ideal France, which is often passionately loved, and the colonial France, which based its domination on force and discrimination, became glaringly apparent. By its very logic or, if one prefers, by force of circumstance and often contrary to the intention of those engaged in it, the war, as repression, tended to reveal both its own nature and the nature of the colonial system and to show up France as a colonial power.

So it is that even today the Algerians often distinguish between "the true Frenchmen" or the "Frenchmen of France" and the "French of Algeria" or, better, "the Europeans of Algeria." By the latter expression and by the insistence with which they recall the Spanish origin (and more rarely the Italian origin) of the *pieds noirs* (descendants of the pioneers), they mean to underline the fact that they refuse to ascribe to these people the qualities of the true Frenchmen. All these stereotype phrases, which are based to a certain extent on actual experience (particularly among those who formerly worked in France) but whose main function is to express the distinction they wish to maintain between ideal France and colonial France, were called into question by the actual fact of the war in which all Frenchmen indiscriminately participated, and in which the soldier "of France" sometimes behaved as the worst of the *pieds noirs* would (or would not . . .) behave. Having learned by experience that the members of the Home Army (*métropolitains*), when placed in the colonial situation, would be converted very rapidly to the colonialist and racist attitude—is it not true that the great majority of the leaders of the extremist movements were from metropolitan France?—the Algerians have felt (without always stating it explicitly or admitting it) that this attitude was not attributable to individual malice or to a congenital disposition peculiar to a certain ethnic group, but rather to a special situation and the conditioning it imposes.[5]

[5] In the colonial situation, collective pressure and social determinants acquire exceptional strength and intensity. The social conditioning of the individual is going on constantly. The refusal to adopt the racist and colonialist attitude on the part of the European means that he is cutting himself off from his own group and exposing himself to being rejected as a traitor. That is why there is a good deal of unfairness in the attitude of those Frenchmen who make the *pieds noirs* their scapegoats and blame all the tragic happenings in Algeria on their racism. When dealing with the French of Algeria, one can adopt two points of view, which must be sharply distinguished from one another: by adopting the standpoint of formal morality, one can condemn racist dehumanization, or, by considering the fact that it is the colonial situation that makes the racist and, more precisely, that it is the colonial Algeria that has produced the *pied noir* and not the reverse, one can conclude that all ("Frenchmen of France" and *pieds noirs*) are equally responsible for the colonial system which has given rise to racism. While there is no question of denying that racism in the absolute is a crime, one cannot help thinking that the virtuous indignation displayed by those whose main concern is to relieve themselves of any responsibility in the matter has all the appearance of pharisaism.

Thus the war carried the colonial system to its extreme limits. Generous actions prompted by an ethic of pure good intention stood out as ridiculously weak palliatives when viewed against the background of this system of oppression. The display of a false solicitude that is intended to hide the reality of the colonial situation appeared either as a contradiction or as a cynical method of reconquest. The ideology that favors assimilation, the last resort of those who had fought with the utmost violence against any attempt to give equality of rights to the Algerians, appears as a rather crude effort to obscure the issue at a time when the infernal logic inherent in terrorism and repression was tending to reveal the schism between the castes in the most clear-cut manner. In such circumstances, any attempts at trickery or subterfuge are at once revealed in their true light. The war helped to bring about a heightened awareness.

The effectiveness of terrorism lies in the fact that it causes a violent break between the members of the two castes by creating an atmosphere of mutual fear and distrust. And repression cannot fail to produce the same effect. The reason for this is that those engaged in repression cannot help considering all the members of the dominated caste as being suspect, even when they try to discriminate between them. By the mere fact of regarding them all as suspect, it separates them from the members of the other caste and develops in them an awareness of the existing schism. One of the objectives of the war of subversion was precisely to make Algerians aware of this schism, and thereby to strengthen the solidarity between the members of the dominated society. Terrorism, then, increases scission and provokes repression; this, in turn, further increases the scission which it is supposedly intended to prevent.

On the one hand, certain Europeans claimed that the war of liberation was being carried on by a handful of conscienceless killers directed by cynical ringleaders who sought to stir up against France, by ruse and terror, populations that had really remained faithful to her, but, on the other hand, the behavior of these same people appeared to be based, consciously or unconsciously, on their real feeling that all "Arabs" were in league with one another and were supporters of the army of the National Liberation Front. The result was that this type of behavior merely strengthened the solidarity of the Algerians. The general attitude of suspicion, the methodical searching of cars whose passengers are wearing the veil or *chechia,* the identity checks, the arbitrary arrests, the daily vexatious measures (to cite only the minor ones) are all examples which illustrate the existence of racial discrimination and which force all members of the dominated caste to become aware of their opposition to the dominant caste and their solidarity with the other members of their own caste.

Moreover, every war, carried along by a sort of dizzy momentum, tends to go to extremes and become a total war. And this is even more true in the case of a war in which the civil population is both the prize that is at stake and the plaything of the opposing forces, a war without a front line or without frontiers, a war in which the enemy is everywhere and nowhere, in which neutrality, or the adoption of a wait-and-see policy or a policy of indifference, are practically impossible, in which the army charged with repressing the revolt finds itself besieged and surrounded and inevitably distressed by the collective conspiracy with which it is confronted.

The chain of violence causes the adversaries, who are placed in an inevitable concatenation of acts and counter-acts, to be driven inexorably into making unlimited use of every available weapon. There seems to be a spiral movement, in which any increase in the size of the forces of repression leads to increased tension and a corresponding increase in the revolutionary forces and vice versa. No doubt our abstract argument as to the normal evolution of a war of liberation was not strictly fulfilled by the turn of events, and the actual war, however atrocious it might be, still remained short of absolute war. However, this spiral movement tends to lead not only to a quantitative increase in the opposing forces and in the intensity of their employment, but also to a qualitative transformation, a mutation in intentions and sentiments. The hostile intention, that is to say, the objective that one desires to attain through war, and the feeling of hostility, the hatred that one feels toward the enemy, tend to develop in inverse ratio. The hostile intention, in this case the abolition of the caste system—an intention which, when considered in its pure form, excludes all hatred towards those who, whether they like it or not, benefit from the system one desires to destroy—could very well be replaced by a passionately emotional feeling of hostility directed against an enemy who is not distant and abstract, as in other wars, but who is intimately, closely and familiarly known.

War as Cultural Agent

Thus the Algerian war, by its mere existence as well as by its special form and its duration, transformed the situation in which and by which it was brought into being. The social setting in which the acts of everyday existence are carried on was radically changed and, with it, the attitude of the individual. How are we to describe and understand this complete and sudden transformation, this revolution within the revolution?

One explanation is that the war of liberation constituted the first really severe challenge to the colonial system, and, above all, constituted the first challenge which was not, as in the past, symbolic and, to a certain extent, magic. The adherence to certain traditions, to certain ways of conduct, to certain beliefs and values, could formerly be considered as a way of expressing, through forms of behavior which were implicitly or explicitly endowed with a symbolic function, the refusal on the part of the Algerians to adhere to a Western civilization that was identified with the colonial order, their will to affirm their radical and irreducible difference from the Europeans, their resistance to any attempt to make them deny their own way of life and their desire to defend their besieged identity. In the colonial situation any renouncement of their original way of life would have meant, in fact, a renouncement of themselves and the acceptance of an allegiance to the other civilization, that is to say, to the colonial order. And such is, indeed, the meaning that the supporters of the colonial order gave to what they termed "the signs of evolution."

Colonial traditionalism had come to replace the traditionalism of the traditional society. As a result, ways of behavior which in appearance had remained unchanged were really endowed with a very different meaning and function, because of the fact that they were now set in relation to a totally new frame of reference. The veil and the *chechia,* for example, had been in the traditional context mere vestimentary details endowed with an almost forgotten significance, simple elements of an unconsciously devised system of symbols. In the colonial situation, however, they take on the function of signs that are being consciously utilized to express resistance to the foreign order and to foreign values as well as to pledge fidelity to their own system of values.

In a society whose self-knowledge is obtained exclusively by reference to itself, the cultural models, although conventional and therefore arbitrary, are yet considered normal and natural. With the discovery of a foreign cultural system, however, their hidden essence is suddenly revealed. Traditional traditionalism meant following a tradition that was considered, not as the best possible (which would have presupposed the awareness and knowledge of other possibilities), but as the only possible tradition. The discovery of the existence of another tradition leads to a new understanding of one's own tradition as being only one among several, or, in other words, as being just as conventional and arbitrary as all the others. When this happens, it means the end of traditional traditionalism, which can only continue to exist on condition that it remain in ignorance of its true nature—that is to say, that it remain as a choice not between but of. The colonial situation favors the emergence of a new traditionalism. All those forms of behavior which, in a society that constituted its own frame of reference, were felt to be quite natural, and whose conventional character became evident only by comparison with other forms of behavior characteristic of different cultures, are now being purposely adopted and chosen in opposition to a whole series of other possible choices that the dominant society proposes and whose adoption it often imposes by the mere fact of its existence and by the compulsion inherent in the colonial order.

Such is the significance and the function of all the forms of
resistance which seem to have been accumulated consciously or
unconsciously, the significance and function of all the apparently
aberrant and absurd forms of refusal. It is as if this society had
chosen to remain tightly closed upon itself, as if it had taken
great pains to set up a thousand invisible, impregnable barriers
against the intrusion of new methods and ideas. Feeling that
they were constantly exposed to the critical eye of the Europeans,
anxious not to give them any pretext or reason for their unfavorable judgments, the Algerians, by their behavior, their clothing
and their whole way of life, created a language of refusal. Such
a refusal, to be sure, could only be expressed in a symbolic
fashion.

Consequently the existence of a revolutionary organization
capable of standing up to and attacking the colonial order, the
existence of an effective form of negation of the system operating
within the system itself and recognized as such—whether they
liked it or not—by those who were going to great lengths to
deny its effectiveness, was enough to make valueless many of the
forms of behavior by which the dominated caste had expressed
its refusal to be dominated. The war, in itself, constituted a
language; it gave the Algerian people a voice, a voice capable
of saying "No!" Between the members of the dominated and
the dominant castes a new presence, a third man, was interposed:
the charm of the straightforward conversation ended; the dialec-
tic between humiliation and contempt broke off. The context in
which personal relations formerly were established is now quite
different and the relations themselves have changed. Understand-
able now is the extremely important role performed by the
clandestine radio broadcasts and by the passage of information
by word of mouth. Through these media each Algerian was able
to catch an echo of the language of the combatants, spokesmen
whose very existence constituted a language.

Each Algerian may henceforth assume full responsibility for
his own actions and for the widespread borrowings he has made
from Western civilization; he can even deny a portion of his
cultural heritage without denying himself in the process. Because the negation of the system remains, permanent and un-

changed, a negation made up of the sum total of all the refusals on the part of individuals, any innovation introduced by the West can be adopted without its acceptance being considered as an expression of allegiance. An Algerian once said: "The war has killed off a good many phantoms." He meant by this that the war had allowed a number of traditions, institutions and beliefs, which they had tried to keep alive by artificial means, to be finally considered as dead and buried. It made possible a self-confession that had been impossible previously. One often hears them say, "Times have changed." By this they mean that, with the change in situation, ways of behavior that had meaning in a different context have now lost their significance.

This total change in attitude reveals itself in different spheres. The most obvious transformations have occurred in the traditions endowed with an essentially symbolic significance, such as the customs pertaining to dress. A second function has been added, for example, to the traditional function of the wearing of the veil. Like the *chechia* (distinctive cap worn by the men), the veil has the role of a symbol that expresses both an alliance and an exclusion; it is primarily a defense of the inner self and a protection against any intrusion from without. But in addition to this, by the wearing of the veil, the Algerian woman is also creating a situation of non-reciprocity; like a cheating gambler, she can see without being observed; and it is through her that the whole of this dominated society is symbolically refusing to establish any reciprocal relations, is looking on without letting itself be observed. The veil is the most obvious symbol of this closing in upon oneself, and the Europeans have always obscurely felt it to be such. In this way it becomes evident why all attempts at assimilation have taken the discarding of the veil to be their primary objective. The demonstrations of May 13, 1958, in the course of which several Algerian women removed their veils or "burnt them symbolically" (as the newspapers reported), amid the applause of the crowd of Europeans present, was tantamount to a ceremonial magic rite by which the whole of Algerian society was offering itself, naked and willing, to the embrace of the European society.

This symbol of refusal, like many others, can now be aban-

doned. The girls and even the married women who have given
up the veil are every day becoming more numerous in the
cities. And if, as a result of the demonstrations of May 1958, there
was a slowing down and even a regression in this movement,
it was because the wearing of the veil once again was taking on
its meaning as a symbolic form of negation and because to discard
the veil might appear to be a sign of adherence to the policy of
integration.

This total transformation in attitude can also be noted in
other domains. Certain institutions, such as education or the
medical services, which were instinctively felt to be part and
parcel of the colonial system and which, because of this fact, provoked ambiguous and ambivalent attitudes towards them on the
part of the Algerians, are now ascribed quite a different significance because the tie linking them to the system of colonial
domination has been broken.[6]

This change is particularly noticeable in the field of education. There was originally a good deal of resistance to the first
attempts at making education available for all children, particularly for girls. The school, it was said, produced renegades
(m'turni), individuals who had broken with their community
and their ancestral traditions. The first teachers, who, with much
zeal and devotion, came to teach in Algeria about the year 1885,
were astonished at the swift progress made by their pupils, who
were eager to acquire a general education and even more eager
to obtain technical or agricultural training. But the years that
followed brought nothing except cries of disappointment and
acknowledgment of failure. It seemed that once the children had
gone back to their home environment they forgot everything
they had learned in school. One of the reasons for this was that
the relation between master and pupil (like the relation between

[6] The fact that the army of the National Liberation Front (F.L.N.) took
over responsibility for these institutions and techniques by levying taxes, by
taking over the verification of vital statistics, by occasionally opening up new
schools, etc., has been a major factor contributing to this disassociation.
Similarly, ways of behavior which, in another context, would have been considered an absolute denial of the Algerian way of life have become possible,
because they have been authorized or prescribed by orders of the F.L.N. Thus
modern institutions and techniques have been assigned a change in symbol
and may now be adopted without hesitation or reserve.

doctor and patient) was set against the background of the colonial situation, so that the teaching of the schoolmaster or the instructor in agriculture was intuitively felt (without there necessarily being any conscious awareness of the basis for this feeling) as an attempt to impose the norms of a foreign civilization. During the past few years, however, there has no longer been any resistance to education. In all social classes, in the rural as well as the urban communities, an extraordinary desire for education has become evident. Teachers are besieged by parents coming to demand an education for their children. It is becoming more and more frequent for poor families to undergo great sacrifices in order that their children may be allowed to continue their studies. This devotion to education is undoubtedly the clearest possible indication of an over-all adherence to the modern world, a world to which education opens the door.

But it has gone even beyond this. What was considered to be an imposed restraint or a gracious gift up to a few years ago is now regarded as a due right or as a prerogative won by right of conquest. This was noted in the demanding attitude of the parents who came to ask that their children be enrolled in the schools or in the attitude of the women who crowded about the doors of the free medical dispensaries or welfare centers. Everywhere the same consciousness of their rights is now in evidence: the right to work, the right to decent housing, the right to the different social benefits (social security, family allowances, etc.). For the attitude of the beggar who comes humbly to solicit a charitable gift there has been substituted a demanding and revolutionary state of mind which is inducing the Algerians to insist on their rights to social benefits and services.

The image that the individual of the dominated caste had formed of the individual of the dominant caste was composed of certain basic concepts. On the one hand the Algerian, particularly the Algerian of the poorer classes, tended to identify the European with all social superiors. And on the other hand he tended to perceive all the members of the dominant society— teacher, colonist, doctor, engineer, foreman, policeman and administrator—in an indistinct or syncretic fashion, in other words, as having solidarity with one another and indissolubly connected with the colonial situation. The attitude of dutiful obedience was linked confusedly to an attitude of resignation, prompted by an awareness of the real obstacles which made it actually impossible to imitate or equal the European. Roughly, then, the social order was such that the experience of the relation to the boss or the superior was superimposed upon, and identified itself with, the experience of the relation to the European. As a consequence the Algerian tended to play the role of the Arab-as-seen-by-the-Frenchman. The man who is going to apply for a certain job knows that he must speak a certain language, that he must arrive on time, and that he must adopt a specific attitude and so on. Relations between the members of the two societies, therefore, were generally based on misunderstanding. The Algerian's answer to the European's protective paternalism was to assume an attitude of dependency tinged with aggressiveness. The relations between the administration and those being administered were formed on the same pattern.[7] The war revealed to everyone that the position of the dominant caste can be brought into question and with it the situation of the dominated caste. The European and his whole world no longer cast a spell over the Algerian, now resolutely penetrating into this world and seeking to take it over for himself. The discovery that the dominant caste can be held in check and that the order over which it reigned can be shaken led the Algerian to set a higher value on his own situation. He no longer felt ashamed of the inferiority of his social condition; he rather regarded as scandalous injustice all that he formerly endured as an ineluctable and inescapable necessity. The sense of shame that one could

[7] Medicine and, generally speaking, all forms of social service have often been utilized (especially since 1954) as "instruments for the penetration and conquest of populations," to adopt a certain officialese, that is to say, as a means employed for the maintenance of the colonial order. Thus it may be understood why it is that members of the dominated class have trouble in conceding that the acts of the members of the dominant caste can ever be inspired by an ethic based on pure intention only—that these actions can constitute an end in themselves. They are always inclined to see them as merely a means to an end, because the action that is most generous in intention is interpreted against this background of the colonial situation and hence receives a quite different meaning than that which its author wished to confer upon it. Thus it is that the Algerians attribute all the social measures from which they have benefited for several years to the action of the F.L.N.

note in certain individuals has been replaced by pride in themselves and a shame at having been ashamed. Because he no longer
looks on his condition as being an inevitable destiny but rather
as a situation that can be changed, the Algerian can at the same
time accept himself as an Algerian and can ignore his status as a
dominated member of society; he can adopt the techniques and
institutions introduced by the colonizer without accepting the
position of the colonized.

The relations between the members of the dominated society have also been modified. The war was, at the beginning,
a rather episodic affair that each Algerian lived from day to day
within the confines of his own village. Gradually, however,
through exchanges of information, through the reading of newspapers and listening to the radio, each person began to realize
that the same events were going on throughout all the regions
of Algeria. The feeling of being engaged in a common adventure,
of being subject to a common destiny, of confronting the same
adversary, of sharing the same preoccupations, the same suffer-
ings and the same aspirations, widened and deepened the sentiment of solidarity, a sentiment which was undergoing at the
same time a veritable transformation as the idea of fraternity
tended to lose any ethnical or religious coloration and became
synonymous with national solidarity. The village, the closed
microcosm in which the country dweller once lived, was now
in contact with the whole of Algeria. Through the press, through
the radio, through wider contacts, through the action of the
political commissaries, each Algerian communicated with and
was in communion with a wider social unit; he participated in
a national existence.[8]

The war provided this people, kept so long on leading
strings, with an opportunity to demonstrate that it can be adult,
sensible and responsible. It allowed them to gain a true experience of a self-discipline that was voluntarily adopted because imposed by their own freely recognized authorities; in other words,

[8] This deep solidarity finds expression in many different ways: usurers
have practically disappeared, whether because they were the object of popular
sanction, or because loans are now being made without demanding any security; to demand the payment of any debt contracted before 1954 is considered,
in certain cases, dishonorable.

the Algerian people have experienced autonomy. Thus, for example, in various regions a very definite reduction in the number of repudiations was noted as a result of the instructions issued by the F.L.N. It was also reported by the cadis that the number of lawsuits had greatly decreased. The instructions issued by the F.L.N., which were of all kinds and concern all aspects of daily life, quickly put an end to what was formerly considered an unshakable resistance to change on the part of the Algerian people and induced them to accept efforts, sacrifices and behavioral changes which one hundred and thirty years of "civilizing influence" had never been able and never would have been able to bring about. Thus the war created a profound alteration in the situation, and there is not a single aspect of the social system that has not been modified as a result of this change in context. With the outbreak of war, there began the process of decolonization.

To this total mutation that the war provoked through the fact of its existence and through the resulting awakening of consciousness it produced, there must be added the upheavals and disturbances which are the direct consequence of the conduct of the war or of the political and economic measures that were adopted to meet the emergency. By reason of its special form and its duration, this war affected all aspects of reality: the economy and the vital statistics as well as the social structures, the religious beliefs and observances, and even the system of values.

The Resettlement Policy

The Algerian people have been subjected to a veritable diaspora. The forced or voluntary displacement of peoples assumed gigantic proportions. The number of persons who no longer inhabit the home in which they were living in 1954 may be roughly estimated at about 3 million, if one takes into account the moves that occurred as a result of the resettlement of communities and the exodus to the towns and cities. This means that approximately one Algerian out of three is no longer living in his former place of abode. While the regroupings of communities are only one aspect of these internal shifts in population, they are undoubtedly the most important.

After having first been carried out in the most troubled regions, in order to facilitate the conduct of military operations, these regroupings or resettlements of population later became much more frequent, particularly during the years 1958 and 1959 (and often in spite of the instructions issued by the civil authorities), until finally they were being carried out as a systematic policy. In addition to the purely military reasons and the desire to cut off the forces of the F.L.N. from the civil population who were giving them much-needed support, new reasons were put forward in favor of this policy, reasons inspired mainly by the integrationist doctrine resulting from the demonstrations of May 13, 1958, and by a strategy for waging counter-revolutionary war that was very popular in military circles, particularly among the readers of Mao Tse-tung and the veterans of the war in Indochina. Communities which had formerly lived in widely scattered dwellings or in remote regions, and who as a result were naturally difficult to administer, to educate and to control, were to be settled in villages that would be run on a collective basis and would be located along the great communication routes. It was hoped thereby to effect a reconstitution of the social structures and to set in motion a movement of accelerated social evolution.

From the standpoint of the total society, there has resulted from these measures an upheaval without precedent in the history of Algeria (see Fig. 15): the mountainous regions (Aurès and Nemenchas, Kabylia and the Tellian Atlas) and the zones bordering the frontiers have been almost completely cleared of their inhabitants. These people were either resettled in the plains of Piémont or have gone to the towns and cities. As a result of this migration the cities have all had an increase in population varying from 50 to more than 100 per cent.

The most severely disturbed regions are those which had been relatively spared up to the outbreak of war because they had been partially sheltered from the colonizing enterprises. It was in the mountainous zones, those that were most affected by the war and the policy of resettlement, that the little rural communities, leading a secluded way of life and remaining obstinately faithful to their past and to their traditions, had been able to safeguard the essential features of a civilization which can henceforth be spoken of only in the past tense. This situation prevailed among the Kabyles and in the Aurès, where the Berber-speaking societies had maintained themselves relatively unchanged, in spite of the sequestrations of their property that were made after their early insurrections, in spite of the creation of new administrative units (see Chap. 6) and many other hostile measures (see Fig. 16). Doubtless the contact with the European civilization, particularly the influence of emigration (especially important among the Kabyles) and also that of the school (the first classes having been opened in Kabylia about 1880), had resulted in great changes in the economic sphere and the social structures as well as in the system of values. However, because of their isolation, because also of the extremely powerful integration of the cultural system, the Kabyle and Shawian societies, and to a lesser degree the societies of the other mountainous regions, had conserved the main essentials of their ancestral traditions. Indeed, only the coherence of the social structures, the intensity of the collective sentiment, and the force of tradition could cause these peasants to remain attached to a land that was becoming less and less capable of supporting them, particularly when they were exposed to the powerful attraction of the high wages being paid in the cities of Algeria or of France.

Thus the war and its aftermath merely finished what colonial policy had begun. Only the great land acts and the introduction of large-scale colonization into the areas of the plains and hills —the effects of which were to create a sub-proletariat of agricultural workers, cut off from their geographical and social environment and from their traditions and way of life—have been able to cause any comparable upheaval in Algerian society.[9]

One is struck by the fact that, when confronted with identi-

[9] The comparative study of two groups who had a very different history during the nineteenth century—on the one hand, the populations of regions situated on the border of the areas of large-scale colonial development (in the plain of the Chéliff, for example) and who thereby escaped the forces of disintegration, and on the other hand, the agricultural workers employed on the great European properties, a class resulting from an analogous, al-

cal conditions, although a century apart, those responsible for framing colonial policy have resorted to measures that are identical in both form and spirit. Everything that has already been said about the *Senatus Consulte* and the motives behind its formulation of policy is also true of the policy of resettlement. Originally conceived as a means of "taking in hand" and "controlling" communities by placing them in close proximity to a military post, the resettlements were also supposed to "assure the emancipation of the Moslem masses" according to the army theorists. The confusion between the two objectives was increased by the conviction that in order to break down the resistance that this society opposed to the French order and to the modern world, it was necessary to destroy its social structures.

Although the widest powers of initiative had in most cases been granted to the minor officials in charge, the villages constructed for these resettlement projects all had a basic similarity, because they were created in pursuance of this implicit or explicit policy, and because Algeria has been the experimental ground to which the military mind, as in a projective test, has applied its own structures. Often, in point of fact, granted an absolute authority, the army officials decided on everything—

though less brutal and less complete, upheaval to that which is being caused by the policy of resettlement—can provide a basis for forecasting the consequences of this policy.

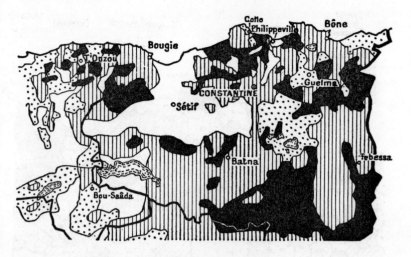

Fig. 15. The Military Situation in 1957

This map, which distinguishes (1) the "rotten *douars*" (the regions in which "90 to 100 per cent" of the people have rallied to the nationalist cause), (2) the "very heavily contaminated *douars*" (50 to 90 per cent), and (3) the "contaminated *douars*" (20 to 50 per cent), was drawn up by the army at the end of the first year of the war. If one sets aside the frontier zones, the regions in which the army of the National Liberation Front entrenched itself most strongly and most rapidly were the mountainous regions, the most difficult of access and, consequently, the most favorable for the conduct of a revolutionary war. But these are also the poorest regions, in which 75 to 100 per cent of the farms owned by Algerians are less than 25 acres in size. They are the regions in which the Berber-speaking societies have maintained their way of life, strongly integrated societies which have been relatively spared the disintegration that has been the lot of societies in the regions of large-scale colonization (as in the High Plains of Constantine, the valley of the Chéliff, the Plains in the Oran District, for example). Finally, they are regions (particularly the Kabyle regions) in which the French influence has been most deeply felt through the effects of schooling and emigration (it is in Kabylia, for example, that the most acute awareness of conditions of unemployment has been noted: cf. the commentary accompanying Figure 13). These characteristic features of the regions in which the revolution has been most strongly rooted may appear contradictory; in reality, because of the fact of their strong integration, the mountain peoples have remained highly conscious of their own originality, while at the same time contact with French civilization has helped to make them aware of their poverty and has supplied them with the revolutionary ideologies through which they can express their revolt against a situation which gives them an inferior status, both in the economic and in the social domain.

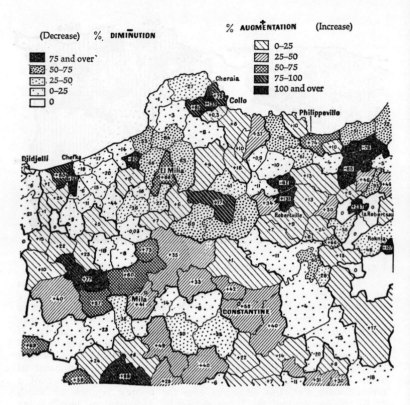

Fig. 16
Population Shifts in the North
of the *Département* of Constantine

A detail drawing of a portion of the map indicating the population shifts taking place in Algeria between 1954 and 1960 (Fig. 14), this map gives a more exact idea of the upheavals that have taken place in Algeria since 1955 (the figure placed within each commune, or district, indicates the rate of increase or decrease). However, it fails to indicate the sometimes very large-scale movements which have taken place within a single commune, such as the shifts in population resulting from the resettlement carried out by the military authorities in the region of Collo (see Figure 19).

168

the site of the villages, the layout, the width of the streets, the interior arrangement of the houses and many other details. Either unacquainted with, or willfully ignorant of, the traditional structures and standards, little inclined to consult the people involved, and being placed in a situation such that, even if they had sought it, this cooperation would have been tacitly refused them, they went ahead and imposed their own arrangements, generally without noticing the distress caused by the measures they initiated. Convinced that they must make men happy in spite of themselves, persuaded that they knew the real needs of others better than the latter did themselves, assured of belonging to a superior civilization that was absolutely good in itself, the officials were unable to conceive of the customary life of the people as being anything other than a primitive and barbarous survival, and concluded that any resistance offered to the order they wished to impose was the mere expression of an obstinate and absurd routine way of thinking.

Thus, through either a deliberate or an unconscious ignorance of the human realities involved, the local authorities charged with organizing these new settlements usually imposed, without any regard for the desires and aspirations of those being resettled, an order that was absolutely foreign to them, a way of life for which they were not suited and which was not suited to them. Animated by the feeling that they were carrying out a great plan, were "bringing about the evolution of the masses," exalted by their passion for putting things in order, and often devoting all of their enthusiasm, good will and resources to the performance of their activities, the officers indiscriminately put into practice plans whose implications had not been thought out. They began by attempting to discipline space, as if through it they hoped to discipline men. Everything was characterized by uniformity and straight lines. Built on prescribed sites in accordance with set standards, the houses were laid out in straight lines along wide streets, which could serve equally well to outline the plan of a Roman camp or a colonial village. In the center is the square, with the characteristic triad of the villages of France —the school, the town hall and the war memorial.[10] It is as if the

[10] On the war memorial of a resettled village in the region of Collo there is a single name, that of a caïd who was killed by the F.L.N.

authorities thought that they could create village life by creating its outer symbols. A census would be taken, a municipal council and a mayor chosen, a group organized for defense of the village, a commercial center set up preferably in the main street, with a grocery store, a butcher shop and a Moorish cafe, and the most loyal villagers would be granted as a reward and a favor the authority to set up shop; an infirmary would be built, to which the military doctor came to give consultations and administer to the sick once or twice a week. And they would consider that they had accomplished the main part of their task when they were able to show the visitor a village with well-laid-out houses and wide, clean streets, with the basic essentials of collective equipment and with a rudimentary administrative organization. They seemed to have been faithful to the revolutionary principle of all or nothing. But this was only in appearance. The resettlements might really have been (and still could be, in another context) the occasion for a true revolution of the agricultural society, if they had been accompanied by an agrarian reform, by a redistribution of land, and by a concerted attempt to improve agricultural methods; but that would have presupposed a challenge to the very foundations of the colonial order.

All these villages, even those that appear to be the most "successful," now have the desolate aspect of dead cities. Those who live in them, even when they are enjoying a standard of comfort previously unknown (and this is sometimes the case) express in their whole attitude a profound discontent and inner disturbance. The mere fact of a change of residence (by emigration to the cities, for example) is known to be sufficient to bring about a complete change in the attitude toward the world. In the case of the resettled populations, the sharp break with their familiar environment and their customary social world, in which the traditional ways of behavior were felt to be the natural ways, led to the abandonment of these forms of behavior, once these people had been cut off from the original soil in which they were rooted. The extended family, clan or village broke up once it was placed in a resettled community. The change in environment really requires a complete change in conduct. But the feeling of having been uprooted from their accustomed surroundings was usually so strong that disgust, anguish and despair almost always triumphed over the desire to invent the new ways of conduct required for the adaptation to radically new conditions of existence.

To understand the full extent of the upheavals brought about by these resettlements of population, it is first necessary to realize that they affected peasants almost entirely, and it is also necessary to recall that group of characteristics that is almost inseparable from the peasant condition in its traditional form. It is his attachment to his land and to his animals that makes the peasant. The quality of his work is determined by the strength of his devotion to his occupation as farmer, a devotion that is much more mystical than rational in character (see Chap. 5, para. 2). The true peasant identifies himself with his farm: his whole existence and all his thinking are turned toward his land and his flock; his property possesses him much more than he possesses it. The house is often the center of his domain. It is important, indeed, to be as close as possible to the plots of land that he owns. In Kabylia the most prized lands are those which immediately surround the village, and this preference cannot be explained merely on economic grounds. Does not the peasant have the habit of going, as they say, "to pay a visit to his field?" The work of the farm is carried on within the domestic group, as well as on familiar land in the immediate vicinity of the house. The interior arrangement of the house itself is the best indication of the interpenetration of home life and of the life of the farm. In the Kabyle house, composed of a single room, the section reserved for the animals is separated from the part lived in by the humans only by a low wall, on which are placed the earthenware jars containing the wheat from the last harvest. Thus the field, the animals, the implements, the farm products and all the preoccupations connected with these things have taken their place at the center of the home and family life. But the peasant enjoys great autonomy. Whether a small farmer or a sharecropper, he determines his own working conditions; he himself, decides on the nature of his tasks, on the time to do them and the rate at which they will be carried out; he disposes of his produce as he sees fit. But the independence it assures him cannot be considered as the real cause of the peasant's devotion to his calling, this complete and utter adherence, not to a trade, but to an art of living that is inseparably linked to the peasant attitude of mind. It is indeed this peasant spirit or attitude of mind that makes the peasant, but this spirit, like any other passion, must be able to feed on the object of its devotion and fares badly when separated from it.

Removed from their lands, which were often inaccessible because situated in forbidden territory, removed from their houses, which they were almost always obliged to destroy with their own hands before leaving to join the resettlement project, sometimes separated from their animals for hygienic reasons, compelled to place the whole of their cereal crop in the storehouse of the military authorities who allocated a set amount each month for their use, these peasants felt their forced removal to be a separation in the strongest sense of the term; stricken to the core of their being, they gave vent to their indignations and despair (the word is not too strong) in a voice of wretched suffering.[11]

The peasant can exist only when rooted to his land, the land where he was born, which he received from his parents and to which he is attached by his habits and memories. Once he has been uprooted there is a good chance that he will cease to exist as a peasant, that the instinctive and irrational passion which binds him to his peasant existence will die within him. No doubt there are degrees of deracination, and the monographic study of different resettlement villages has shown that there are also degrees of "deruralization." Before the resettlements took place, the rural population was almost entirely composed of work-

[11] The analyses put forward here are the result of investigations undertaken during the summer of 1960 in different Algerian centers. In the villages in the region of Collo, of which a study was made, the persons who had been resettled were compelled to ask for a pass in order to go and work their fields; they turned over the whole of their crop to the S.A.S. (Section Administrative Spécialisée). Many had given up cultivating their farms, either because these were situated in the forbidden zone, or because they had been overrun by prowling animals and wild boars, since the farmers could no longer watch over their fields. At Djebabra, a center in the region about Miliana, the greatest cause of indignation was the fact that these people were separated from their animals, which were now all being kept together in a collective stable some 50 yards removed from their *gourbis* (houses).

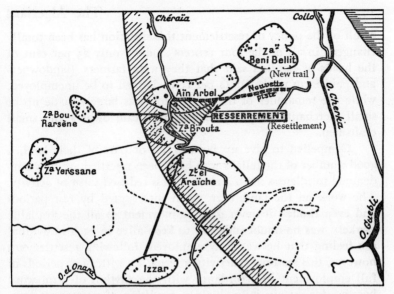

Fig. 17. The "Resettlements" in the Territory of Aïn Arbel

Situated to the east of Collo, on the territory occupied by the *zariba* of Aïn Arbel, the new village groups together about 2,500 persons belonging to groups (*zaribat*) that were formerly settled at distances varying from a half-mile to two miles from one another. Situated in the center of a farming area on land that had been carved out of the forest, each *zariba* (clan) grouped together all the descendants of a common ancestor, that is to say, there were some seventy persons in the smallest *zariba* and some 420 persons in the largest. Having abandoned their houses, most of these resettled persons have also given up farming their lands (all those that were situated to the east of the hachured line). It is not so much the fact that it takes from half an hour to an hour and a half to walk to them (resulting in the abandonment of the farms), as the fact that the owners could no longer live surrounded by their fields.

ers who made their living directly from agriculture—fellahs, farm workers, sharecroppers—while the unvaried and generally similar nature of farm work tended to give rural society its unity. Living in the same district as the peasants, engaging in dealings with them and often doing farm work themselves, the small merchants, the owners of cafes or cheap restaurants, and the artisans did not stand out in contrast to the farm worker because, in general, their activity was still very much the same and was at any rate complementary to the agricultural activities. As a result of the policy of resettlement this situation has been totally changed: in all of the four centers studied, only 25 per cent of the heads of families said that they were farmers (landowners and paid farm workers); 44 per cent claimed to be unemployed, while the remainder of the population was largely made up of small merchants, shopkeepers, peddlers, cafe owners and small craftsmen.

Compelled to give up farming all or part of their land, a good number of the fellahs who have been resettled are now condemned to idleness or to a more or less reduced form of activity. The work on the land, even when interrupted by rest periods and even though it never gave employment to all the available workers, was no doubt sufficient to keep alive in each individual the feeling that he was fully employed; following resettlement, however, this seasonal inactivity alternating with busy periods of full employment in accordance with the rhythm of farm work became, for certain individuals, a condition of permanent inactivity, and hence was felt to be abnormal and not to be endured.[12] But generally speaking, because it is interpreted as being the consequence of a situation to which they are absolutely opposed, an ordinary reduction in employment, even when very slight, is sufficient to bring about a radical change in the attitude to work and a realization of their condition of chronic underemployment that has often only been made worse by resettlement.

No doubt the fellahs had already gone through more or less long periods of inactivity in the past. But these fitted in with an accustomed cycle that was fixed by tradition and linked to the

---

[12] Here are two examples: "Formerly, when my children were here, I got along, I was well established, I used to work my fields with my brothers and my children. We could manage. Now here I am in the resettlement village"; "I used to sell whey in Collo, now I only have four goats left. I used to take two hours to make the trip to Collo. All that has become impossible today, we have nothing left. Since I was moved to this center, I haven't done a single day's work." To the partial or total abandonment of the farms there has generally been added considerable reduction in the amount of livestock. The consequences of resettlement evidently are particularly serious when the move is one that concerns the nomads (200,000 of them approximately are said to have been resettled) whose sole wealth consisted of the flock and for whom the sedentary life means a complete change in their mode of existence.

rhythms of nature. With resettlement, however, these cycles and these rhythms changed; as a consequence, what was being questioned was not only the actual amount of employment provided, but the actual schedule of employment and unemployment as well. Henceforth, the fellah had a different outlook on both his present and his past occupations. "All these people," one of them said, "are beginning to find out what work really is and to realize that what they used to do before, digging away at the ground, was not really work at all." The peasant now regards as busywork what was formerly his lifework. The total devotion to his peasant existence which enabled him to endure often wretched living conditions is now a thing of the past.

Although their love of the land was sometimes expressed through the nostalgic recall of the way of life they had had to abandon, all the peasants who were questioned in the resettlement villages in the Collo region said that they did not like their occupation. No doubt this must be regarded as an effect of the tendency to project into all spheres the discontent roused by their forced settlement. It remains to be seen, however, whether this attitude was the result of special circumstances and will disappear entirely with the return of their usual way of life, or whether there is a possibility that it may have become firmly entrenched—in which case one could prophesy that, with freedom of movement restored, a good number of these "deruralized" country men will go to increase the population of the city suburbs rather than return to their farms and their ancestral pursuits. "Once peace has come," said a butcher of Kerkera (Collo), "I shall not go back to the *zariba* [a quarter in which are grouped together the members of the same clan]; I shall go instead to Tamalous or to some other city, but not back to the *zariba*. Wherever I find a job, that will be my country. We've had enough of 'hard' life; we want a 'soft' life, an 'easy' life. Anyone who wants the life in the mountains, let him go there. He can have it."

The awareness of their lack of employment, combined with the feeling of rebellion against their forced displacement, dominated the whole of their existence. Partially or totally deprived of their old occupations, many of the former fellahs aspired to become wage earners. In those areas in which a tradition of emigration existed, they departed for France when they could obtain the necessary authorization, which generally presupposes their obtaining a certificate that they have a job waiting for them or a letter from a relative who is willing to give them board and lodging.[13] Certain individuals succeeded during the war in finding employment in local concerns or factories or in the building yards opened up by the army. But these were usually only temporary means of support, and the feeling of insecurity persists.

It is this context that explains the excessive growth in the number of very small businesses and of manual trades. What are they waiting for, these merchants without customers, whom we see sitting all day long in front of their shops that stretch out in a row along the main street of certain resettlement villages? What can be the function of these pretended trades for those engaged in them? They cannot be considered as merely a means of livelihood, because their material result, or the profit to be gained from them, only partially explains their real significance. It is as if, because these pseudo-tradesmen have been unable to have access to work as a means of obtaining a wage or an income, they have ended, through force of circumstances, by disassociating work from its economic result, and now look on it, not so much as being connected with its product, but as being opposed to no work at all. Is not this multiplicity of small shops and businesses particularly illogical at a time when the drop in buying power, correlative to the drop in the standard of

[13] A new fact that has been observed is that more and more frequently entire families are leaving for France as a result, primarily, of the prevailing insecurity. It often happens that the emigrant returns to get his family as soon as he has the means to assure them decent living conditions. Thus in Aghbala, for example, a village of about 2,000 inhabitants, only six families had gone to France before 1954. By early 1962 eighteen families had moved there, and four of these include, in one case, the mother and sister of the head of the family and, in the other cases, his nephews and nieces. About twenty families have moved to neighboring small towns, Sidi Arch and El Kseur, or to Algiers. The exodus would have been on a still larger scale, if it had not been checked by the mayor, who would grant authority to leave only in return for the payment of a large sum of money. At Kerkera a whole clan, comprised of about one hundred persons, emigrated to Philippeville as a consequence of the policy of resettlement.

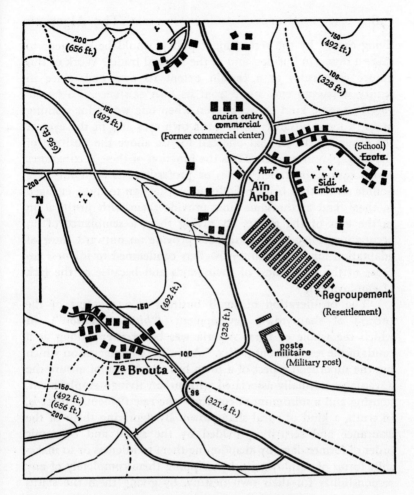

Fig. 18. The "Resettlement" of Aïn Arbel (detail)

The black squares represent the site of the houses that formerly belonged to the members of the *zariba* Aïn Arbel and the *zariba* Brouta. These people have now been resettled in the new village. Each group of houses sheltered a single social unit and was surrounded by the lands cultivated by the group.

living caused by the resettlement policy, would be sufficient to
cause a slump in business and in the manual trades? Work of this
nature constitutes to a certain extent its own end, since in
reality it has no end apart from its own existence. To be engaged in some kind of work, even when one works for nothing
or for a mere pittance, is, in one's own eyes and in the eyes of
the group, to do all that one can to rise above the position of
the unemployed worker. Thus the function of these occupations,
which cannot be called trades or professions, is symbolic in a
double sense: they bring a fictitious satisfaction to those engaged
in them, and at the same time provide them with justification
in the eyes of the group. By giving them a semblance of an
occupation, these small businesses provide an outward show of
adaptation for these country dwellers condemned to idleness because of the remoteness of their lands and because of the lack
of employment.[14]

The proliferation of small business is one aspect of the
process of shantytown development ("*bidonvillisation*"), in
which the whole of rural Algeria was being swept along as a
result of the resettlement policy.[15] A soulless agglomeration which
has the superficial aspect of a town but which cannot ensure the
advantages normally associated with urban living—employment,
housing and a minimum of comfort—the resettlement project is,
in truth, a kind of rural shantytown. By depriving them of the
assurance and security provided by the social and economic
order of former days, by abandoning them to idleness or to makeshift forms of employment, by stripping them completely of any
responsibility for their own destiny, by giving them the status

[14] The country districts have always been the scene of a sort of pendulum
movement: driven from the land by a poor year, some of the fellahs and the
agricultural workers would go and seek a livelihood in the cities. A promising
year would bring back to the agricultural life this particular portion of the
rural population. The resettlement has given full scope to this movement
of deruralization, to such an extent that it has perhaps made the latter
irreversible.

[15] The large-scale resettlements, like all great social upheavals, favored the
appearance of a class of profiteers, who were often supported by the army
by reason of their "loyalty," who held a majority of the administrative responsibilities (the mayoralty functions, for example), and who were allowed to run
the principal business concerns.

of persons on relief, the authorities transformed these deruralized country dwellers into a sub-proletariat who had lost all memory of their former ideals of honor and dignity and who wavered between attitudes of meek resignation and ineffectual revolt.

The whole of their existence was lacking that which normally constitutes its main framework: the daily work at one's customary occupation, with its temporal and spatial rhythms, the demands it imposes, the security that it offers, the future that it allows one to envisage and plan for. The tragedy of unemployment does not lie solely in being deprived of real opportunities to work, but in being deprived of a regular daily occupation and the stability guaranteed by the assured product of one's labor. For individuals placed in this catastrophic situation, what is threatened is their whole psychological balance and, more particularly, their emotional balance. They gradually lapse into an apathetic attitude of fatalistic resignation. They inevitably become reconciled and accustomed to a parasitic and vegetative form of existence. Is it not a fact, for example, that, after two years of idleness and misery, the inhabitants of a resettlement project in the Collo region refused the chance to move to another place where they were assured of finding farms that could be worked? Is it not likely that familiarization with prolonged unemployment and the habit of pretending to be busy at poor trades will produce parasites who are lacking in dignity, complacently resigned to being on relief and imbued with a vague and peevish feeling of resentment rather than with any truly revolutionary ideas? There is a good chance that such may be the fate of the populations of certain centers who, as a result of the lack of any farm work, were placed in a situation of absolute dependency on the administration or the military authorities, and had no other means of support than their periodic allotment of semolina, their pay as auxiliary police, and the wages they were able to earn in the workshops that had been opened up by the army.

Moreover, the constraints, persecutions and unfair manipulations to which they had been subjected finally broke down their resistance. At Cheraïa, in the Collo region, the people came a long distance (from two to four miles) to build at their own

Fig. 19. The "Resettlements" in the Kerkera Region (Collo)

In the whole of the *arrondissement* (administrative district) of
Collo, some 33,000 persons—or more than a third of the total population—have been resettled. The resettlement center of Km 10 (kilometer 10) was comprised of 3,264 persons (about 589 families) to which
were added in September 1960 the 1,091 inhabitants (205 families) of
the *zariba* Kerkera, situated about one-half mile away from the resettlement center on the side of the hill which overlooks the valley of
the Wadi Guebli. At Redir, 371 families, comprising 1,894 persons,
were resettled. Finally, at Km 19 the authorities grouped together the
zaribat Lazilet, el Afia, Outaïet Aïcha, el Hammam and Bourguel.
Whereas at Aïn Arbel the new village was established in an area already
occupied by one of the contracted groups, the site of the resettlement
project of Kerkera, at the edge of the Wadi Guebli with its dangerous
spring overflows, had been occupied by only a few scattered houses. By
reason of its size and the arbitrary way in which its site was selected,
the Kerkera project, which brings together formerly separate groups,
is the prize example of the rural shantytown (*bidonville*).

(See map on opposite page.)

expense houses in which they were to live—and they were aware
of this—only until such time as the definitive site of the village
could be acquired. At Kerkera the inhabitants of a *zariba*, situated half way up the slope of a hill, were obliged before the
end of summer to leave their houses, which were almost all
solidly built and very comfortable, to go and live in *gourbis* situated in a part of the valley that was regularly flooded in winter
by the Wadi Guebli. Thus, gradually, they get used to an unstable existence. And each one experiences in his inmost heart all
the tragedy of having his customary existence and way of life
shattered about him.

Groups of different origins were brought together, a fact
which tended to weaken the old communal ties. A new type of
solidarity now made its appearance, quite different from the
former solidarity and closely linked to a feeling of revolt against
commonly shared conditions. The real and sometimes terrible
material misery they had to endure was, however, nothing compared to the moral misery of these men who had been torn from
their familiar world, their home, their lands, their customs, their
beliefs, everything that helped them to live.[16] Placed by force in

[16] As a consequence of the depressed condition of agriculture and stock
raising, there may be noted in nearly all cases a drop in the standard of living

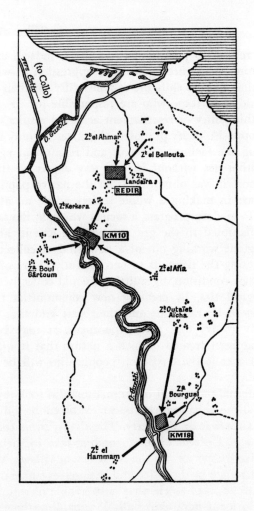

a situation they detested, prevented from taking control of their own destiny, they could not turn their thoughts to devising methods of developing a cooperative movement that would be based on the common interest and on deliberate participation in a common effort. Rather, they demonstrated in a great many

---

that is difficult to evaluate properly. In such conditions any available capital—flock, poultry, reserves—is rapidly consumed. Life becomes a hand-to-mouth existence, a sink-or-swim affair. The physiological condition of these people leads to a very high death rate, particularly among children.

ways their refusal to participate.[17] Is there, indeed, any better way of gaining vengeance against the oppression of which they are the victims than to shift the responsibility for their own fate to the shoulders of those who are responsible for it?

Thus this policy of resettlement achieved results which are the direct opposite of its proposed objectives. It only succeeded in increasing the feelings of revolt and resentment against the colonial authorities without in any way depriving the F.L.N. of the support it was obtaining from the native population. It played a part in making a whole society adopt an attitude of opposition to modern progress, a society which, at the same time, had been disrupted to the greatest possible extent. Finally, by encouraging the working out of a new kind of collective existence, by causing the peasants to become fully aware of the true nature of their condition, by splitting the old collectivities based on genealogical ties, by creating new communities that have broken with their traditions and their past and that are, as a result, ready to try any new experiment, it may be that a situation has been created of such a nature that it will impose solutions of a collectivist type on people who will be ready to accept them.

The internal movement of population also took the form of an exodus to the cities, which appear to the country dwellers as a refuge against war and poverty. The shantytowns continue to increase in size. Citizens of long standing take in their country relatives. Like the persons in the resettlement villages, those who have sought refuge in the cities find themselves suddenly thrown into an unaccustomed world that is incapable of assuring them steady employment and, above all, of providing them with the security that could give balance and stability to their existence. This will be seen in the following typical statement:

I have been in Constantine since March 1959. Before that I was at C. du R. . . . . I came to the shantytown at H. They destroyed our *gourbis* and they found us a new home in the city

[17] This may be seen, for example, in the fact that the people who have been resettled rarely make any modification to their houses or attempt to beautify them in any way, and hence do not display any real feeling of ownership.

of El Bir. The house belongs to the S.A.S. [*Section Administrative Spécialisée*]. There is neither water nor electricity. There are eight of us in two rooms, one for my brother and his family, the other for me. My father was a day laborer, "a pick-and-shovel man," and a fellah before that. I used to work as a *"trabadjar"* [the pejorative name for a farm worker]. Now I am unemployed. Every day I go looking for a job in several work yards, but I haven't found one, either in B. or elsewhere. I would do anything at all if I could find a job, provided I could bring home a bit of bread to my children. But I have no trade [no specialty]. The specialist, he gets a job right away. He's never out of work. I'd do any work at all, but I haven't any trade. The man who hasn't a trade is always unemployed.

Characteristic of the class of rural dwellers who had recently come to the city to flee from war and poverty, driven from pillar to post, not understanding very clearly what was happening to him—either when the powers that be demolish his tin-can hut to find him a new lodging in the city or when they refuse him work in yard after yard—he had been able to obtain only a few days' employment here and there since his arrival in the city over a year before. He was able to exist only with the help of his brother, a little candy peddler whose income is completely dependent on chance.

Unemployed worker, unskilled laborer, unlicensed peddler, all may be successive occupations of the same individual; in any case they are three callings that are easily interchangeable. There was nothing solid, nothing stable, nothing permanent for all these men who were ready to do any kind of work and were conscious of their ignorance of all trades; who were always available for employment and completely at the mercy of external forces; who were condemned to live a hand-to-mouth existence and who craved security; who had no real trade and so were forced to engage in all kinds of pseudo-trades; who were compelled to gain a knowledge both of the technical world and of city life—to become acquainted with work regulations, to learn the French language, to learn the use of tools and measuring instruments, and to acquire certain skills. Their whole life appeared to be a series of temporary jobs. Poorly adapted to an urban society in which they seemed quite out of place, cut off from the rural society and its reassuring traditions, they went about, persons without a past and without a future, desperately trying to gain a hold on a present which irremediably escaped them.

The man of the rural communities, held in the powerful grip of community ties, placed under the strict guidance of the elders, and supported by a whole group of traditions, has been replaced by the isolated, defenseless and gregarious man, torn from the organic units in which and through which he formerly existed, cut off from his group and his home soil, often placed in such material conditions that he is unable to recall his former ideals of honor and dignity.

End of a World

No one is unaware of the fact that a deep gulf now separates Algerian society from its past and that an irreversible change has taken place. The important thing is, however, not so much the break with the past as the feeling that such a break has occurred. The result of this realization has been to raise doubts and questions about the values which gave meaning to the former existence. The permanent state of insecurity, the experience of a way of life constantly unsettled and threatened with sudden change, has made these people consider the traditions and beliefs which were formerly held sacred to be futile. The strictest prohibitions have been violated.[18] The revolutionary situation has upset the former social hierarchies, now associated with the system of outmoded values, and has substituted for them new men to whom authority was granted for reasons other than birth, wealth, or moral or religious ascendancy. The former values based on honor have crumbled as a result of the cruelties of the war. The ideal image these people had formed of

[18] To take a single example: at the time of a large-scale military operation in 1959, the wives of a marabout, from a village near Michelet, fled in the middle of the night to a neighboring village where they had no acquaintances. This conduct, which would formerly have been considered scandalous, since the wives of a marabout rarely leave their home, was looked on as being almost normal.

their society and the values they associated with it have been put to the cruelest kind of test. As witness of this, we have these words of an old man of the Kabyles: "At the end of all this, there will not be a man left who can say 'I am a man.'" There are the cases of rape and abduction of women, of army interrogations during which the husband was slapped or knocked about in the presence of the women. This renouncement of traditional values took place in an atmosphere of despair and great moral anguish.

Like some infernal machine, the war has made a clean sweep of the social realities, grinding up and scattering to the four winds the traditional communities of the village, clan or family. Thousands of men were in the underground movement, in the internment camps, in prison, or living as refugees in Tunisia and Morocco; others departed for the cities of Algeria or France, leaving their families behind in the resettlement projects or in their home villages; many others have died or disappeared. In entire regions there are practically no men left. In these deserted villages will there remain even a memory of the former traditions? For this enforced separation interrupted the transmission of the traditional civilization, which, because of their adherence to new values, tend to be no longer regarded with reverence by the young people. The women and the old men have remained behind in the villages with the children. The young men, thrown into an urban way of life, no longer learn from their elders the precepts, the customs, the legends or the proverbs which formed the soul of the community. The teaching of the elders has been replaced by a kind of political education imparted by those who are able to read. The maintenance of tradition presupposes a continuing contact between the successive generations and a respect for the elders on the part of the young. The patriarchal family, the primordial community which had escaped disintegration to a much greater extent in the country areas than in the cities, and which remained the keystone of the whole social structure, now is sometimes dispersed and is split by the conflict between the different generations, which is really the expression of the conflict between the old and the new systems of value.

The young men of the great cities are no longer subject to

the traditional controls and the pressure of public opinion, the principal means of enforcing respect for law and order in the village communities. Moreover, through the absence of a father or of an older brother, they are often left entirely to their own devices. A good number of them, especially in the cities, are now in the position of the young man whom the Kabyles call "the widow's son," that is to say, the one who has been deprived of a past, of traditions and ideals, because he has not received any paternal education. The authority of the father, although it still makes itself felt, is often weakened. In any case the head of the family is no longer regarded as the fountainhead of all values and the director of all family affairs. This is because the war has upset the scale of values which gave precedence and authority to the elders. The revolutionary values are those of the younger generation. Schooled by the war, turned towards the future, and completely ignorant of a past to which their elders cannot help remaining attached, the adolescents are often animated (and the part they played in the revolutionary war bears witness to this) by a spirit of radicalism and negativism which often separates them from their elders.

The traditional patterns for the relations between the sexes have also been altered. With the departure of the men from the villages, the women themselves gradually became more and more affected by the war. In many cases they now find themselves responsible for matters which traditionally devolved upon the men. Often they must work to support the family, even when they are receiving aid from a brother, a brother-in-law or an uncle. Their former severely restricted field of action has now been greatly enlarged. They go about in the European city, enter the big department stores, undertake business ventures and carry out administrative formalities. They are now breaking out of their closed and secret world to take part in activities formerly reserved for the men. They are sharing in the political preoccupations and aspirations which, in the traditional society, were the prerogatives of the men. Engaged in the war, either directly or indirectly, as actor or victim, driven by the force of circumstances to take on totally new roles, the Algerian woman has acquired a greater independence and, at the same time, a keener pride in her tasks and responsibilities.

Thus, combined with other influences such as education, which has increased the demands of the young and their desire for emancipation, the wider acquaintance with other cultures that has been produced by the shifts in population, the urbanization and political indoctrination of the masses which has led to a widening of the "intellectual outlook," the war situation has upset the entire cultural system. However, contrary to what one might think, a state of open warfare is less unfavorable to cultural exchanges than a situation in which resistance is underground and disguised. Paradoxically, open conflict brings the two sides together just as much as it places them in opposition, because, in order to win the war, it is necessary to borrow the most efficient weapons of one's adversary, and perhaps, also, because war remains a dialogue when all is said and done.

To express the present state of affairs the old Algerians often say: "We are now in the fourteenth century." To them the fourteenth century is the century of the end of the world, at which time everything that was the rule will become the exception, when all that was forbidden will be now permitted, a time, for example, when children will no longer respect their parents, the wife will go to the marketplace and so on. The mind of the people thus expresses its experience of a topsy-turvy world in which everything works backwards; it sees in the disorder and chaos which surround it the final state announcing the end of the world. And indeed, in Algeria, we are witnessing the end of a world. But the end of this world is felt by the people to be the announcement of a new world to come.

Algerian society has been undergoing for 130 years—and is undergoing today—a great upheaval. No domain has been spared. The pillars of the traditional order have been shaken or overthrown by the colonial situation and the war. The urban middle class has been broken up and dispersed; the values that it represented and protected have been swept away by the eruption of new ideologies and by the appearance on the scene of a new elite, of new leaders who often come from the common people and who are armed with an authority that has been forged in the struggle for independence. The great feudal chiefs, often compromised by the support that they gave to the French administration, and hence associated in the eyes of the masses with the system of oppression, have lost in most cases their material power and their spiritual authority. The great mass of peasants, who opposed their deeply rooted traditionalism and conservatism to any innovations offered by the West, have been carried along in the whirlwind of violence which is sweeping away even the vestiges of the past. Because it has been disassociated from the magico-mythical practices and beliefs that kept it rooted to the soil, because for a time it was more or less deliberately used as a revolutionary ideology capable of mobilizing the masses and enlisting them in the struggle, Islam has become progressively changed in meaning and function. In short, the war, by reason of its nature, its special form and its duration, was accompanied by a radical revolution. One could forecast with some assurance that the return of peace would reveal an Algeria quite different from the Algeria at the outbreak of war, an Algeria highly revolutionary because it has been highly revolutionized.

Of all the countries of North Africa, Algeria is undoubtedly the one in which the influence of Western culture, techniques and ideology has made itself felt most strongly. It is significant that during the years of war Algeria found the replies to its questions in French newspapers and French books and formulated its problems, its anxieties, its feelings of revolt and its hopes of revolution in the very terms employed by Western thought. It must not be overlooked that the number of children entering the schools is steadily increasing, that more and more of the male and even female population can now express themselves in French, and that the provision of modern housing for an increasing number of city dwellers has led to a profound change in habits and attitudes. Equally significant is the fact that the efforts of the administration and the army, whatever one may think of them, did have an effect in all domains—basic education, professional training, agricultural training, etc. Another important fact is that the revolutionary situation awakened a political conscience in all Algerians, of all classes and of all ages, and at the same time led to a new attitude toward society and toward the future that is featured by a great thirst for learning, understanding, information and material progress. One can see a manifestation of this awakening of the political conscience in the appearance of an oral literature composed principally of popular songs which exalt the revolutionary struggle. Usually anonymous and inspired by precise events, they sing of the atrocity of the war, the heroism of the combatants and of hope for peace. Simple and naive, these poems in Berber or Arab language, sung in accordance with the modes of the traditional music, are both chronicle and *chanson de geste*.

There has been an infiltration of traitors into the Army of Liberation—
They almost succeeded in shaking it to its foundations;
De Gaulle is beginning to boast about it, happy at his success,
He continues to watch more and more closely, thinking that his seeds of discord have taken root,
Whereas we have sworn that Algeria will live, even should only one man survive.

The numerous students [who have joined the F.L.N.] have been forced by traitors to abandon their post.
If they slumber, they dream, but if they are awakened, they will say "All right, count on me."
At the bottom of his heart, he wishes to betray his brothers.
On the man who goes astray from his duty the eagle will pounce and he will be carried off.
The flag is unfurled by the wind and dawn has risen over it.
And on the day when Algeria lives again, the orphan will once more find his father.

(Recorded in Kabylia in 1958.)

Listen to this story.
Be attentive and in order to hear
And understand what I say,
Be sure not to fall asleep.

Wherever the Frenchman goes,
He leaves behind bloody traces;
No one is spared,
Even the old are struck down.
He has despoiled the trees which were laden with fruit.
He has poisoned the waters of the streams.

Wherever the Frenchman goes,
Bullets pierce the walls,
The wheat fields are destroyed by fire.
To feed the people even acorns are becoming hard to find.
And as for the honor that has been violated,
Words are not sufficient to describe it.

From one generation to another
The message will be transmitted
So that it will never be forgotten—
How the people were seized by the throat.
Every day each village can count one more person who has died.
Poor child who weeps without understanding
The stiffness of the body of its mother.

Everywhere the Frenchman goes
The fields are left burned behind him,
The cattle that were tied up
Have died burned to a crisp.
They even burn the swaddling clothes
In which are wrapped the new-born babes.
No tomb will be opened for them—
Only the common grave
Will receive the dead.

                                        (Recorded in Algiers in 1960.)

Finally, it must be remembered that the Algerians feel
themselves to be affected by the experiences of all the countries
that were formerly colonial possessions, and that the Chinese
venture, of which they are generally ill-informed, has aroused
ambivalent attitudes of mingled interest and distrust. Algeria
has now become resolutely open to the world.

The size and duration of the colonial enterprise, the numeri-
cal importance of the European population settled in Algeria
and the influence it has exerted through the power of example,
the setting up of a capitalistic economy, the prolonged control
of the civil and military administration in a great many fields,
the unusual appeal and deep penetration of French culture, the
severity and long duration of the war of liberation, which had
a direct or an indirect effect on all spheres of existence and on
all social classes—all these are factors which have led to a complete transformation of the old Algeria. The economic and social

structures, the system of values, and the categories of thought have also been greatly altered. Contrary to what has happened in other new countries, it will be impossible for any future political regime to draw support from the former social structures, such as the tribe, or from the old social hierarchies, such as the great landed proprietors or the educated bourgeoisie of the cities; nor will it be able to base itself upon the old rural traditions or even upon the common religious beliefs of the people. Because of the development of a capitalistic economy in which a constantly increasing proportion of the Algerian population is finding employment, and because of the diffusion of education, a new elite has come to the fore. Together with an enormous sub-proletariat of unemployed workers, day laborers and peddlers, there has appeared in the cities a proletariat made up of permanent employees in the public and private sectors, qualified tradesmen, employees of the railways, of the large trucking companies and of the Public Works Administration, etc. Both a modern lower middle class—composed of minor government employees and administrative officials and of a section of the shopowners and factory workers—and an upper middle class—which includes members of the liberal professions, the higher officials of the public and private sectors, commercial and industrial contractors—have been added to that small portion of the old middle class which survived because it was able to adapt itself to the modern economic system. While the conflicts between classes are not consciously felt or explicitly expressed, and while they remain hidden or attenuated because the general feeling of the dominated society was one of opposition to the dominant European society, these conflicts nevertheless potentially exist. In this connection, too, the war favored an awakening of consciousness. The proletarianized and uprooted rural dwellers, as well as the sub-proletarians and proletarians of the cities, are conscious of having played a decisive role in this war, and it could be expected that with the termination of the war of national liberation they would insist on a true social revolution.

It is not only the interests of one social class but the whole economic and social situation that will make mandatory the adoption of a revolutionary policy. A society which has been so greatly revolutionized demands that revolutionary solutions be devised to meet its problems. It will insist that a way be found to mobilize these masses who have been freed from the traditional disciplines and thrown into a chaotic, disillusioned world, by holding up before them a collective ideal, the building of a harmonious social order and the development of a modern economy capable of assuring employment and a decent standard of living for all. Algeria contains such explosive forces that it could well be that there now remains only a choice between chaos and an original form of socialism that will have been carefully designed to meet the needs of the actual situation.

Glossary of Arab and Berber Terms

The French system of orthography for the following terms is employed in this book because it reflects the local dialect in a way the standard orthography does not; also, since almost all works on the subject are in French and use the French orthography, it was deemed advisable for convenience of reference to follow the practice in the field.

French Orthography	Standard Orthography	Definition
achoura	'āshūrā'	(Arabic.) Religious festival.
acils	aṣīl	(Arabic.) Descendants of the first city inhabitants in the Mzab; see *nazils* (nazīl).
adab	adab	(Arabic.) Education, culture, courtesy.
adainin	adaynīn	(Berber.) Part of Kabyle house situated on the lower level, serves as stable.
adekuan	adukan	(Berber.) Little wall. Protrusion of gable wall serving as shelf or cupboard for utensils; see *tadekuant* (tadūkant).
adroum	adhrūm	(Berber.) Clan; pl. *iderman* (idharmān).
akham	akhām	(Berber.) The "large house." Both a social unit (extended family) and collection of buildings where this same group lives.
akharroub	akharrūb	(Berber.) All the families whose members are descended from the same ancestor to the fourth or fifth generation, generally having the same name and considering themselves as "brothers"; see *takharroubt* (thakharrūbth) and *kharrouba* (kharrūbah).

193

French Orthography	Standard Orthography	Definition
akoufi	akūfi	(Berber.) Large jar of dried clay, placed either in the upper part of the house near the entrance, for important food supplies (grains), or on the protruding wall that separates stable from living quarters, for smaller provisions (dried figs, meal, beans and other leguminous foods, seeds). The latter jars, much smaller, are also called *tikoufiyin* (tikūfīyīn), sing. *takoufit* (thakūfith).
amin	amīn	(Arabic, Berber.) Representative and responsible person of village.
ârch	'arsh	(Arabic, Berber.) Tribe, group of villages. *Ârch* land is land belonging in an indivisible manner to tribe as a whole and is not the personal property of individual members.
azriya	azrīyah	(Local Arabic.) Woman without a husband, widowed or repudiated. In the Aurès region she conducts herself as a veritable courtesan (azrī: single).
baraka	barakah	(Arabic, Berber.) Mysterious and beneficent power favoring selected persons. Can be transmitted through heredity, initiation or name-borrowing; can be withheld by gift of nature or divine power.
berrou bat'el	barrū baṭāl (or tina-brawth baṭāl)	(Berber.) Act by which husband sends wife back to her parents, pronouncing the traditional formulas and refusing to accept the equivalent of what he paid at the time of marriage. This repudiation without return of the marriage payment is particularly offensive because it shatters the system of reciprocity—giving without receiving in exchange—which is contrary to the logic of honor.

Glossary

French Orthography	Standard Orthography	Definition
chebka	shabakah	(Arabic.) Net, netting.
chefâa	shafā'ah	(Arabic.) Right of redeeming real estate or of pre-emption, whose development received great impetus from Berber custom in order to keep strangers or foreigners away from the property.
cheikh	shaykh	(Arabic, Berber.) Local head of religious life.
çoff	ṣaff	(Arabic.) Moiety. Political and agonistic alliance (pl. sufūf).
çohba	ṣuḥbah	(Arabic.) "The company." Patronage. Protection assured by a powerful family to poorer families in exchange for fidelity and allegiance.
diia	dīyah	(Arabic, Berber.) Blood money. Compensation paid by murderer's family to family of victim.
djelf	jalf	(Local Arabic.) Hollow, soil of which is cultivated by nomads.
djemâa	jama'ah	(Arabic.) Assembly of all male members of village; see *tajmaât* (tajma'th).
douro lahlâl	dūrū laḥlāl	(Arabic.) *Douro* piece or sum of money) of sale by auction among Touaba; see *haqd-dkhoul* haqq-dūkhūl).
fellah	fallāḥ	(Arabic.) Fellah, peasant.
ferqa	firqah	(Arabic.) Division, fraction (social unit).
freda	farīḍah	(Arabic.) Act by which a cadi (Moslem magistrate) establishes the share of each of the parties entitled in the inheritance.
gandoura	gandūrah	(Arabic.) Man's robe of linen or wool.

French Orthography	Standard Orthography	Definition
gourbi	gūrbī	(Arabic.) Roughly built dwelling, often consisting of single apartment made of mud or boughs daubed with earth.
guelâa	qal'ah	(Arabic, Berber.) Granary—citadel, castle—fortress; small town or village situated on plateau or steep rock. The defensive site encourages the group to store their provisions here for safekeeping.
habous	ḥubūs	(Arabic.) Religious foundation; donation made to religious establishment consisting of property, the revenue from which is kept for oneself and heirs.
hachouma	ḥishmah	(Arabic.) Shame, modesty. Dignity, reserve.
halqa	ḥalqah	(Arabic.) The "circle"; assemblage of learned persons in Mzab.
hammam	ḥammām	(Arabic, Berber.) Moorish bath.
haouch	ḥawsh	(Arabic.) "Farm." Continuous property with building in the center. Court of city dwellings.
haouita	ḥawīṭah	(Arabic.) Generally a small, roofless, stone enclosure, encompassed by a high wall around the tomb of a marabout. In the Mzab, an ellipse of 26 tombstones laid out in the market place, where questions of a secular nature (legal deliberations, financial transactions, political debates) are discussed under the protection of the dead.
haqd-dkhoul	ḥaqq dūkhūl	(Arabic.) Wedding present from sale by auction consisting of one *douro* among the Beni-Bou-Slimane in the Aurès region.
harfiqt	harfīqth	(Berber.) Clan, group unifying several extended families; pl. *hirfiqin* (hirfīqīn).

French Orthography	Standard Orthography	Definition
h'orm	ḥūrm	(Local Arabic.) Sacred territory, site of the five towns of the Mzab, where the observance of the true religion, free from all contamination, is maintained.
h'orma	ḥurmah	(Arabic, Berber.) Honor by oposition to point of honor.
iderman	idharmān	(Berber.) Clans; sing. *adroum* adhrūm).
ikufan	ikufan	(Berber.) Large jars; sing. *akoufi* (akūfī).
ittifâqât	ittifāqāt	(Arabic.) Collection of Mozabite written customs.
kanum	kānūn	(Arabic, Berber.) Entrance, hearth consisting of a hole hollowed in the ground in upper part of house and daubed inside with clay.
kharrouba	kharrūbah	(Arabic.) See *akharroub* (akharrūb).
khouan	khūwān	(Local Arabic.) "Bothers." Members of a religious brotherhood.
kitmân	kitmān	(Arabic.) Act of veiling, hiding, silencing; arrangement permitting Mozabite austerity to adjust to religious prescriptions.
ksar	kasr or qaṣr	(Local Arabic.) Oasis gardeners' village; the houses of stone or dried earth cling to the shelter of the ramparts as a protection against nomad incursions; pl. *ksour.*
lâada	al'ada	(Arabic, Berber.) Custom, tradition, rule. *Lâada imezwura* (al'ada imazwūrā): "the custom of the fisrt," or "the custom (established) by the first ones." The ancestral tradition.
lhara	al-ḥārah	(Berber.) "The house." Dwelling place. Collection of houses shelter-

French Orthography	Standard Orthography	Definition
		ing Berber family, cattle leased out and food supplies.
matmoura	maṭmūrah	(Arabic.) Underground silo, property of family or group.
mçalla	muṣallā	(Arabic.) Slab raised up on and supported by a parallel-faced block where prayers are said.
mechmel	mashmal	(Arabic.) Common lands of the clan or village, generally serving as pastures.
mechta	mashtā	(Arabic.) At first, winter encampment of semi-nomads of eastern Algeria, eventually a village.
meddah	madaḥ	(Arabic.) Popular singer, kind of wandering troubadour who recites poetry, narrates religious history of Islam or relates local legends.
mektoub	maktūb	(Arabic.) Fate, or what has been written.
nazils	nazīl	(Arabic.) As opposed to acils (aṣil), recently arrived inhabitants of towns in the Mzab.
qanoun	qānūn	(Arabic, Berber.) Collection of customs, usually oral, belonging to each village.
rahnia	rahnīyah	(Arabic.) Mortgage of revenues of a property in payment of interest on a loan.
souq	ṣūq	(Arabic, Berber.) Market.
srir	sarīr	(Arabic.) "Bed"; elevation constructed of earth, in the form of a bench on which is spread bedding, particularly of important personages.
taâricht	ta'rishth	(Berber.) A sort of loft. Apartment, or room, situated under the same

Glossary

French Orthography	Standard Orthography	Definition
		roof as the rest of the house, above the stable, *adainin,* and connecting with the living quarters (taqa'at). Reached by ladder or by "adhab-dhar," a small built-up elevation supporting little *akoufi* (akūfī).
taddart	thaddarth	(Berber.) Village. Can be made up of a single clan, *adroum,* or several.
tadekuant	tadūkant	(Berber.) Small *adekuan.*
tadjadit	tajaddith	(Berber.) Literally, of *jadd;* grandfather, ancestor. Consanguinity; lineage. All the descendants of the same ancestor, real or mythical.
tajmaḏt	tajma'th	(Berber.) See *djemḏa* (jam'ah).
takharroubt	thakharrūbth	(Berber.) See *akharroub* and *kharrouba.* Little *akharroub;* pl. *tikharroubin* (tikharrubīn.)
takiya	taqīyah	(Arabic.) Prudence in supplying dogmatic justification for adjustments made with traditional conservatism.
taleb	ṭālib	(Arabic.) Scholar, student in general. One who seeks knowledge: by extension, a wise man, virtuous, pious, uncomplicated, detached from the world's goods and devoid of all passion.
tamaouokt	tim'awāqth	(Berber.) Literally, "the woman who is put in distress, left in a state of hesitation." Woman who, by the fact of *barrou batel,* or by refusal of dowry settlement and its counterparts, finds herself in an ambiguous situation, without a settled social status and thus even excluded from the cycle of matrimonial exchanges after the manner of a gift refused to which no counter-gift can be made.

French Orthography	Standard Orthography	Definition
t'amen	ṭāman	(Berber.) "Spokesman" of takharroubt, its representative in the assemblies, of which it is the guarantee because it is the depository of the confidence (amen) of all its members.
taousa	tāwsah	(Arabic.) Gift in kind made by guest to host and publically proclaimed on the occasion of festivals and ceremonies.
taqaat (adainin)	taqa'at (adaynīn)	(Berber.) Part of house contiguous with stable and specifically reserved for human beings. Habitable part of house.
taqbilt	thaymat	(Berber.) Confederation of tribes.
taymat	thaqbilt	(Berber.) Literally, of ayma: brother. Brotherhood, all the brothers.
tikharroubin	tikharrūbīn	(Berber.) Sing. takharroubt (thakharrūbth).
timechret'	timashraṭ	(Berber.) Apportionment of meat among all the inhabitants of a village on the occasion of agricultural ceremonies (festivals of the first autumnal plowing, rain ceremonies, etc.), or of religious festivals ('īd-assghir, Mūlūd, etc.).
tiouizi	tiwizī	(Berber.) Collective work; see touiza.
toufiq	tūfiq	(Local Arabic.) Territorial unit where clan or "confederation" of clans has taken root.
touiza	tūwīzah	(Arabic.) Collective work; see tiouizi.
umma	ummah	(Arabic.) Moslem community; modern sense of term: nation.
zaouia	zāwiyah	(Arabic.) Establishment for instruction attached to a religious brotherhood.

Glossary

French Orthography	Standard Orthography	Definition
zariba	zarība	(Arabic.) Village of mountain dwellers in the Collo massif, grouping within an enclosure of thorns and shrubs the members of families descended from a common ancestor (pl. zarā'ib).

Selected Bibliography

BERNARD and LACROIX. *Evolution du nomadisme,* 1906.

BERQUE, J. *Etudes d'histoire rurale maghrébine,* Tangiers, 1938.

———. *Les Arabes,* Robert Delpire, Paris, 1959.

BIROT and DRESCH. *La Méditerranée et le Moyen-Orient,* Presses Universitaires de France.

CAPOT-REY. *Le Sahara français,* Presses Universitaires de France, 1953.

CHARLES. *Le droit musulman,* "Que sais-je?" series no. 702, Gallimard.

CHOURAQUI. *Les Juifs d'Afrique du Nord,* 1952.

DEPONT and COPOLANI. *Les confréries religieuses musulmanes,* 1897.

DERMENGHEM. *Le culte des saints dans l'Islam maghrébin,* 1954.

DÈSPARMET. *Ethnographie traditionnelle de la Mitidja,* 1918.

———. *Coutumes, institutions, croyances des Musulmans d'Algérie,* 2d ed., 1948.

DESPOIS. *L'Afrique du Nord,* Presses Universitaires de France, 1949.

DOUTTE. *Magie et religion dans l'Afrique du Nord,* 1909.

EMERIT. *L'Algérie a l'époque d'Abd-el-Kader,* Algiers, 1951.

E.S.N.A. *Cahiers nord-africains,* Paris.

Fichier de Documentation berbère, Fort-National.

GARDET. *La cité musulmane,* Vrin, 1954.

GAUDEFROY-DEMOMBYNES. *Les institutions musulmanes,* 3d ed., 1946.

GAUDRY. *La femme chaouïa de l'Aurès,* Geuthner, 1929.

GAUTIER. *Le passé de l'Afrique du Nord,* Payot, 1937.

———. *Moeurs et coutumes des Musulmans,* Payot, 1931.

GOICHON. *La vie féminine au Mzab,* Geuthner, 1927.

HANOTEAU and LETOURNEUX. *La Kabylie et les coutumes kabyles,* 3 vols., 1873.

ISNARD. *Algeria,* trans. by O. C. Warden, Oxford, 1955.

——. *La réorganisation de la propriété rurale dans la Mitidja,* Algiers, 1948.

——. "Vigne et structures sociales en Algérie," *Diogène,* September 1959.

LARCHER. *Traité élémentaire de législation algérienne,* Algiers, 1903.

LETOURNEAU. *L'Islam contemporain,* Ed. Int., Paris, 1950.

——. *Les villes musulmanes de l'Afrique du Nord,* Algiers, 1957.

MARÇAIS, G. *Les Arabes en Berbérie du XIe au XIVe siècle,* 1913.

MASQUERAY. *Formation des cités chez les populations sédentaires de l'Algérie,* 1886.

MAUNIER. *Mélanges de sociologie nord-africaine,* Alcan, 1930.

——. *Coutumes algériennes,* Paris, 1935.

MERCIER. *La civilisation urbaine au Mzab,* Algiers, 1922.

MILLIOT. *L'association agricole chez les Musulmans du Maghreb,* 1911.

——. "Les institutions kabyles," *Rev. ét. isl.,* 1932.

MINER, H. M., and DE VOS, G. *Oasis and Casbah: Algerian Culture and Personality in Change,* University of Michigan Press, 1960.

RAHMANI. *Coutumes du Cap Aokas,* 1936.

Revue Africaine, Algiers.

Tables on Algerian Economy, *Statistique générale de l'Algérie,* 1958.

TILLION, G. *Algeria: The Realities,* trans. by R. Matthews, Knopf, 1958.

——. "Dans l'Aurès," *Annales,* July-September 1957.

——. "Les sociétés berbères de l'Aurès méridional," *Africa,* 1938.

YACONO. *Les bureaux arabes,* Larose, Paris, 1953.

——. *La colonisation des plaines du Chéliff,* Algiers, 1955.

Index

Abadhite doctrine, 38-42, 44, 45-48, 50
Abadhites, 38. *See also* Mozabites
Abodaoui, 33
Abderrahmane, Ouled, 36
Abdi, Ouled, 25, 35
Abdi, Wadi el, 25
Abiod, Wadi el, 25, 34, 35
Achoura, festival of, 79
Acils, 43
Adab, 112
Adroum, 3, 12
Aggregation, tribal, 87-91; power of name in, 88-90
Aghbala, 176n
Agnatic principle, 3, 5, 7-8, 10-12, 17, 23, 32, 44, 82, 83, 97, 102. *See also* Family organization
Agouni-n-Tesellent (Aït Akbil), 20n
Agriculture, decline of native, 128n. *See also* Resettlement policy; Fellah, dispossession of
Ahmar Khaddou, 27
Akham, 3
Algeria, topography, xiii
Algiers (city), 59, 62, 65n, 66, 124, 125n, 176n
Algiers (*département*), 97n
Algiers, Sahel of, 125n
Almsgiving, 30, 47
Amin, 3
Arab culture, interchange with Berber, xii-xiv, 5, 27, 30, 56, 92, 93. *See also* Bedouins
Ârch, 3, 32, 36
Assimilation and dissimilation, principle of, 90-91, 93, 94n
Athbedj, 84
Atlas: Saharan, 66; Tellian, 164
Aurès, topography, xiii
Autoconsumption, 26, 103
Azriya, 30-31

Banishment. *See* Ostracism
Bank of Algeria, 123
Baraka, 90, 115, 116
Bedouins, cultural interpenetration with Berbers, 56, 57, 93
Beni-Bou-Slimane, 10, 35
Beni Isguen, 40
Beni Melkem, 35
Beni Menna, 76
Beni Merzoug, 76
Berber culture, interchange with Arab. *See* Arab culture
Berriane, 39, 40, 49
Berrou bat'el, 10
Bône, 57, 125n
Bordjia, 78
Bou Noura, 40
Bourdieu, P., 105
Bourgeoisie, in Arab cities, 64
De Broglie, A., 120
Burial customs, 12, 35-36, 41
Business success, Mozabite, 51-54

Cadi, 7, 30, 42
Caïds, 140
Cantonment of 1856-1857, 120
Capital, 9, 39, 48, 64, 72, 73, 103
Capot-Rey, 67n, 69
Cereal growing, 27, 58, 66, 67, 70-72, 73, 80; colonial, 123
Chebka, 37
Chechia, 154, 156, 158
Chefâa, 5, 6, 75, 82
Chéliff, 56, 57, 78, 165n
Cheraïa, 179
Citrus growing, colonial industry of, 123-126
Clan, 1, 2, 4: Arab, 67, 82, 83; Kabyle, 12-13, 17, 22; Mozabite, 41, 42, 48; Shawian, 31, 32-36
Classes, urban, 64, 191

Climate, effect on economy, 57, 65, 68, 72, 73, 103

Çoff: Arab, 90-91; Kabyle, 13-16; Mozabite, 42, 43; Shawian, 29, 34-35

Çohba, 78

Collo, 169n, 172n, 174n, 175, 179

Colonists, alienation of, 132

Colonization and French rule, xiv, 44, 57, 64, 65n, 84, 117-118. *See also* Resettlement policy

Commensality, 3, 4, 13

Comte, 109

Confederations, tribal, 83-84

Constantine, 124, 182

Constantine, High Plains of, 56-57, 64, 65n, 125, 135. *See also* Woman

Corporations, urban Arab, 60-62

Crime and punishment, 20-23, 41, 43, 47

Curse, 3-4

Dahra, 57

Daoud, Ouled, 25, 35

Despois, 84, 86

Diia, 33

Divorce, 29-30

Djebabra, 172n

Djebel Bous, 26

Djelf lands, 67

Djemâa, 42, 43n, 70, 140

Djerba, 45

Djurdjura, 1n

Douars, 35, 59, 71, 139-140

Douro, 10; *lahlâl*, 10

Doutté, 87

Dresch, 135

Education, 48, 51, 95, 165. *See also* War, effects of

El Arab (Bou Okkaz family), 84

El Ateuf, 39, 40

Emigration, 39; and group ties, 11, 45, 46-47, 49, 50-51, 78-82, 165

Excommunication, 43, 49

Family organization, 3-5: Arab, 60; Kabyle, 5-12; Mozabite, 41; Shawian, 27-32; of business, 48, 60; as structural model, 97-98: Kabyle, 12-24; Shawian, 35-36

Family solidarity, as social factor, 97: Arab, 60; Kabyle, 12; Mozabite, 49, 51; Shawian, 28; breakdown of, 141-142. *See also* Social Structures

Fatalism, Islamic, 103, 109-111

Father, role of, 3-4, 102, 186: Arab, 83; Kabyle, 10-11; Shawian, 25, 27-28, 31

Favrod, 147n

Fellah: attitude to life, 103-106; dispossession of, 64, 126, 129, 135, 139, 171-176; religion, 115-116

Ferhat Abbas, 147n

Ferqa, 83

Financial Delegations, 123

Fort National (*arrondissement*), 1

France, images of, 151-152

Freda, 74

Front de Libération Nationale (F.L.N.), 147n, 154, 159n, 161n, 163, 164, 169n, 182

Gandoura, 79

Gautier, E. F., 38, 45-46

Gentilitial family. *See* Family organization

Ghardaïa, 40, 68

Gourbi, xi, 63, 172n, 182

Gours, 37

Granary, as social institution, 33-34. *See also Guelâa*

Great family, 78; and power of name, 88-90

Guebli, Wadi, 180

Guelâa, 33, 40, 104

Guerrara, 39, 40

Habous, 5, 6, 74, 75, 82

Hachouma, 96

Halqa, 41, 43n

Hamada, 37

Hammam, 62

Hanencha (Harar family), 84

Hanotreau and Letrouneux, 7-8

Haouita, 42

Harfiqt, 32-34, 36

Haqd-dkhoul, 10

Hillalian Arab invasions, 56, 89

Home Army, 152

Honor, 96, 112: Kabyle, 3, 6, 10, 17,
   20-23; Shawian, 28, 33; decline of,
   184; as guarantor of sharecropper
   pacts, 78-81
Honorable exchange, 9, 16n, 81, 103
H'orm, 40
H'orma, 87
Hospitality, 28
Humboldt, Wilhelm, von, 113

Inheritance customs, 3, 5, 102; Ka-
   byle, 5-6; Shawian, 28
Irrigation, 67, 68
Islam, conversions to, 56, 62
Islamic law, 6, 13, 38, 42, 74, 92;
   cultural influence, 107-118
Isnard, 126
Ittifâqât, 39, 42-44, 47

Jews, 63, 93, 111

Kabylia, topography, 1
Kerkera, 176n, 180
Khammès, 138n
Kharedjites. *See* Abadhites
Khelouf, Ouled, 78
Khouan, 109
Khouidem, Ouled, 78
Kinship, fictitious, 84-86
Kitmân, 54
Koranic schools, 43, 48, 60
Kouloughlis, 62
Ksar, 67n
Ksourien, 67-68, 69

Lâada imezwura, 95
Laghouat, 66, 68
Landholding, 5, 102: Arab, 66-67,
   70, 74-76; Kabyle, 1-2, 5; Mozabite,
   34-36; a basis for social unity, 82-83;
   colonial policy on, 120-122; sale
   of nomads' lands, 58. *See also*
   Resettlement policy
Lartique, 35
Law, 20-23, 92. *See also ittifâqât*
Lévi-Strauss, 91
Little Kabylia, 56

Madhi, Ouled, 84, 86, 89, 90
Magic, 10, 118; and woman, 29, 30-
   31, 49, 93, 95, 98

Mao Tse-tung, 164
Marabouts, 4, 27, 89, 93; tribes of
   89. *See also* Priests
Marçais, G., 85, 89
Marçais, W., 62
Marcy, G., 92
Markets, xiii, 26, 40, 59, 62, 68
Marriage compensation: Kabyle, 8-10;
   Shawian, 29-30
Marriage customs, 4: Kabyle, 5-10;
   Shawian, 29-30
Matmoura, 71
May, 1958, demonstrations of, 149n,
   150, 158-159, 164
Mechmel, 1
Mechta, 71
Meddah, xiii, 94
Médéa, 62
Médersas, 60
Medina, 67n
Medjana, Ouled (Mokran family),
   84
Mektoub, 109
Melika, 40, 47
Melk, 121n
Menaâ, 35
Métayage au quint. See Sharecrop-
   ping
Michelet, 184n
Miliana, 62, 172n
Mitidja, 57, 125n
Mohammed Dib, 148
Montesquieu, 20-21
Moors, Andalusian, 62
Moroccans, 84
Morocco, 60, 185
Mosque, 40-42, 49, 59, 60, 114n
Mouloud Mammeri, 95
M'turni, 159
Mutual aid, 2, 11-12, 28, 48, 60, 75,
   112; pacts, 76
Mzab, topography, 37
Mzab, Wadi, 37, 40
Mzira, 36

Naïl, Ouled, 84, 86, 91
Nazils, 43
Nedroma, 62
Negroes, 63
Nemenchas, 164

Nomads, Saharan, 76; Shawian, 27, 32-33

Oases, paradox of, 37-38
Oath, collective, 22-23, 33
Oil, 54n, 69
Oran, 57, 60, 65n, 66, 125n
Oranie, plains of, 57
Ostracism, 17, 22, 43, 45
Ouarsenis, 57

Pacts, 76, 78-82, 103
Past, idealization of, 94-95. *See also*
    Traditionalist society
Pastoral society, decline of, 69
Patrimony: legalized break-up, 58,
    82-83; as social factor, xii, xiii,
    33, 82-83
Personality, concealment of, 96
Philippeville, 125n, 176n
Piémont, 164
Pied noir (pioneer), 130n, 152
Politeness, 95
Population: growth, 63n, 119, 128,
    134-135; ratios, 67n
Population growth, European, 123
Priests, 42-44. *See also* Marabouts
Proletariat, in Arab cities, 64, 191

Qanoun, 13, 20-23

Racism, 133-134, 150
Rahnia, 105
Ramadan, fast of, 113
Rechaïch, Ouled, 121
Resettlement policy: economic ef-
    fects, 164, 170-179; failure, 182;
    motives, 164, 166; procedures, 169-
    170; social effects, 164-165, 171-176
Resolutions of 1748, 6
Richard, Captain, 76
Rivière, T., 36

Sahara, xi, 25, 27, 60, 64, 67, 68, 69
Saussure, Ferdinand, de, 90
Section Administrative Specialisée,
    172n, 183
Senatus Consulte of 1863, 33n, 35, 58,
    82, 120, 122n, 139, 166

Sersou, 69
Sétif, 64, 65n
Shantytowns, 178
Sharecropping, 2, 78-82
Sheik, 42, 83-84
Social structures: continuity of, 66-
    67, 98; decline of, 139-144
Souq, 62
Speech, conventions of, 96, 107
Standard of living, 135, 177-178
Stock raising, 57, 58, 65, 70-73, 128,
    134-135
Swing-plow, 67, 72
Synœcism, 44

Taddart, 3
Tajmaât, 3, 12, 17, 22
Takharroubt, 3, 12
Takiya, 54
Taleb, 47
Tamaouokt, 10
T'amen, 3
Tamesroit, 31n
Taousa, 9, 106
Taqbilt, 3
Tell region, xi, 45-49, 58, 65n, 66,
    68, 69, 76, 84
Terrorism, 153
Theocracy, 43
Thresholds, 12
Tiaret, 69
Tillion, G., 35, 36
Timechret', 3, 12, 22
Tiouizi, 11
Tlemcen, 60, 62, 140
Tolls, paid by nomads, 66
Touaba, 10, 33
Touaregs, 31n, 91n
Toufiq, 13
Trabadjar, 183
Traditionalism, colonial, 155-156
Traditionalist society, 94-96; atti-
    tudes toward work, 104; and eco-
    nomic planning, 104-105; sources,
    109-114
Transhumance, 25, 35, 71, 334
Tribe: Arab, 82, 83-84, 86-87; Kabyle,
    3; Shawian, 32, 36
Tunisia, 185
Turks, 62

Umma, 112
Unemployment, 129, 174-176, 182-183, 191
Usury, 39, 111-112

Vaissière, Captain, 88, 121, 122n
Veil, 154, 156
Village, Kabyle: layout, 1; social unit, 3, 13

War, Algerian: causes, 145-147; and cultural exchange, 187-188; and decolonization, 163; and native view of dominant culture, 159-162
Warnier law of 1873, 120-121

Weber, Max, 104, 114
Wife, role of, 1, 4, 95: Arab, 83; Kabyle, 7; Shawian, 25, 27-31. *See also* Woman, status of
Winegrowing, colonial industry of, 123-126
Woman, status of, 97-98: Kabyle, 5-10; Mozabite, 49; Shawian, 29-32; change in, 186-187. *See also* Wife, role of

Yacono, 78

Zaouïa, 89, 116
Zariba, 175, 180